ISBN 978-1483971223

Manufactured in the United States of America

Strategic Decision Mastery

How to build an Effective Decision Culture in any Organization

A. Brent Pulsipher

© 2008

For executive managers, the leadership and organizational principles advocated in this book may represent the right solution for establishing a *performance excellence* culture in their organization. It may be that readers find the one idea they have been looking for, but without the complicated philosophies and entanglements that so often prevent the practical and timely implementation of good ideas.

Contents

I

Section Three

Section Four

Section Five

Appendix Materials

Foreword

Pass it on – Many senior executive leaders, especially as they complete their active careers, believe that their leadership and lifelong experiences are meaningful. Too few are inclined to pass on the significant knowledge and lessons they learned. I am one who believes the practical lessons and learning's of a 40 year career are of value. Consequently, I have chosen to 'pass it on' by writing this book about a subject of significant importance to organizational success. In the broadest sense, the subject is decision making and how to make it more effective. The premise is that decisions, the good ones and the bad ones in all their variations, are too often made ineffectively by people at all levels of an organization. Given an actual set of circumstances people either rely too much on so-called standard operating procedures, insufficient experience with the situation, and/or too little information about possible outcomes. More importantly, an abundance of critical decisions are disconnected from the strategic intent and objectives of the organization. Further, an awareness of the difference between a routine and a critical decision is often lacking, except for the most repetitive situations and actions. The result of disconnected decision-making varies from inconsequential to catastrophic. It is perhaps the greatest cause of suboptimal performance and can be the cause of total failure. Since decision outcomes depend on time, which can vary from seconds to years, there is an urgent need for a means to recognize decision results in time to minimize their unintended consequences and maximize the intended and unintended benefits, especially for the most critical and important decisions. The early chapters provide thoughts, information, and facts from relevant experience to make the case for why improving decision-making is important and worth more attention than it gets, especially from organizational leaders.

Personal background information – After graduating with a master's degree in Economics in 1967, which was essentially an MBA, I began a career in business that spanned 38 years. I worked for six different companies and had a short period with a large government agency as a regional financial management officer. My career goal was to become a chief financial officer (CFO) as a natural culmination of being a financial analyst, consultant and accounting officer. I was able to achieve that goal when I was 35 years old. From there my business career progressed to being the COO of a privately held corporation while concurrently serving as the CFO of a publicly traded company that was over 50 percent owned by the private company. With a taste of enterprise management from the smaller company I next found myself accepting a position as the president (CEO) of a $400 million division of $2.3 billion NYSE Corporation. For a period of years following this role I worked with a number of businesses, both large and small, as a consultant. My primary consulting emphasis was on assisting senior executives to improve operational and financial performance by more effectively utilizing a specific enterprise-wide software solution that I knew inside and out. From there I served as the CIO of an apparel company and was hired specifically to manage the installation of the apparel and footwear version of a sometimes infamous ERP software solution. I completed my career as the executive vice president responsible for logistics and technology of a $1.0 billion dollar national distribution company.

During my diverse career I worked for two manufacturers, three wholesale/retail distribution companies, the federal government, a software company, and a big four consulting practice. I was tutored by some very capable business leaders, particularly in my first company. They taught me principles and concepts that have stood the test of time. I worked for people in executive positions for whom the *Peter Principle* should have been invoked much sooner. And I worked with some people who were merely place holders and master defenders of the status quo. As an executive I participated in taking a company public, identifying and completing acquisitions, leading a leveraged buyout effort, and seeing my division sold out from under me to a leverage buyout firm. I worked on a grass roots effort to design fully integrated enterprise software. I worked for 15 months with the largest software company in the world to install their solution only to see them withdraw with an admission that their software wouldn't work as represented for our company. I could add many more instances that were high and low points in my varied business experience, but these involvements provide the insights that I believe are valuable and relevant to an effective discussion of decision-making and how to improve it.

Not all of these experiences turned out the best for me, but they provided invaluable understanding. During my career the explosion of personal computing capabilities happened and I learned to take my analytical ability from the pad and pencil to the personal computer. I worked with masterful human relations people who understood the value of people and taught me when and how to promote the achievers and dismiss the underperformers. I have suffered the consequences of ineptitude in the managers and executives at the highest levels. I have also been the beneficiary of high level executives who saw my talents and mentored me to succeed more than I could have done on my own. I have suffered from the subtle efforts of people whom I managed to undermine my objectives and initiatives. Conversely, I have greatly benefited from people who worked with me and not only caught the vision of what we were trying to accomplish, but sometimes expanded it beyond my initial view.

My father was a truck driver-owner. He worked hard all his life. Beginning at age 12 my brothers and I worked with him by helping manually unload 12-13 tons of cinder blocks and concrete pipe each time we went with him. All of us learned to drive trucks and most worked in our teen years driving trucks and doing hard labor to earn money for our educations. A secondary lesson from this experience was that we knew we wanted to find a better way to make a living. Perhaps best of all we learned one very valuable lesson, *how to work until the job is done*. We couldn't unload only part of the truck. Those early-life experiences taught me that the most certain way to succeed is to *do the job in front of you* as well as you possibly can. I firmly believe that and have taught my own children this lesson. Throughout my career I found that when I did this, my managers would notice and when opportunities for more responsibility came along I was considered. That is how it worked for me and I am confident the same approach will work for most people. I know that I was offered two of my executive positions because I did the job well for my clients. I also found that some skills and abilities that I first learned and applied in high school and college have worked to my advantage. The two specific abilities, which have served me well, are an ability to speak and make presentations in large public gatherings; and the ability to write to the understanding of your audience. On two different occasions I was offered an executive position based on a presentation that I made. I accepted one and passed on the other. Consequently, if it was up to me, presentation and writing skills should be included in every business school curriculum at the undergraduate and graduate levels.

While I recognize that I am not a high profile publicly known business leader of which there many, I believe I have something worthwhile to say. I am one of a far greater number of senior business leaders whose leadership and experience provides the insight and background sufficient to espouse meaningful, practical and relevant organizational ideas. There is a common thread that spans all of my experience. It is that there are principles for doing business and managing results that do not change. Most of them existed long before so-called modern management philosophies came along. As an executive I was able to reinforce my belief that the principles for living a successful life can and should be applied in the workplace. I learned, often by trial and error, how to apply character-based principles to business and organizational environments. And, I was able to translate them into meaningful approaches for delivering positive results for my employers and clients. Needless to say I would not be writing this if I did not believe that there are some valuable treasures and principles from my life's experience that are worth passing on. I am confident that they will ring true to many people and will initiate meaningful changes to organizational results if applied.

In this book I have put together some of the most enduring and practical tools for understanding and succeeding, particularly in business environments. Many of the ideas and concepts can be applied on a personal level and the person who embraces them can accelerate their track to greater responsibility and the compensation that comes with it. For executive managers, the leadership and organizational principles advocated in this book may represent the right solution for establishing a *performance-excellence* culture in their organization. It may be that readers find the one idea they have been looking for, but without the complicated philosophies and entanglements that so often prevent the practical and timely implementation of those good ideas. Throughout the book I believe you will find good ideas, sound practices, ways to communicate what you may have always been thinking, and, most importantly, a set of tools for building an organizational culture where strategic decision-making is understood, embraced and practiced by everyone in your organization.

The intent is to provide a framework for a better and more practical approach for effectively managing an enterprise by successfully linking business objectives, and the strategies for accomplishing those objectives, to actual process level operating behavior. I have chosen to call the methodology *Strategic Decision Mastery* (*SDM*) because the title adequately captures what I believe is the essence of the primary task of executive leadership. In my view the executive leadership role is to establish appropriate objectives, determine and set the strategies for the achievement of those objectives; and then cohesively lead a diverse group of people with dissimilar functional responsibilities toward the achievement of those goals. The SDM approach can be applied in any type of organization. Strategy should be the prerogative of organizational leaders. However, strategic decisions, even though they are companion to the setting of objectives and strategies, are not always made at the executive level. People throughout an organization can make decisions that seem to be tactical or operational, but

4

turn out to be strategic because of their unforeseen outcomes and consequences. This happens most often when there is a lack of understanding about how everyday operational and tactical decisions affect the entity's true goals and strategy. I believe *SDM* [as we shall call it going forward] corrects this problem and builds a unified decision-making structure from top to bottom that will enhance performance, identify where strategic decisions need to be made, and ensure that tactical and operational decisions promote the accomplishment of the entity's goals and objectives by being consistent with strategies.

Having said that, it is important to make a case for why better decision management needs to be a primary focus of organizational leaders. Implied throughout this book is the allegation that the connections between strategic decision-making and decision-execution are broken in far too many organizations. Further, that most performance management systems are not sufficient to successfully communicate strategic direction at the operational levels. Despite choosing to challenge the traditional well imbedded hierarchical leadership structure; and the often incorrect assumption that higher ranking managers possess unilaterally superior ability to make sound decisions, I do offer an alternative solution. The early chapters establish a foundation for the *SDM* methodology by introducing and explaining some principles, concepts and ideas that are essential for understanding and adopting the *SDM* approach as an enterprise-wide pathway to strategic achievement. Of necessity adopting *SDM* requires some procedurally detailed concepts in the later chapters. To the potential practitioner this is a good thing. To "big picture only" individuals reading too much detail may divert their attention; but not reading it will increase the risk that they will overlook some good ideas and the potential benefits these ideas might bring. Nevertheless, the need for sufficient detail to facilitate adoption of the *SDM* concept is essential to confirm that it can work.

Section I
Decision-Making
Principles and Concepts

Chapter 1

Leadership, Management and Decision-Making

Leadership – an Essential for Effective Strategy

Early in my business career I used a few concepts and ideas that I originally "found" during undergraduate school. I discovered the ideas to be helpful years later, in the mid-1970's, as a consultant with DeLoitte Haskins and Sells (now Deloitte & Touche) where my expertise and focus was on financial planning and control systems. In that era there were no personal computers, so we developed our concepts and ideas for clients by writing them down and then having someone type them. If we needed presentation overheads (prior to Harvard Graphics and MS PowerPoint) they were produced manually and then copied in black and white to plastic sheets on a Xerox copier. Despite the lack of polish compared to today's tools, these simple documents were an effective method for working with executive leadership teams in both the public and private sectors. In combing through my personal business archives I found copies of some of those early documents. Upon reviewing them, I determined that those ideas continue to be relevant to business leaders who are interested in better understanding their role and excelling in their performance. They survive because they are not just ideas, they are sound principles; and like truth, they endure.

To help build the foundation for *SDM*, I have elected to recount several ideas that are taken from the book *Leadership in Administration*[1] by Philip Selznick, which was first published in 1957 and was a text book in my senior year for a management leadership class. I recently discovered that the book was republished in 1984 and can still be purchased. In the following paragraphs are some of the most relevant statements from the book that will increase understanding of the leadership role as it should be. Additionally, they support the purpose of *SDM* as will become clear as we progress into the methodology.

Selznick's book is written as a treatise on institutional leadership and thereby encompasses and makes examples of leadership in government,

---

[1] *Leadership in Administration*, Philip Selznick, University of California Berkeley, Harper & Row Publishers, copyright 1957

military, education and business. However, the point is that true principles of leadership apply to whatever type of organization an individual has the opportunity to lead. To my way of thinking, the logical sequence for developing strategic leadership starts with setting *objectives, or goals*, then devising appropriate *strategies* that will lead to the achievement of those goals. The simplest definition of strategy is "a *set of major goals and policies*". Once strategies are set for the organization they must be transitioned to the execution phase which should include three things. First, a set of *action strategies* that define what must be done at the transaction level of the enterprise. Second, *process goals* must be established for every process that is linked to each action strategy. Finally, *process measures* are essential for each process goal to be able to determine the level of achievement, or success. When all five layers of what I call the "*achievement structure*[2] of an enterprise are in place and cohesively determined, all successes at the lowest level of operations will contribute to the achievement of the highest level goals and objectives of the entity. Likewise failures can be tracked to each level. It is the combination of successes and failures, as measured at the process-level that determine the overall achievement of enterprise goals.

Another way to think about the five layers of an achievement structure is in terms of so-called *key performance indicators (KPI)*. Most corporations are accustomed to identifying a limited number of KPI's to measure their success in terms of profitability and asset/investment management. Each KPI is typically connected to several process level measures. Some process measures will affect more than one KPI. The complexity of this hierarchy from KPI's to process-level measures depends on the nature of the entity. A rule of thumb when KPI's first became popular was to limit the number to no more than fifteen (15). However, for each KPI there could be from four to eight process measures resulting in 60 to 120 meaningful process-level measures. This is more than enough for most organizations. Crossing the bridge from KPI's to process-level measures is where the concept of a balanced scorecard was often lost in the translation between executives and the people working at the process level because of the lack of appropriate process-level goals and measures. It takes time to create meaningful process-level measures and then effectively connect them all the way to enterprise goals, or KPI's. Even after they are initially defined it usually takes several iterations of the reporting cycle to validate the measures and their links to the right goals. As a result, when leaders were not willing to

---

[2] In a later chapter these five layers are presented in much more detail as *The Layers of Decision Execution*.

burn the time doing it right, they defaulted to having financial analysts develop their KPI measures. Without connectivity between entity goals and processes, those same analysts will spend the majority of their time trying to explain what happened to KPI performance with limited and inconsistent success. This is especially true when negative results are reported. Worst of all is that there will be little ability to connect results to the decisions that caused them. This oft repeated disconnection between objectives, processes and decisions is a primary reason for recognizing the validity of Selznick's ideas. Furthermore, it supports the case for adopting a decision-making methodology like *SDM* to eliminate the sub-optimization of the strategic decisions that are made by executives, managers and employees.

I have separated the quotes from Selznick's book into three groups that match the essential roles of leaders, which are establishing goals (objectives), determining strategies, and paying attention to process execution. All of these tasks are an important, not to be neglected, responsibility of organizational leaders.

Roles of an Effective Leader

*L**eaders set Goals** —This concept seems intuitive. Nevertheless, when most people assume a new leadership role, they are often quickly caught up in the day-to-day activity of the business instead of focusing on evaluating the strategic direction of the entity. Equally at fault, no matter how long they have been in the leadership role, are those who only focus on the more glamorous part of their job and completely ignore the execution processes. It is a fact that people tend to be most comfortable with what they know. Typically, newly appointed leaders arrive in their roles with a good tactical understanding of the business and only an informal feel for the need to address objectives [goals] and strategy. Selznick offers these leadership cautions to place emphasis on setting goals and strategy while not ignoring process-level execution.

"The tendency to emphasize methods rather than goals is an important source of disorientation in all organizations. It has the value of stimulating full development of these methods, but it risks loss of adaptability and sometimes results in a radical substitution of means for ends."[3]

"When institutional leadership fails, it is perhaps more often by default than

---

[3] Ibid, page 12

by positive error. One type of default is the failure to set goals."[4]

"Leadership sets goals, but in doing so, takes account of the conditions that have already determined what the organization can do, and to some extent, what it must do."[5]

The ideas in these quotes require little clarification and should induce personal reflection by every leader about how well they perform the important task of establishing goals and objectives. Nevertheless, the last quote is such a short statement about a very large pitfall that prevents many leaders from being as successful as they could be. Just as the NFL football coach who inherits a team with a losing record cannot expect to win the super bowl in the first year, business leaders cannot achieve beyond the capabilities of the people and processes that already exist in their organization when they take over the leadership role. Therefore, it should be a logical preoccupation of business leaders, particularly new ones, to assess and address the talent and abilities of the people they must rely on to be successful as it is a critical element of goal setting.

*L*eaders evaluate and determine Strategy – One of the sayings I have always enjoyed says, *"Even when you are on the right track you will be run over if you stand still."* A companion statement is, *"Everyone is in favor of progress, its change they can't stand"*. In 1984 as a newly appointed president of a $400 million division of a larger publicly traded company, my executive supervisor gave me the following statement to give me some guidance and understanding about the task that I had before me. In subsequent years of consulting I probably used the phrase more often than any other as a preface to my presentations to get people thinking about what they are up against when they undertake to be a champion of change. As I learned years later from my research oriented librarian daughter, it is really a paraphrase of a statement by Machiavelli. It had obviously been modified to make it more compact and business-oriented without losing the meaning of the original statement. Here is the modified statement:

"It must be remembered that there is nothing more difficult to plan, more uncertain of success, nor more dangerous to manage than the creation of a new order of things. The initiator has the enmity of all who would profit by

---

[4] Ibid, page 25
[5] Ibid, page 62

the preservation of the old institutions; and merely lukewarm defenders in those who would gain by the new ones." (Niccolo Machiavelli – 1469-1527)

To be certain the development of strategy almost always connotes change, especially when it challenges the comfort level of the existing leaders in an organization. Keeping strategy current and focused on addressing the right competitive direction is very difficult even without leadership changes. There are great examples of once stalwart companies who have in recent history seen their imbedded strategies for success turned upside down. One only has to look at the historical challenges of General Motors, Chrysler, Ford, IBM, etc. to find classic examples of the need to rethink strategy. In more recent times Linens-and-Things, Blockbuster and others are examples of the lack of an appropriate strategy for self-perpetuation and business success. Another almost daily example is the proliferation of companies being bought by private equity firms and other investors. These companies have been identified as buyout targets because their would-be owners can see that the operating status quo has lead to under performance. The buyout firm's entire objective is to leverage their investment by changing operations to improve profitability and then either sell or go public with a hopefully more profitable entity. Selznick makes these important points about the leader's role to develop appropriate and dynamic strategies.

"A valid strategy will yield growth, profit, or whatever other objectives the managers have established. It can gain extraordinary results for the company whose general level of competence is only average. And conversely, the most inspiring leaders who are locked into an inappropriate strategy will have to exert their full competence and energy merely to keep from losing ground.[6]

"A wise leader faces up to the character of his organization, although he may do so only as a prelude to designing a strategy that will alter it."[7]

"Leadership fails if it permits a retreat to the short run."[8]

The summation of these three statements is that a business leader has to have a valid strategy that fits the character and abilities of the entity;

---

[6] Ibid, this quote is a compilation of several thoughts from the book rather than a specific sentence from any one page.

[7] Ibid, page 70

[8] Ibid, page 81 – As you think about this simple statement, consider how many companies have failed because they have focused on short term earnings.

and it must be focused on the long-term. There is no such thing as a short-term strategy. Whatever needs to be done in the short-term can be expressed as an *action strategy*[9] that supports longer-term leadership strategies.

*L**eaders pay attention to Everyday Activity* – Whenever a new leader takes over an existing organization it essential that they "learn the business" and not take more than 90 days to do it. This means they spend time with every executive leader, and selected key managers and employees to learn what they do and particularly, how they think. The most astute new leader will want to get into and understand the primary business processes. For example, they should learn how many ways revenue (sales) comes into the entity and how it flows through to settlement (payment). They should learn how procurement is accomplished including how people determine what goods and services to buy, when and how much to buy, and how payment is made to suppliers. Essential knowledge also includes how the company controls and manages inventory and physical assets. During this process of digging into process details new leaders will learn how the business works. It may not be necessary to get into nitty-gritty detail, but this learning process should be sufficient to understand the operational priorities that drive the organization. Consider the following statements.

"Within broad limits, we sometimes say, these large corporations "run themselves"; yet we understand that this holds only for routine activity. And the proper tooling of everyday activity is a legitimate, and necessary, preoccupation of management."[10]

"The more limited and defined the task, the more readily can technical criteria prevail in decision-making."[11]

"...we must distinguish problems posed by the task at hand, which do not call for organizational changes, from problems that are set for an organization by the stage of growth in which it finds itself."[12]

"A creative task of leadership is to 'shape the character of the organization', sensitizing it to ways of thinking and responding, so that increased reliability in the execution and elaboration of policy [strategy] will be

---

[9] The concept of layers of performance management is explained later.

[10] Ibid, page 35

[11] Ibid, page 41

[12] Ibid, page 103

achieved according to its spirit as well as its letter."[13]

Without process knowledge leaders will more easily make strategic decisions that cannot be accomplished within the framework of the existing process infrastructure. If they attempt to make changes that will significantly affect process they will likely jeopardize the probability for success; and surely be disappointed by the complexity of instituting the change not to mention that it will take longer than they want. In all likelihood an inappropriate strategy will also disrupt operating performance and, in the worst case, negatively affect customer relationships. Pay particular attention to the last quotation above. It directly addresses the essential need for building a decision-making culture that allows people throughout an organization to "think and respond" in ways that support goals and their related strategies.

With this introductory discussion of leadership and the leader's role we can now consider how to apply these ideas to the management of an enterprise, whether it is business, institutional or government. These thoughts and ideas provide a foundation for initiating meaningful change within an entity that is focused on appropriate decision-making. These introductory ideas and concepts should be reviewed often to reinforce an individual's ambition to adopt, in some way, a more effective decision structure such as is elaborated in the pages that follow.

---

[13] Ibid, page 63

Chapter 2

The Essence of Management

When business leaders are asked to define management, most of them would either have a ready definition, or be able to at least express what they think it is. Our individual descriptions of the management role are, for the most part, based on a combination of our experience, what we read, and the perceptions and views we have gleaned from the respected people that we have worked with during our careers. It may be influenced by the discourses and writings of management gurus like Peter Drucker, Tom Peters, Stephen Covey, Clayton Christensen, or any other well-known business author. No matter how management is defined it should always include something about moving people toward a common goal. Since each individual's personal definition of management will be inclined toward what that person's actual experience has been, it may not apply to different situations. All leaders are heavily influenced by how they have been taught to manage. How effective they are is influenced by their personality and demeanor, and how they interact with and value people as co-workers. Typically, as people gain more experience and have a few successes, along with some failures, they will modify their definition and improve it by making it more people-oriented.

It is important to work with a common definition of management as a basis to help me make the case that there is a need for more effective strategic decision making and process execution. Therefore, I turned my effort to writing a definition that makes sense to me. After considering my own experience, including my mistakes, and applying everything I have seen, done, and learned I propose that the following is a valid definition of management. It captures the complexity, some of the futility and everything about the ambiguity of what it means to successfully manage anything, and particularly a business enterprise.

> *"Management is the Art of creating a Predictable Result by making Valid Assumptions, based on old information, about Random Factors and Future Events, while Depending on People."*

It should be beneficial to elaborate on the key words in this definition to make an attempt to keep us on the same page throughout the balance of the book. If the definition is at the back of your mind as you read and try to understand the proposed solution as it is presented; it will make it easier to see why each element of *Strategic Decision Mastery* is an important aspect of the total concept. The important points to understand about this definition of management, especially as it applies to decision-making, are expanded in the following paragraphs.

Management at the executive level is more of an **art** than a science. This may be a contrary opinion because most business people are taught that empirical evidence will determine consistency in decision-making. If this were true then the same information and circumstances provided to a group of people with similar backgrounds and experience would lead to the same decision a high percentage of the time. But, it does not[14]. Consistent decision-making only occurs for tactical process-level decisions where policies, procedures, business rules and guidelines have been clearly defined, are well known and understood, and have been imbedded in the data structures and process settings of computer systems. When the right infrastructure is in place organizational transactions can be accurately executed by well defined, system-based, decision criteria. Such a structure eliminates the need for most process-level decisions.

This is not so for strategic decisions, which are the focus of our discussion. Strategic decisions are far less precise and truly require thoughtful consideration among alternative solution opportunities. The longer the period of time required to validate decisions the more strategic they are. Finally, the *art of management* not only requires the application of factual information and an understanding of the cause and affect dynamics of an enterprise, it requires the application of judgment to uncertainty. The level of uncertainty increases both with the time-to-resolution and the complexity of the proposed solutions and accelerates as more people, competitors, regulations and other external factors are involved in determining the right approach.

The heart of successful management is the ability to make *valid assumptions about random factors*. Successful managers must be aware of all of the information relevant to a decision; and be able to decide what matters and what does not. Decision-making assumptions are always based

---

14 Easily accessible demonstrations of this idea are the monthly "case studies" that are presented in the *Harvard Business Review*. Every month a business situation is presented to a panel of experienced and capable executives who offer their advice about how to solve the dilemma presented in the case. In most cases, while there is an element of consistency and respect between the participants, their solutions are rarely the same.

on old information even if is as current as possible. It is what has happened as the result of a given set of circumstances. Information does not represent what will happen with an every changing set of circumstances. It is still about the past and there is no certainty that the future will look or behave the same way.

Not long after Alan Greenspan stepped down as chairman of the Federal Reserve an article appeared in the *Wall Street Journal*[15] that articulated how challenging it is to establish good management, or decision making. To quote:

"He [Alan Greenspan] portrays himself as a "Bayesian." Thomas Bayes was an 18th century British Presbyterian minister who had early insights into making decisions when key determinants of the outcome are unknown. A Bayesian makes a decision based not on the most probable outcome but on a range of possible outcomes."

The article goes on to outline that Mr. Greenspan did not work from a recipe for success regarding the management of monetary policy in a free enterprise environment like the United States. In fact, he and his fellow governors *made decisions based on circumstances and applied the right criteria to the situation*. Thus, the logical decision was not always the decision that came out of their meetings. He said,

"At the Fed, he and his closest colleagues describe their work as "epistemology," the science of identifying what is known, what is unknown and what is unknowable".

This is where the element of science does come to bear for successful decision makers. Understanding what is *known, unknown and unknowable* relative to the decision at hand, especially if it is strategic, is the foundation for the *valid assumptions* that form the starting point for every strategic decision that executives will make. In all cases, the best available information in the right quantities is essential; and the more critical the decision the more important it is to have the right information available as early as possible.

Creating a predictable result about future events is obviously burdened with uncertainty, since there is no guarantee about what occurs in

---

[15] "Greenspan's legacy Rests on Results, Not Theories", Wall Street Journal, January 31, 2006, front page

the future. The impact of random factors that drive decisions tends to classify all decision makers, according to the Greenspan article, as either "hedgehogs" or "foxes".[16] Philip Tetlock, who is quoted in the *WSJ* article said,

> "Experts [for our purposes these are executive decision-makers]...who have a single, unified view of the world are more likely to be wrong, and badly wrong. Such "hedgehogs"...are less prone to self-doubt, more likely to dismiss evidence that contradicts their vision and less likely to admit to mistakes. "Foxes"...accept ambiguity and contradiction as inevitable."

Obviously, the executive decision-makers that stand out tend to be "foxes", especially when their performance is measured over time and across a spectrum of varying economic business climates. Tetlock also said, "*We insist on looking for order in random sequences.*" Further, Greenspan admitted in the article that he had no ability to project or forecast events when he was quoted as saying, "*One of the few things an economic forecaster can count on is that a company's inventories can't go below zero.*" That is an example of a certainty. Managing the process of strategic decision-making is about dealing with uncertainty, knowing when trends based on history will be perpetuated, and when to rely on data versus expertise, which is sometimes no more than gut feel. Whenever someone uses their "gut" it really means they are applying experience to their decision-making.

Finally on this point, in the article Mr. Greenspan described his form of decision-making as "*risk management*", which "*amounts to deliberately risking small mistakes to avoid much bigger ones.*" It is my opinion that the differentiating attribute of successful decision-making at the executive level is to know if you are on the verge of a small mistake, or a large mistake. An implied characteristic of successful decision-makers is that they are collaborative. The bigger the risk or the more strategic the potential impact of a decision the more know-how should be brought to bear. And, that means getting the cross-functional view and advice of executive peers before arriving at a final decision. Besides creating the feeling of involvement, collaboration has the added benefits of eliminating second guessing and establishing a pattern for cohesive management among senior executives and their managers.

---

[16] *According to the same WSJ article, "The hedgehog and fox labels come from philosopher Isaiah Berlin, who in turn traced them to ancient Greece."*

Depending on people constitutes another highly unpredictable random factor that impacts the probability for making successful decisions. The level of risk depends on how well roles and responsibilities are defined throughout the organization; and the level of awareness that people at the transaction-process level have about corporate objectives and strategies. The more ambiguous the definition of roles and responsibilities, or the lower the awareness of objectives and strategies, the higher the risk of failure to execute and manage even simple decisions. Ambiguity is born from inconsistency in decision-making. The people factor is really about the culture of the enterprise. It is less about size and more about how enabled people are at every level of the enterprise. Enabled people are more knowledgeable about their role and aware of its impact on others and how they impact the success of the enterprise. It follows that the more enabled people are the higher the probability is for people to make uninterrupted successful strategic and operational decisions.

My recommended definition of management, as well as any other I can imagine, is a highly summarized version of what actually takes place in the day-to-day transactions and activities of any business, institutional or government enterprise. It also does not address the time and effort spent structuring the processes and related information that are essential to successful transaction processing. After all, transactions are where the execution of decisions takes place and from which financial results are the outcome. Process structure and information management are necessary components of management responsibility. Our purpose should be to develop a methodology for decision-making and decision-execution that focuses on _accelerating successful performance through effective strategic decision-making_.

Now that we have a working definition of management let's transition to putting managing into the context of our dominant theme, which is _strategic decision mastery_. It is important to understand that successfully making and executing strategic decisions assumes that reasonably sound business processes are in place. [In many organizations this may be an inaccurate assumption.] A sound business process contains the mechanisms for manipulating process, procedure and data to successfully support established strategies. Without it the difficulty of realizing the projected outcomes of strategic decisions increases geometrically, if not exponentially. The degree of difficulty will depend on the complexity of the business, the response timeline, and the economic conditions relevant to the entity.

Chapter 3

Strategic Decision-Making

The most visible and practical mechanism for performing the management role is decision-making. It happens on an hourly, daily, weekly, monthly, and yearly basis as choices are made between competing solutions and alternatives. The decision-making process is about evaluating the reasonableness and probability of the outcome of alternative choices regarding future events after considering the information that is presented about those choices. Management success is achieved and so-called "good" management occurs when actual business results approximate predicted or planned outcomes. Failure to achieve success and the breadth of the gap between expected and actual results tend to define the degree of mismanagement. Up to a point, the more information that is available to a decision maker the higher the likelihood for a successful outcome for any decision.

Most decisions are highly influenced by the most recent past events, and the information about those events, that created the need for a decision in the first place. Some decisions are critical and therefore strategic to the success of the enterprise. Some decisions are guided by the similarity of current conditions to past circumstances and experiences. Unfortunately, the outcome of past decisions made under comparable circumstances may have resulted in favorable or unfavorable results, but people don't tend to keep track. Therefore, actual relevant circumstances and results are not easy to recall or compare to the current decision. The tendency of the decision-maker will be to replicate their good decisions. However, for the decisions that failed, they will be forced to consider new solutions just to avoid making another decision that leads to an unacceptable result. Most day-to-day decisions should be routine for everyone in the organization, including managers, when the culture of the enterprise is based on effective leadership communication[17] throughout. There are a number of ways to ensure that decision-making at all levels of an organization will occur consistently and in general accord with the goals, strategies, policies and direction provided by executive leaders. Some methods for accomplishing this are discussed later in the book.

---

17 The topic of leadership communication is discussed in a later chapter.

In the traditional hierarchical structure of most organizations it is implied that the higher a manager is in the structure the more difficult and impacting are their decisions. This is not always a valid assumption. A recent edition of the *Harvard Business Review* was entirely devoted to decision-making[18]. The subject was discussed and elaborated from many points-of-view, some of which challenged the institutionalized approach that is in use by most corporations today. Some of the significant points from the articles that are relevant to this discussion are provided below. They are included because they help explain some of the barriers and challenges associated with creating successful strategic decision management within an enterprise. The questions raised by some of the statements are directly addressed and can be resolved by applying the *SDM* methodology that is elaborated in this book. The titles of the articles from the HBR issue are shown in bold italic type followed by the author's names followed by the relevant quote(s).

A Brief History of Decision Making[19] - Leigh Buchanan and Andrew O'Connell
   "...the costs of acquiring information lead executives to make do with only good-enough decisions."

Evidence-Based Management[20] - Jeffrey Pfeffer and Robert I. Sutton
   "The challenge is, quite simply, to ground decisions in the latest and best knowledge of what actually works."

   "...when managers act on better logic and strong evidence, their companies will beat the competition."

   "Like medicine, management is learned through practice and experience. Yet managers (like doctors) can practice their craft more effectively if they relentlessly seek new knowledge and insight ...so they can keep updating their assumptions, skills, and knowledge."

Stop Making Plans; Start Making Decisions[21] - Michael C. Mankins and Richard Steele
   "...strategic planning most often acts as a barrier to good decision making and does little to influence strategy"

---

18 Harvard Business Review – Special Edition, January 2006
19 Ibid, Page 32
20 Ibid, Page 62
21 Ibid, Page 76

"...strategy decisions...are neither constrained by the calendar nor defined by unit boundaries."

Decisions without Blinders[22] - Max H. Bazerman and Dolly Chugh
"Collecting too much information for every decision would waste time and other valuable resources."

Competing on Analytics[23] - Thomas H. Davenport
"At a time when firms in many industries offer similar products and use comparable technologies, business processes are among the few remaining points of differentiation."

"...analytics is central to strategy...and quantitative activity is managed at the enterprise level."

"...this article...lays out...some of the very substantial changes...companies must undergo in order to compete on quantitative turf. ...the transformation requires a significant investment in technology, the accumulation of massive stores of data, and the formulation of company-wide strategies for managing the data."

"But, at least as important, it also requires executives' vocal, unswerving commitment and willingness to change the way employees think, work, and are treated."

The Hidden Traps of Decision Making[24] - John S. Hammond, Ralph L. Keeney, and Howard Raiffa
"The <u>anchoring trap</u> leads us to give disproportionate weight to the first information we receive."

"The <u>status quo trap</u> biases us toward maintaining the current situation – even when better alternatives exist."

"The <u>sunk-cost trap</u> inclines us to perpetuate the mistakes of the past."

---

22 Ibid, Page 88
23 Ibid, Page 98
24 Ibid, Page 118

"The <u>confirming-evidence trap</u> leads us to seek out information supporting an existing predilection and to discount opposing information."

"The <u>framing trap</u> occurs when we misstate a problem, undermining the entire decision-making process."

"The <u>over-confidence trap</u> makes us overestimate the accuracy of forecasts."

"The <u>prudence trap</u> leads us to be over cautious when we make estimates about uncertain events."

"The <u>recall-ability trap</u> prompts us to give undue weight to recent, dramatic events."

"The best way to avoid all the traps is awareness..."

I was pleased to read these articles because I thought the information and insights to be highly relevant to the problem that I expect to address. The *SDM* methodology is a framework of concepts that form a viable solution for eliminating many of these pitfalls to making sound strategic decisions. The application of the *SDM* approach will produce consistently more successful operating results. These thoughts are important to understanding why it so important to take a new and different approach to strategic decision-making. Naturally, they are supportive of the approach taken in this book and, of course, lend credibility because of the reputation of the source publication. Additionally, they represent contemporary insight into some of the dilemmas that regularly confront executive decision-makers. Each executive/manager can interpret the ideas in the context of the existing performance management structure under which they operate; and especially as they consider *SDM* as a new approach to solving some of the issues that confront them on a regular basis.

Much of the insight evident in these quotes makes it relatively easy to conclude that several currently popular methodologies for managing decision-making, and particularly strategic decision-making, lack the ability to tie the primary decision-making processes to the realities of operational challenges and therefore what should be the strategic focus of most organizations. Most management teams are unaware that there is a chasm between how decisions are made and how they should be made to optimize enterprise performance regardless of how it is measured. This *decisional-*

operational gap[25] provides an opportunity to offer a new approach to strategic decision-making, including how to successfully transition to compatible decision execution at the operating level.

In the following sections the methodology for building, applying and utilizing each of the *SDM* components is explained. The chapters are organized to first present concepts and principles that are the foundation of the practical techniques and elements for building a *strategic decision mastery* framework for performance reporting. It should become evident that the consistent application of *SDM* concepts, throughout the management ranks of an enterprise, will drive "same page" operating performance at each of the following five levels of performance management.

1. ***Business objectives*** lead to
2. ***Strategy*** which determines
3. ***Action strategies*** that establish
4. ***Process goals*** with appropriate
5. ***Process measures***.

Each of these layers of performance management and execution are elaborated and illustrated in the following sections, including how *SDM* addresses each level of performance accomplishment.

---

[25] The idea of a *Decisional-Operational Gap,* or DOG, is not a bad way of expressing what could be considered the essence of the organizational issue that can be solved by applying the principles in this book. If it were to catch on I can imagine companies would begin to measure and monitor their "DOG" more closely. The size of the gap could be compared to the length of the leash. It might be logical to include it as a measure of performance and certainly as something that should be considered when evaluating entities for acquisition.

Chapter 4

Elements of Good Decisions

It seems that everyone understands what a "good" decision is. It is the one where the outcome at least meets or exceeds the expectation. Unfortunately, time is required to determine outcomes and in some cases the timeframe is quite long. Operating decisions in business tend to have a shorter _result timeframe_ because any changes brought on by a decision can be measured by the outcome of the next instance of the activity, or by multiple instances in a short period of time. Strategic decisions on the other hand, take longer to demonstrate outcomes. Where the results of operating decisions are typically measured in hours and weeks, strategic decision outcomes are normally measured in months and years. In addition, operating results are completely under the control of the enterprise, while strategic decision results are heavily impacted by some forces and influences which are beyond the direct control of the enterprise. These include forces exerted by the economy, the marketplace, competitors and outside decision-makers. The longer the time from the point of decision-making, the more uncertain is the outcome because the information considered relevant to the decision when it was made will change. This is particularly true of strategic decisions.

An additional problem with business decision-making is that too few decisions are defined in terms of their expected outcome. Therefore, except for the most important and dollar significant decisions, little effort is applied to capture the costs of implementing the decision, or to definitively quantify the expected benefits in terms of dollars. Even for the "big" decisions that may require some version of an ROI or EVA calculation to obtain executive approval; the assumptions behind the cost and benefit numbers are seldom documented sufficiently to measure future outcomes at the same level. In addition, the results of multiple strategic decisions accumulate, but each specific decision is seldom tracked independently. Therefore, without incremental cost and benefit tracking of major initiatives, it is impossible to define unambiguous outcomes for each decision that can be tied back to the original decision assumptions and quantified to determine if any decision was a "good" one. The _Standard Performance Measurement_ component of _SDM_, which is discussed later on, has been designed to resolve this dilemma by applying the concept of _cumulative decision impacts_. It simply prevents one decision from borrowing the costs or benefits from a prior decision by modifying the financial base for each new decision "as if" prior decisions occur as anticipated. This approach is assumed to be effective in the illustrations and examples later in the book. It is easy to understand that the more strategic decisions that are in play the more complex the tracking and reporting. Nevertheless, if it is not accurately done, the decision outcome learning curve for decision makers is significantly compromised.

Assuming that there is an almost universal interest in not only making, but also measuring and validating "good" decisions; every decision-maker should be interested in considering and adopting the fundamentals for making good decisions, which are outlined below. To increase their decision-making success rate, decision-makers should insist on having these elements of decision information before they make strategic decisions. In some cases, where the outcome is critical to success, even tactical short-term decisions should be determined with the same level of thoroughness. Prior to making a strategic decision, every executive decision-maker should require the following.

A clear definition of the circumstances - that require a decision to be made. It is important to fully understand what one person or group of people has discovered that leads them to advocate a change of course that requires a decision. Clear understanding may lead the decision-maker to forego making a decision and change nothing. When all the relevant facts and assumptions arc known, better decisions will be made, and only when they are necessary.

An understanding of all of the reasonable alternatives – from which to choose in making a decision. One of the primary reasons that there are organizational layers in business is because the level of understanding about outcomes varies for those who manage at each level. Subordinate managers seem to intuitively recommend decisions that are either protective of the status quo at their level, or that minimize their organization's need to change. They may not fully understand the cross-functional impact, and even if they do, they will lean to their own self-interest. Executive managers should more fully comprehend decision impacts. Only when they consider all of the reasonable alternatives will they make their best decisions. The more strategic the decision the more exhaustive should be the search for alternatives.

Accurate and comparable information about each alternative – is essential to be able to comprehend the complete costs and benefits of each reasonable choice. The minimum requirement for decision information should include the quantification of all incremental costs for each realistic alternative both in terms of money and resources (people and assets). This should include a clear statement of all of the analytic assumptions and how the relevant costs are calculated and accounted for within the accounting and financial structure of the business. Equally important is the quantification of all incremental benefits of each alternative in terms of financial gains and organizational improvements to the business. The validity of assumptions and how they are quantified also applies to purported benefits. Finally, a statement about the time required to realize the benefits from start to finish. The estimation of the project's duration is particularly important. Executive decision-makers armed with timing information must be able to not only make a decision about what is being proposed, but also put it into the context of other decisions that may have already been made which will be competing for resources and time over the projected timeframe of the proposed solution.

An understanding of the cross-functional impact – of making the decision to be able to determine the proper level of collaboration that will be required between organizations in order to produce a successful outcome. Most strategic decisions will impact multiple organizations even though the decision requirement may be presented by a single functional manager. An explanation of the concept known as _The Strategic Forces of Profit_ is contained later in this book because it explains the potential for cross-functional impacts in more detail.

Insight into the communication plan – for letting affected company employees at all applicable levels know about the decision and its probable impact on them. Strategic decisions require that this be as detailed as is required to ensure that the decision is implemented at the process-level for every affected organization. Anything short of this will jeopardize the delivery of the expected benefits and will increase planned costs. Ideally, changes to policies and procedures resulting from the decision will have been determined in advance of the communication at a level that will answer most of the intuitive questions people are prone to ask.

Having the above information available for the decision-maker does not necessarily require a lengthy amount of time to compile. Some decisions, such as changes in statutory requirements, are thrust upon the enterprise and the decision information is accumulated to logically respond rather than to decide, as there is no option[26]. Other decisions will be supported by readily available data from a sound performance management system, which can be quickly and reliably gathered and presented. When outside information is required the timeline for developing sound decision information will be extended. Nevertheless, once the decision-maker has the decision information in hand, in sufficient detail to satisfy their needs, the decision should be made, communicated and executed as quickly as time and resources will allow. Normally, significant tactical decisions are made every day and will have varying impacts on day-to-day activities. However, strategic decisions should occur with more preparation, deliberation and reflection because of their long-term impact.

This introductory discussion about the importance of decision-making and process execution provides a basis for the remainder of the book. It is intended to set a foundation for understanding *Strategic Decision Mastery* as it is explained in later chapters. Prior to presenting the essentials of *SDM* the next few chapters explain some very important concepts relative to decision-making that further construct a framework for *SDM.* Based on experience, *SDM* is a performance management and decision-making solution that should be easy to understand, straightforward to accept and embrace, uncomplicated to implement, and simple to communicate. As a performance measurement system it can release the untapped synergy that can be realized when decision-making is consistently applied at the process-level in support of strategic achievement and thereby the realization of enterprise objectives and goals. It remains for individuals to decide if they can reach the same conclusions.

---

[26] A good example of this is the Sarbanes-Oxley legislation. It included a timeline that determined when it would be adopted by most publicly held corporations. What it did not include were the specifics about what was required for compliance. Therefore, most companies sought and responded to the advice of consultants who tried to guide the compliance initiatives for their clients without knowing what the final guidelines would be. The result was that too many companies spent too much money establishing compliance.

Chapter 5

Principles of Reliable Decision-Making

Executives and managers often make an assumption that everyone they manage knows what they are talking about when they give instructions and directions. They further assume that their people have been hired because they have a fundamental understanding of organizational and business concepts and not just the function-specific tasks they are hired to perform. I have never been comfortable that either one of these assumptions[27] is correct, particularly the second one. The next four chapters are written in an attempt to "level the playing field" regarding the minimum level of understanding that is essential to applying an effective performance management approach that will lead to successfully executing strategy through decision-making. The concepts outlined in these chapters are essential information if executives are to get everyone rowing in the same direction and ensure that dependable decision-making is reasonably cohesive and an inherent part of the desired operational culture.

Simply stated, decision management can be defined as providing executive/manager-level people with the information they need to make informed choices among competing alternatives, and particularly for the more strategic decisions. While *SDM* can be an effective tool for information delivery, it is still important that management teams have a fundamental understanding of the business principles that are relevant to their strategic decisions. When they do, these principles become a foundation for understanding and deploying a more effective approach to decision management. Like most business leaders, the writers of almost all business books assume that their readers have some basic level of understanding about economics, business concepts, and financial principles so they can comprehend at least the essence of the concepts presented in their books. Too often, this is also an incorrect presumption. Within most organizations, people do not have a consistent or uniform understanding of the basic

---

[27] Some years ago I bought one of those daily calendars with sayings and advice for each day. As I worked my way through the year I came upon several that I liked so as I tore them off and kept them. One of the most applicable to much of the consulting and management work I did in subsequent years is *Wethern's Law of Suspended Judgment*. It is that "_Assumption is the Mother of all Screw-up's_". While I had no idea who Wethern is I admire the simple insight into what I believe is one of the biggest reasons for failure in organizational decision-making.

business concepts that apply to their roles and tasks. As soon as they do, it enhances their understanding and increases their ability to solve business problems. This is particularly true when they set about to learn and apply new concepts, or implement innovative processes.

I have outlined below my perspective about four specific business concepts that can provide a foundation of understanding between decision makers at all levels. Once individuals take the time to get comfortable with these concepts they should be able to make decisions with a reasonable assurance that they have made right choices. Decision teams, meaning the executives and key managers in any enterprise, should be able to absorb the concepts into their organizational culture and develop appropriate decision guidelines as a starting point for creating unity in decision-making across the organization's decision spectrum. You may remember that we earlier alluded to the fact that what an organization is has a big impact on what it can do; and may determine what it must do. As you read about each of these decision-making principles take the time to assess where you believe your organization is relative to each of them regardless of where you fit in the organization. You might ask yourself, on a scale of one to ten, "How able to make decisions are the people in our organization with confidence that each of these principles has been taken into account, especially where the decisions affect the successful execution of strategy?"

The Costs of Strategic Decisions

One of the most overlooked reasons that decisions become strategic is when they significantly impact how the available resources of an enterprise will be deployed over a specified period of time. The longer the period of time a resource is expected to be encumbered the more critical, and therefore strategic, is the decision to utilize that asset for the intended initiative. The resources of all business enterprises are limited during a specific timeframe; and no entity has an unlimited supply of any one resource. Therefore, if an entity's resources are already committed, there will be none available to allot to new desirable initiatives. As the proportion of an enterprise's resources that are committed increases the less opportunity there is to initiate new meaningful projects. Many executives have a problem with this idea because it constrains them. Consequently, such business leaders will regularly over commit limited resources by pushing more initiatives than can be accomplished within the designated timeframe. I have lived in this environment. The inevitable outcome of an over-committed resource environment is that few projects are done well and, even fewer are done on time. Principally, failures occur because of the disruption of people's abilities when their work time is extended and they are forced to stop and start while waiting for constrained resources to be available.[28]

This illustration highlights the four primary resources available to an enterprise and some of the ideas that apply to solving the strategic resource

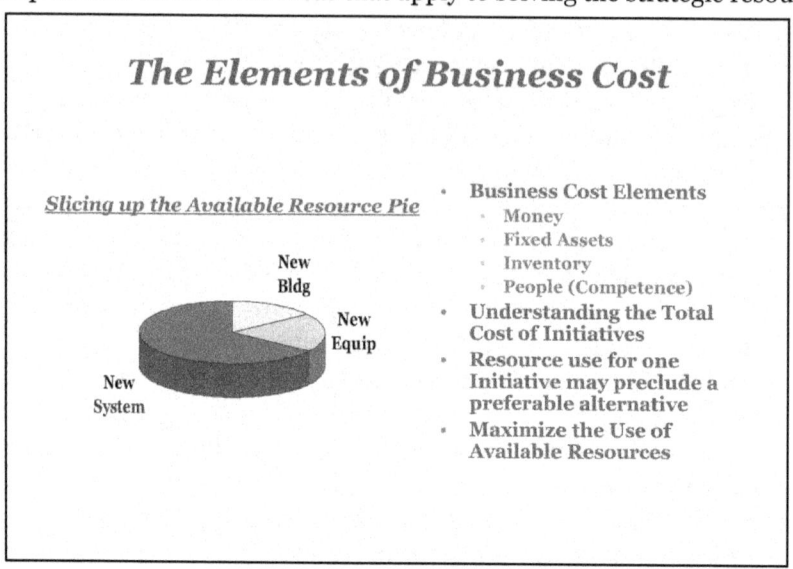

The Elements of Business Cost

Slicing up the Available Resource Pie

New Bldg

New Equip

New System

- Business Cost Elements
  - Money
  - Fixed Assets
  - Inventory
  - People (Competence)
- Understanding the Total Cost of Initiatives
- Resource use for one Initiative may preclude a preferable alternative
- Maximize the Use of Available Resources

allocation issue. The four resources available to any enterprise are *people*, or competence; *money*, or the ability to access funds; *fixed assets*; and *inventory*. Almost all projects and initiatives take some or all of these resource types. It is certain that people [competence] will be required. I use the refining word competence when addressing people as a resource because all people are not equally competent. Further, some tasks, especially when they are more technical and challenging, require a higher level of competence. It is also true that many highly complex tasks that require highly trained and experienced people cannot be accelerated by adding more people to the task. Conversely, less challenging, labor intensive tasks can be completed more quickly by having more people involved.

The money or financial resources required to launch and sustain strategic projects can be significant. The amount of necessary funds is just one dimension of the money resource allocation. Another equally important factor is the length of time the spending will continue and when the funds

---

[28] Another part of the problem is that executives fail to prioritize among initiatives that compete for constrained resources. This subject is covered later.

will be needed along the timeframe. In other words, what will be the cash flow requirements of the project including the in-flow of cash when the profitability benefits of the project begin to be realized? Most companies try to quantify the use of money resources by preparing some version of a return on investment calculation as part of their capital budgeting process. Unfortunately, capital budgets tend to only include larger projects where funding requirements are significant. As a consequence smaller projects, which may have significant strategic impact on resources, are left out of this process. When executives and managers come to understand how their decisions affect resource allocation and utilization, they will become better decision-makers and promote a more complete approach to financial resource utilization.

The fixed asset resource can be a constraint or an advantage depending on the existing capacity and physical location of those assets. The need for additional fixed assets must factor in the time required to add or change fixed assets, which include plant, equipment and land. In the typical definition, an asset is fixed if it cannot be changed or created in less than 12 months. Over the years more and more flexibility has been introduced into this part of the resource pool because there are a number of companies whose only business is to provide on-demand fixed asset capability in a number of variable locations. These companies not only rent or lease buildings and equipment they can provide the people resources to perform necessary work tasks as part of facility and equipment agreements. This type of fixed asset flexibility applies particularly for warehouse and distribution needs, as so-called third party logistics (3PL) firms abound in the United States. Such services allow companies to more quickly launch major initiatives that cannot be accommodated with existing company-owned facilities and equipment.

Finally, inventory as a resource, particularly for manufacturing enterprises, includes production capacity, raw materials, work-in-progress and finished goods. For a distribution enterprise it is the amount of saleable product on hand. For a services enterprise it is the number of people and their capabilities that are available to deploy. Like the other three resources, inventory is either an asset or liability depending on its composition and the relative contribution it makes to the business. The traditional measure of the effectiveness of inventory is how often it turns over. The higher the turnover the higher the profit contribution because each time inventory turns it contributes value, or profit to the business. Consequently, the objective is to increase turnover and any project initiative that requires inventory should be judged by its ability to improve inventory turnover[29]. Naturally the more complex the products, competence or technical specifications of the components of inventory the higher the need to commit them to the right projects. And, by definition, once fixed assets are committed to existing projects they are not available for other initiatives.

As an anecdotal comment, inventory is often the most abused of the resources because most entities lack any emphasis on ensuring that all components of inventory are contributing to the business as they should. Competence as inventory (people) should be considered in the same way as products because there are so many parallels in how they contribute to business success. In a service business, such as consulting, the inventory of talents and capabilities in people is similar to the options and characteristics of products. If you have a green product, but the customer wants red and you don't have it you have the wrong inventory. Likewise, if your customer wants an accountant and you only have engineers you have the wrong inventory capability.

A primary task of executives should be to quantify and understand the resource "cost" for every significant[30] decision that they make. Prior to making a strategic decision, they should have the best estimate of the total resource costs that are likely to be incurred before making any decision that would launch a new initiative, or expand an existing one. There a number of ways executives can develop a feel for the utilization level of current resources and therefore their probable cost if allocated to new initiatives. Ideally, internal measures of resource use can be enhanced to provide more relevant detail for decision making. One idea is to utilize a format similar to a cash flow statement for funds, where beginning and ending values would be defined by each significant resource utilization project. If an executive could know the capacity and utilization level of each of the four primary resources, they would be able to make better decisions, especially when newly proposed initiatives have potentially high resource requirements.

Total project costs should include a reasonably accurate dollar estimate of the amount and value of each of the resources required for any

---

[29] Turnover is the lowest level measure of inventory effectiveness. A higher level measure is so-called turn and earn, which measures the profitability achieved with each turn of the inventory. An even higher level measure applies velocity to account for how many times the turn and earn result is achieved.

[30] The idea of what is significant varies greatly among executives. However, the most astute decision makers will know enough about the state of their enterprise that they will be able to ascertain when a pending decision has the potential to change the course of the company in a material way, particularly in the short term.

significant project or initiative. First, because a decision to use any portion of one or more of the four resources will leave less available for other initiatives that will inevitably come along. Second, because the ultimate challenge is to maximize the use of all resources to accomplish the profit and asset management objectives of the enterprise. There is a legitimate cost-of-capital ingredient to making resource allocation decisions that should be quantified and minimized whenever possible. After a cost is quantified it becomes part of the total requirement for money resources. In a constrained resource situation, whenever substantial new projects come up they will almost always force resource reallocation decisions to be considered. Deciding to introduce a new project may create the resource constraints. When it does there will be two obvious choices to resolve the constraint. First, the constrained resource may be reallocated from existing projects. Or second, an alternative to resource reallocation is to only start the new project when the constrained resource is available, or when more of the needed resource can be acquired. If new resources must be acquired, time will become a more significant factor in making the right decision.[31]

When higher priority initiatives arise and force decisions to reallocate resources, the cost of the suspended project(s) that relinquish the constrained resource will always increase. Resources already exhausted in a suspended project will be lost, or written off, if the project is not reinstated. And, even when a suspended project is reinstated, when resources once again become available, more effort will be required to re-engage the project than if it had continued without interruption. In both cases, the resource cost of suspended projects will negatively impact profitability and should be recognized, not ignored.

One of the greatest fallacies of decision-making is that another initiative (project) can be added and completed with the pool of existing people resources while keeping all other initiatives on course and on time. To take this approach is to assume that current resources are under-employed, or that what they are doing is not as important as the new project. In my opinion, the failure to properly understand the people resource cost of business decisions is the single biggest reason that many initiatives either fail, or flounder from inattention. For example, it is the primary reason that the strategic decision to implement a new computer-based business system

---

[31] A failure of executive decision-makers to acknowledge resource constraints coupled with the pressure to "get things done" has greatly accelerated the growth of the consulting and services industry as such executives clamor for "outside services". Service business now makes up the majority of the profitable revenue for all of the major accounting firms as well as the largest computer providers who have entered the services business.

almost always costs more, takes longer and fails to meet expectations. Too many executive leaders simply assume that the people resource effort required for system changes can be accomplished by the same people without relieving them of at least some of their everyday operational responsibilities. The bottom line is primary decision-makers should "*Know the resource cost of your decisions before you make them.*"

<u>Decision Principle #1</u>: - *Strategic Decision-makers must:*

1. *Understand and quantify the resource impact of their strategic decisions,*
2. *Prioritize resource use among competing alternatives, and*
3. *Adjust the roles and responsibilities of people to allow initiatives to be accomplished.*

Chapter 6

The Dynamics of Resource Allocation

After the business costs have been estimated and considered when making major decisions, it is helpful to have guidelines for understanding how to effectively manage the cost of any new decision relative to the resource requirements of the initiatives that are already underway. The ultimate goal of resource allocation is to maximize the productivity of available resources by setting achievable timelines, utilizing only necessary resources, and supporting only tasks that can be clearly delineated.

The following diagram depicts what I call the _Resource Allocation Triangle_. It contains the three fundamental considerations of resource allocation, namely the amount of time, the quantity of resources and the number of initiatives (tasks). In a resource-balanced condition, the greater

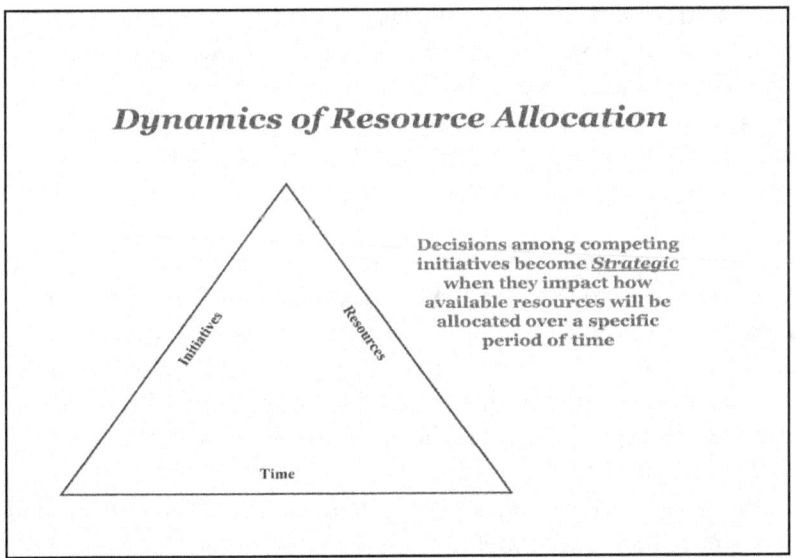

Dynamics of Resource Allocation

Decisions among competing initiatives become _Strategic_ when they impact how available resources will be allocated over a specific period of time

Initiatives

Resources

Time

the value of any of the three factors required by a pending project decision, the more strategic is that decision. All decisions will present themselves to the decision-maker as either resource, time or initiative focused decisions. Invariably one of the three factors will be more critical than the other two and force the decision-maker to recognize and deal with it. There are a number of actions that occur voluntarily and involuntarily in the normal course of business that necessitate resource allocation decisions. One of the most visible and frequent voluntary actions is when executives and managers are considering adding a new strategic initiative. As previously explained, all new strategic initiatives will cost resources at least in terms of money and competence and they will take time. Since decisions are being made all the time and at all levels of an organization, resource allocation is a very active process with an equally dynamic challenge to manage and measure it. Therefore, it is easy to conclude that for all decision-makers *how to manage the dynamics of resource allocation* is an appropriate concept to explore and try to understand. The "how to" is included in this section as a concept, not just a good idea.

Let's consider an example of how to appropriately manage resource allocation. Assume the above triangle represents the current workload of active strategic and major decision initiatives. In this case, the decision choices presented to a management group that is considering launching a new initiative are many. The possible alternatives are outlined below. While all resource decision factors may be involved, one will always take the emphasis because it is the most constrained, or critical resource. For that reason, resource allocation decisions will take their emphasis from one of the following circumstances. These examples assume only one element of resource allocation is changing at a time, which is not always the case. It should also be remembered that resources and projects are the only two flexible elements. The third element (time) is the outcome, which is determined by the number of initiatives and the amount of human and other resources available to employ in their accomplishment.

Resource Decisions present themselves any time there is a change in the number of initiatives; or in the time requirements for completing existing initiatives. These are the most challenging allocation decisions because they affect profitability, the roles and responsibilities of people, and the internal perception about what is most important as prioritized by the leadership team. The following are the possible scenarios that create the need for resource decisions.

- If there is less time and no change to the number of initiatives, more resources will be required.
- If time requirements are the same, but there are more initiatives, then more resources will be required.
- If the time requirements are the same and there are fewer initiatives, then fewer resources are required.
- If the number of initiatives is the same, but more time is allowed for their completion, then fewer resources are required.

- If there is less time and fewer initiatives, then it requires the rebalancing of the remaining initiatives to the resources available during the revised timeframe.
- Likewise, if there are more initiatives and more time allowed, rebalancing of resources to initiatives is required.

As previously discussed, the resources that decision-makers are trying to optimize include people (competence), money, fixed assets and the available inventory of revenue generating products and services. If insufficient attention is paid to the resource reallocation process, especially when major decisions have been made without consideration for their resource consequences, then the likelihood of negative unexpected consequences will go up. The higher the percentage of the entity's total resource pool required to fulfill the expectations of a new strategic decision the greater the risk of a negative impact on business operations and financial performance. This is a reflection of the old dilemma that is caused by putting too many eggs in one basket.

Initiative [project] Decisions are presented any time there is a change in the available resource pool, or in the time expected to complete already scheduled projects and initiatives. In the context of this discussion, an initiative is any project or program that is outside the normal operational and business system process. It can come any time, although in most companies the suite of initiatives is reset on an annual basis during the capital planning, or profit planning (budget) process. Typically, decisions made during a capital planning cycle are incremental to existing decisions and tend to be focused on project timing with a specified priority. The following conditions will require the need to make decisions to either decrease or increase the total number of initiatives.

- When there is less time and the same amount of resource available the number of initiatives must be reduced. An alternative action is to reallocate resources to higher priority initiatives to ensure that they are completed on time. This will decrease the number of projects in the current period, thus extending the completion time for projects that have a lower priority.
- When the same amount of time is allowed and there is an increase in the quantity of resources available, then the leadership team can add initiatives to consume the newly available resources and still meet the time expectations of existing projects.
- When the amount of time does not change, but there are fewer resources available, then managers must reduce the number of

initiatives. Preferably this is done using a prioritization process to postpone the less critical tasks until resources are available.

- Similar to the above, if more time is allowed and the same numbers of resources are available, the number of initiatives can be increased.
- A significant reduction in time or resources will require that the number of open initiatives be reduced to meet the new time and resource constraints. Initiatives and resources must be re-balanced to set realistic time expectations.
- If there is more time and more resources then decision-makers are forced to rebalance the existing initiatives to the new resource pool and timeframe. It may be an opportunity to add initiatives to consume the added time and resources, rather than allow them to be underemployed. An alternative is to eliminate excess resources.

Most collaborative decision making processes in a business enterprise tend to be centered on deciding between alternatives that compete for the same resources. Boards of directors, compensation committees, budget committees and steering committees all tend to be about allocating a limited pool of money, talent and resources to the most promising strategies, people, organizations and system projects. Therefore, these groups by definition are making *initiative decisions*.

Time Decisions can be considered the residue of the resource and initiative decisions because once the resource pool is set and the number of initiatives and projects have been decided and prioritized, the only decisions left are about how much time it will take for their accomplishment. Resource allocation is primarily about managing the number of initiatives and the quantity of resources because time is essentially fixed once all initiatives and their resource requirements have been considered. Nevertheless, time decisions are presented to decision-makers when these scenarios occur.

- The same initiatives with fewer resources will force the decision-maker to allow more time for completion of those initiatives.
- An increase in the number of initiatives, even one more, with the same number of resources will require more time.
- The same amount of resource applied to fewer initiatives should reduce the time to completion.
- More resources applied to fewer initiatives will require less time.
- If there are fewer resources and fewer initiatives it will be necessary to re-balance how the remaining resources are applied to the shorter list of initiatives which will reset the time expectations.

- When there are more resources and more initiatives it will also be necessary to re-balance to determine the time required to complete the tasks on the new initiatives list.

Each of the above decisions assumes that the initiatives have been well defined. If this is not the case, or new information becomes available, it may be possible to redefine initiatives which may adjust time and resource needs. Resource allocation, in most cases, is about how much (number of initiatives) can be accomplished in a specific period of time. Managers are naturally reluctant to add resources, especially people. Therefore, they invariably conclude that what they expect to get done must be done with the existing pool of people resources. Prudent leaders limit their task list to the initiatives that they believe to be essential. New initiatives may be included in a budget wish list and are often submitted as justification for a soft prediction about how much additional human resource will be required to accomplish the tasks on the wish list.

The significance of the resource allocation decisions managers make will depend on their sphere of responsibility and span of control. Typically, the lower the level in the organization the more significant is the manager's perceived need for more "essential" resources during the planning cycle. However, when the total list of essential resources is compiled, senior executives customarily look at the cumulative additional resource request and are appalled at the high totals. Therefore, they find it easy and dutiful to push back and reduce the numbers. Without a valid decision-making culture that incorporates the principles and logic of resource allocation as an essential element of decision-making, managers will achieve less, waste resources, and frustrate the people in their organizations.

<u>Decision Principle #2</u>: *Executives and management decision-makers should embrace the principle of maximizing resource utilization by:*
1. *Only supporting valid initiatives,*
2. *Accurately estimating the resource requirements to accomplish them, and*
3. *Setting achievable timeframes for their achievement.*

Chapter 7

The Strategic Forces of Profit

Profitability and financial success is essential to the growth and vitality of every business enterprise. The incentive for decision-makers to increase profit takes many forms. The certainty that executives and managers can directly affect profitability in a meaningful way, especially in the short-term, is highly unreliable and debatable. There are so many factors that affect the performance of a business enterprise, such as impacts from an unpredictable economy and pressures from competitor's activities. It is difficult to determine whether specific actions taken by decision-makers cause the results that are credited to them, whether good or bad. In an effort to define some profitability parameters for decision-makers, the concept called the *Strategic Forces of Profit* is included in this chapter. It is represented by the chart that follows. This is one of those concepts that too many executives and managers assume

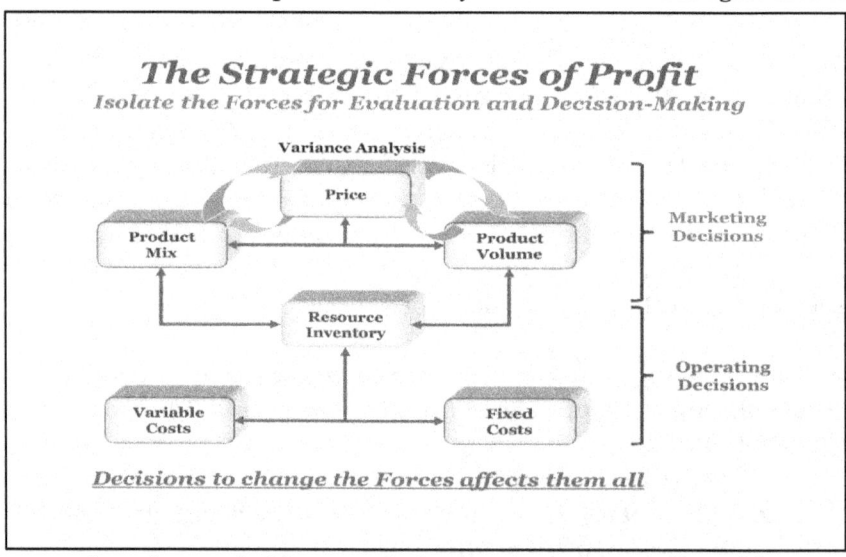

that people understand. Most people do not. An understanding of the dynamics and complexity of profitability is lacking in most decision-makers' repertoire of knowledge and awareness. When it does exist it tends to be one dimensional as in "if sales are up then so is profitability", even though this is not necessarily true. I am convinced that understanding the strategic forces is essential to good decision-making. The forces are important because they encapsulate the primary categories of decision-making that determine the financial performance of an enterprise. While the concepts outlined in the prior two chapters explain how business costs and resource allocation relate to decision-making, this chapter classifies decisions by their logical financial impact, which can be directly linked to accounting categories and financial statements. Understanding this concept helps people understand the *cause and effect* relationship between their decisions and the resulting financial outcomes.

From a financial perspective, decisions can be categorized as either *marketing decisions* or *operating decisions*. Both groups of decisions have an income statement and a balance sheet impact. In a broad sense, marketing decisions relate to the gross profit that is generated by a business enterprise and is the cumulative result of the revenue from sales transactions minus the associated product and service costs. Since gross margin dollars are the only spend-able funds of business, an over concentration and preoccupation with the marketing decision-making process is appropriate. The *resource inventory* block in the middle of this diagram represents the saleable resources of a business, which is normally product inventory for manufacturing and distribution enterprises and people for service enterprises. It is in the middle of the diagram because the quantity of resource inventory is determined by the operating decisions and, therefore, significantly impacts the ability to successfully execute marketing decisions. The operating decisions on the bottom of the diagram determine operating expenses on the income statement and many of the asset and liability values on the balance sheet. The specific definition of the financial elements that tie to each of the categories in the diagram depends on the nature of the enterprise. In an attempt to explain the strategic forces concept more fully I will focus on manufacturing and distribution/retail enterprises, expecting that the reader can adapt the ideas to their specific business situation.

Marketing Decisions directly determine total product/service sales volume, the relative sales volume of competing products (product mix), and pricing or per unit sales. These three outcomes are inseparably connected. For example, any decision to increase price, while intended to increase total sales revenue of specific products, may actually decrease total unit volume and will impact the mix of competing products in the same product line. Major decisions in this category are definitely strategic to the overall profitability of the enterprise in both the short-term and the long-term. There are a number of what can be classified as *hard* marketing decisions including establishing list prices, setting customer discount structures, determining promotional pricing, adding product lines, and selecting sales channels. These are hard decisions because they are critical to financial success and can readily affect customers. Market feedback for hard decisions is typically fast and easily quantifiable. On the other hand, soft marketing decisions are more difficult to measure and have less specific market impacts. Some examples of soft decisions are the design of marketing materials, advertising, packaging and sales training to name a few. Put another way, the primary (hard) market decisions more directly affect the financial rewards that are garnered from the marketplace. The secondary or supportive market decisions (soft) have more to do with how the enterprise is perceived by the customer and how the customer is drawn to contribute to sales revenue.

In an ideal situation, strategic market decisions will be made within the context of a financial and accounting framework that delivers valid decision information. Normally, the outcome of marketing decisions is recorded in the financial statements in the sales and cost of sales accounts. The problem for the decision-maker is that accounting people typically define these accounts from their perspective. Preferably, decision-makers should have input to the structure of the accounting roadmap, or chart-of-accounts, to enable financial reporting to more accurately reflect the results of their operating decisions. Despite a natural reluctance of accountants to break out of what they have been taught, it is possible to change the account structure and retain financial integrity and statutory requirements while supporting improved financial reporting of operating results[32]. Once the leadership team embraces the *strategic forces of profit* as an essential concept for improving their ability to strategically manage an enterprise, potential revisions to the chart of accounts can be easily identified and advisable changes made. It is essential to the education of the decision-maker that enough information about the impact of decisions be gathered within the financial structure of the enterprise to make them accountable for outcomes and more aware of their decision impacts.[33] Accurately measuring decision results against expectations improves decision-making ability, which can then be applied to subsequent decision-making situations. Without it executives will be hard pressed to devote enough attention to the outcome of their marketing decisions to be able to discern what actually happened during and after decision implementation.

---

[32] This is a subject for another time, but it is a vastly overlooked prerogative of operational executives and managers.
[33] A very good tool for accomplishing this is the _Gross Margin Model_ that is illustrated and explained in the Appendix.

Without knowing at least an approximation of the results from making important marketing decisions, such as increasing prices, executive managers will continue to make decisions whose outcome cannot be predicted. For example, the outcome of price decisions depends on a complex set of outcome variables such as market economics, competitive actions, product quality, consumer perception of value, and timing. It is possible to model a proposed price decision based on prior outcomes by making valid assumptions about each of the relevant variables. When this is done, actual results should become more predictable. In addition, the realization of predicted outcomes can be effectively reported in comparison to projected results and allow continuous monitoring to determine whether additional actions should be taken. An additional complexity to delivering reliable measurement of outcomes is that there are multiple actions in play at the same time. Therefore, it is essential to have an appropriate financial and statistical information structure in place so decision-makers will have the tools to effectively document and monitor decision results.[34]

Operating Decisions determine the spending pattern required to support the flow of gross margin dollars into the business predicated on the *marketing decisions*. Where marketing decisions are strategic, the related operating decisions will determine the operational and tactical requirements for supporting the predicted revenue and profit flows. Operating decisions are principally associated with fixed assets, inventory management, inventory control practices, and the acquisition, compensation, and training of people. Some elements of these costs could be defined as institutional because they are determined proportionately by other costs. For example, employment taxes, such as social security and worker's compensation are determined by the relative amount of the salaries and wages paid by the business, but they are a real expense that moves in proportion to other manageable expenses. In the short term, operating decisions directly determine the resource inventory for two of the key business costs namely, fixed assets and people (competence). Operating decisions also have a direct impact on funds and inventory availability. When valid dependencies are established between the revenue, cost and gross margin generating transactions and their associated direct and indirect costs, operating decisions will be more directly aligned with profitability objectives and strategies. The consequence is that a higher

---

[34] Later in this document the concept of *Standard Performance Measurement* will be introduced and explained. It is a tool for understanding, modeling, and projecting decision outcomes based on valid assumptions applied to the financial structure of the enterprise using the principles of the *strategic forces of profit*.

percentage of projected gross margin dollars is retained; and operating income expectations are more likely to be realized.

The importance of knowing the difference between variable and fixed costs is highly relevant for making sound operating decisions and should therefore be part of the financial education of executives and managers. For example, a decision to increase warehouse and distribution capacity to meet an expected increase in sales transactions will create fixed facility costs for the long term, some semi-variable costs associated with warehouse infrastructure and management, and variable costs depending on the actual flow of transactions and the productivity of the order fulfillment process. Consequently, each of these costs should be determined and quantified to make a more informed decision about such a strategic opportunity. It is always advantageous to have a capability for modeling potential results. A valid modeling approach[35] gives the decision-maker the ability to test different assumptions about the interrelationship between revenue transactions and their fulfillment. The outcome should be a reasonably valid projection of the financial impact of operating decisions. Such projected operating costs and expenses can be attached to the gross margin modeling result of marketing decisions to produce pro-forma financial consequences for all major strategic decisions.

Decision Principle #3:

Decision-makers will perform better when they understand the difference between marketing and operating decisions; and that a decision to change any one of the strategic forces of profit will affect them all in a quantifiable way. As a result, because all decisions have a financial consequence, strategic decision making should account for the potential impact on all of the elements of profitability.

---

[35] Building a model for projecting outcomes is a tedious task, however the benefits are significant. The *Standard Performance Measurement* approach can be just such a modeling tool.

Chapter 8

Real-Time Problem Resolution

After the concept of resource allocation is understood, as played out in the context of the inter-connectivity between the strategic forces of profit, the knowledgeable decision-maker will come to understand that most decisions fall into either a "*fix*" or "*prevent*" category. Fix decisions tend to be the operational and tactical day-to-day watching and correcting kinds of activities whose outcome has a short term impact on results. Prevent decisions become apparent when the same types of process problems occur so often that they become symptoms of a business process weakness or breakdown. Some decisions have a fix and a prevent element, meaning that immediate actions must be taken to fix unexpected outcomes, preferably before they become final, but the long-term solution to the problem requires changes to the business process and perhaps improvement in the level of data integrity. For example, a wrong price is a fix problem that is hopefully triggered by system alerts. It can be quickly remedied, perhaps even before billing, by correcting the price in a system price file. On the other hand, if numerous price errors are occurring and they trigger alerts based on low gross margin for example, the problem is likely a prevent problem. Such a condition might suggest a change to the price update programs to identify calculated low gross margins before prices are actually updated. This solution will take more time, but the outcome will be far better than continuing to correct individual price errors.

The illustration that follows demonstrates the effect errors have on business processes, especially if they are not corrected. It is similar to a diagram I have used for years to help people understand the consequence of their process-related decisions. It came about when computer-based systems shifted from batch processing to real-time processing in the late 1970's and early 1980's. It also predates most people's business experience since it occurred before the introduction of personal computers. In the transition to a real-time environment there was no longer an opportunity to stop a bad batch of to-be-processed transactions by pulling a punch card from a nighttime computer run. In a real-time mode, once a person hit the "enter" key things happened and the change was done. In some cases a number of transactions, data files and information streams were affected. The change to real-time processing had a big impact on behaviors and many people found it hard to adapt. The diagram suggests that the impact of uncorrected errors, as they occur during the course of business, can be significant over time. It illustrates the impact of perpetuated errors by comparing the passage of process time to two lines that are drawn one degree apart. When the two lines are only one inch long the distance between them will hardly be

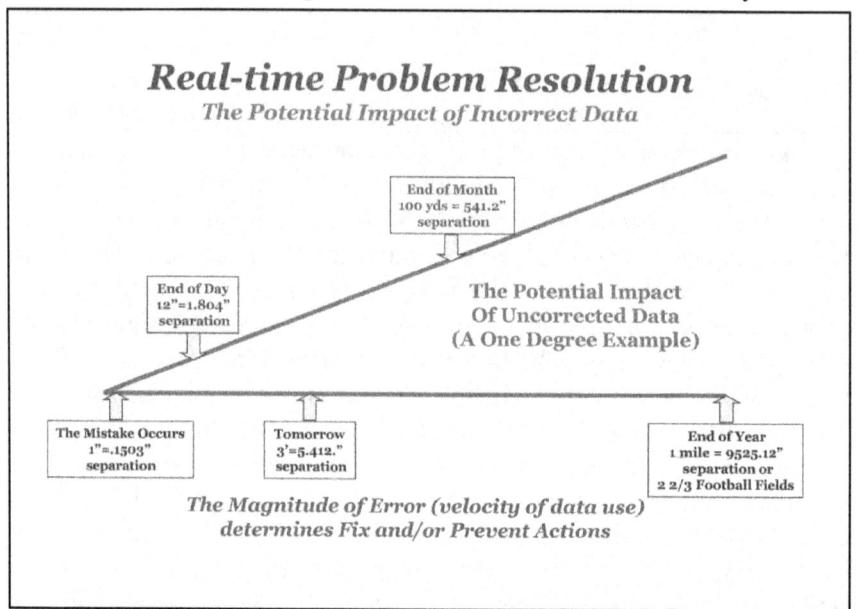

noticeable to the naked eye of the casual observer, and, in fact, they may appear as a single line. To make this analogy applicable to business, assume the straight line on the bottom represents the expected outcome from a business process. The second line, that is one degree off of the straight line, represents a slight error in a transaction outcome. As represented in the diagram, when an error takes place the difference between the resulting transaction's results and the results of an error-free transaction is hardly noticeable. In real-time computer-based business systems minor data and transaction process errors, if not corrected, will impact a number of other transactions in a very short period of time and compound the magnitude of unexpected results. This is particularly true when the data or process error affects high velocity transactions and high use data.

To continue the analogy of two lines one degree apart, the impact of uncorrected errors will exponentially rise, or be compounded, in terms of their negative impact over time[36]. As illustrated in the diagram, the difference between two lines that are one degree apart and 1 inch long is

---

[36] It is always best to correct mistakes as near to when they occur as possible. This is where knowing the difference between fix and prevent situations comes in handy.

hardly discernible. However when the same two lines are one mile long they will be nearly 2 2/3 football fields apart[37]. Similarly, it is illustrative of the fact that uncorrected process errors, if allowed to persist over time, will have a significant impact on results. When there are multiple instances of bad data and poorly conceived process steps throughout an end-to-end process; the predictability and reliability of business results becomes highly suspect. With a higher frequency of errors comes a higher complexity of identifying and implementing the changes that will be necessary to achieve reliable outcomes. The corrective effort will likely involve people from multiple functional organizations and require a comprehensive understanding of the interconnectivity between transactions and data to be able to architect the right remedy. When the frequency of errors gets beyond the ability to make logical corrections across all business systems someone, hopefully a business leader, will call for considering major changes to the business system.[38]

Consider an actual demonstration the one-degree analogy. Assume there is one product with an incorrect cost in inventory. Such a wrong product cost will cause the recording of gross profit in error on the customer transaction, create an incorrect valuation of inventory, and cause gross margin information to flow to the financial statements in error thus misstating profitability, investment and return-on-investment. If the product with the cost error has high usage (velocity) then the incorrect results will occur more frequently and the total impact increases. Such a simple error may cause additional problems when seemingly unrelated decisions are made based on the misinformation created by the error.

One of the great fallacies of business practice is to measure operational and financial results only for monthly, quarterly and annual periods. So-called generally accepted accounting principles and practices are focused on the integrity of financial results over a longer period and the validity of results is defined within fairly broad tolerances. A tolerable "material difference" in financial values between what is reported and what actually occurs grows larger as the total values in the financial statements of the enterprise increase. I suggest that operating managers should not accept financial accounting and reporting as their standard for success, or failure.

---

[37] It brings new meaning to the idea of "straight and narrow" which is a biblical term about adhering to a recommended course.

[38] Business leaders often do not know how bad things are until someone comes along to show them. This is why so-called system consultants and ERP software suppliers are so eager to offer their services. They believe that there was never a business system that could not be improved. So beware of introducing outside forces until you have completed a good self-diagnosis involving your own best people since they are the ones that know your business best. Outside people also "don't know what they don't know", so they should not ignore suggestions from insiders.

They should be provided financial and statistical results, including appropriate variance analysis, in formats that define operational and financial outcomes in terms of the business processes that they manage. Operating managers need daily, if not hourly, results that they can quickly comprehend and understand to be able to provide appropriate response and decisions when anomalies occur. This subject will be given more attention later.

A sound decision support system should have components that allow decision-makers to fix errors quickly and prevent them from reoccurring by adjusting processes and/or correcting faulty data. The decision tasks developed from correct and proper reporting of operational outcomes will almost exclusively focus the decision-maker on data integrity and business processes. Therefore, decision information must be defined at the right level of detail and delivered with the right frequency for process managers to be able to fix data issues and modify business processes early enough to avoid the compounding of errors. In addition, properly quantifying the financial impact of errors provides the details to be able to more easily explain the differences between expected and actual outcomes when financial results are reported after the end of the enterprise accounting cycle.

Finally, when it comes to decision-making related to problem resolution, the education of the decision-makers and their ability to achieve expectations will be increased as they concentrate their efforts on perfecting the business process. Their motivation for taking this approach is enhanced when they understand the importance and dynamics of *Real-Time Problem Resolution*. In the analogy from the book *The Goal*[39] managers must find their "Herbies" and eliminate them. A "Herbie" is a process bottleneck. One of the most effective tools for successful process management is a well-defined and implemented computer-based business system. Nevertheless, when excellent application software is utilized in managing the enterprise's processes; it may underperform or fail because decision-makers are not involved enough in the initial and on-going design and implementation. From my experience, the two most common system implementation errors are the failure by operating managers to review and approve process definitions prior to implementation, and an unwillingness to place emphasis on ensuring that data integrity is assigned to people who are responsible for transaction outcomes. The next chapter provides the guidelines for

---

[39] *The Goal* - Eliyahu M. Goldratt, Second Revised Edition, 1992 by North River Press. In the book, to illustrate the Theory of Constraints the author uses the story of a scout troop on a hike that is constrained in its progress toward the destination by the slowest boy in a single file column. The boy's name is Herbie, thus it is suggested that we all need to find our "Herbies".

determining the effectiveness of a business process. The decision-maker who is seriously involved in managing outcomes should embrace the idea of real-time problem resolution by applying it to their own thinking and insisting that the people in their organization understand it. As they do, people will consistently challenge illogical outcomes and generate new ideas for improving the efficiency and effectiveness of the organization's business processes and the quality of their data. The result will be improved outcomes, higher individual satisfaction with roles and responsibilities, greater confidence in financial outcomes, and a more unified effort throughout the organization.

Decision Principle #4:

Decision-makers need to know, understand and communicate the impact of data and process errors; and then put into practice a mentality where people know the difference between "fix" and "prevent" actions to ensure the early correction of errors in order to produce more predictable results.

Section II
Building Process Capability

Chapter 9

Decision-Makers and Process Improvement

Leadership's Responsibility

In reality, organizational processes tend to be like glaciers. They are broad, deep and move imperceptibly forward. Incremental process change is like the new snow that is added to the deep ice of the process glacier. In this analogy, the ice of the glacier represents the established processes which are made up of a multitude of incremental additions to a base process over a period of years. The entire "process-glacier" has become incredibly large and moves unnoticeably forward in support of sometimes loosely defined organizational goals and purposes. Redirecting a glacier [an enterprise business process] is hard; and building a new one from a new base that is slimmer and faster is even harder. An additional hindrance that gets in the way of the need to improve is the uncomfortable reality that everyone tends to protect the status quo because we are all averse to change.[40] When major process improvement does occur it is most often triggered by the implementation of new software applications. Interestingly today's application software has a heavy emphasis on building effective work flows and, consequently, the process paths that are imbedded in the software as tools for process effectiveness will force the adoptive enterprise to find new ways of working. This is usually a good thing. Only when it is time to blow up the glacier and make wide-ranging alterations to the collective business process are the most important and comprehensive process-level changes made to the benefit of the total enterprise. Without an incentive for major change, organizations will just make incremental tweaks to processes, usually within specific functions rather than more completely across the entity. Whenever there is a comprehensive commitment to initiate enterprise-wide process improvement, for whatever reason, that is the right time to *encourage and strive for process excellence*. This chapter addresses the "resistance to change" issue by suggesting a methodology for process improvement that will work within almost any organization. This approach can be accomplished in a self-directed way with limited outside assistance (consulting) providing there is a high level of executive commitment.

---

[40] Remember Machiavelli's statement:, "There is nothing more difficult to initiate than a new order of things, for it will have the enmity of those who would benefit by the continuation of the status quo, and only lukewarm acceptance from those who would benefit from the change."

One of the most underrated overlooked and frequently ignored roles of decision-makers is their responsibility for the business processes that operate within their sphere of influence. There seems to be an inherent inclination for executives and managers to relegate process definition and management to subordinates and/or consultants. It is as if they feel they have moved beyond what they now consider the mundane nature of day-to-day transaction processing. When in reality that processing is the very key to their ability to succeed, especially in the long-term. New managers, and especially those who are hired from outside an entity, typically inherit a suite of business processes that have their origins in historical company-specific practices whose reasons and purposes may have long since lost their meaning. Nevertheless, except where processes are so badly broken that they demand a true re-engineering effort, outdated processes are generally ignored and remain unmodified when they should be improved to more effectively match the demands of today's business environment. Even when processes are changed, in most cases, only minor modifications [snow on the glacier] are made to accommodate newly identified customer demands or other business needs. Over time this continuous practice of process perpetuation, with only incremental change, tends to create business procedures that are overly complex because they create and accommodate too many exceptions.[41]

Further, the added complexity requires too much human intervention as people monitor transactions from start to finish. Additionally, the hand-offs between independently developed process stages are not clean, there is significant duplication of effort, and the responsibility for outcomes is so difficult to track that no one is accountable. I have yet to review a business process that does not include unnecessary steps. It is a certainty that process indifference is a common occurrence and that process faults exact a bigger blow to profitability than most executives/managers are willing to acknowledge. Despite their reluctance to accept it, organizational leadership has the responsibility for process and part of that role is to be able to identify the symptoms of processes that are in need of improvement. Acknowledging this important leadership role, and then assuming responsibility for it, is the first step in adopting *continuous process improvement*[42] as the organization's best opportunity for establishing competitive advantage.

---

[41] A perfect example is the U.S. Tax Code. Everyone knows it is way too complex, but there are too many people who benefit from not changing it.
[42] This phrase is attached to so many efforts by organizations, and the consultants that tutor them, that it has become somewhat meaningless, except as a marketing tool. Primarily because it is has not become a perpetuated reality within most organizations.

Generally, functional organizations need a strong catalyst to initiate change because the inertia of the status quo is so embedded in the organizational culture. Although it is relatively rare, a strong willed process-oriented manager can identify the need to change, start the process and then see it through to completion. Such an executive/manager is more likely to come from outside the organization or entity because incumbents have such a vested interest in keeping things as they are. A "defending the status quo" mentality can be overridden by the economic weight of consistently poor performance; or by recognition among the leadership team of the need to re-engineer business processes. There must always be a reason or catalyst to initiate meaningful improvement. The change can be initiated by actions that are taken outside an organization such as when competitors and peers make well publicized process changes that have notable positive effects. Suppliers and customers who improve their business processes can force an enterprise to change at the points where they interface with their partners' changes. Finally, changes may be caused by legal edict as occurred with the passage of the Sarbanes-Oxley act. No matter where the reason comes from, forced change is never as effective as logical self-induced improvement. It is best initiated by business leaders who encourage continuous process improvement within an existing well defined and integrated business system.

I have participated in five enterprise-wide business process changes that were all associated with the adoption of new application software. Three of the five were highly successful. One was aborted by the ERP software supplier. And, the last was highly successful at improving productivity and customer-focused effectiveness, but lacked the full transition from legacy systems. From this base of knowledge I recommend that process improvement projects take a clean slate approach in order to produce maximum benefits and ensure longer lasting results. This does not mean completely starting over; it just means everything is subject to change as people are asked to apply their best thinking to the task of improving existing processes.

The objective for process improvement teams should be to minimize or eliminate each of the following conditions that lead to less effective change.

- All efforts to preserve the old methods for the sake of minimizing change,

- Blind acceptance of the so-called 'best practice'[43] processes that are embedded in all new software solutions, especially when adopting such practices will compromise the uniqueness of the enterprise and limit the ability to achieve process excellence, and
- Allowance of functional preferences and sub-processes to dominate the requirements for what should be a new and improved enterprise-wide solution.

Ideally, whenever a major process improvement is undertaken, an open minded and knowledgeable cross-functional group of people should be assembled and given the charter to define the primary business processes from end-to-end including:
- Clearly articulating the essential elements and data requirements for all process steps,
- Defining all points of downstream integration to assure that original process-to-process information drives transactions, and,
- Comprehensively identifying data requirements for transaction processing and information delivery; and then incorporating clearly defined and accountable responsibility for data integrity as an essential element of the total solution.[44]

Preferably the initiative to re-architect an enterprise's business process will be a discovery effort by people within the company who know the business best. It should be organized, managed and completed internally, if at all possible, within clearly defined time limits. As a former consultant and having hired consultants a number of times, I believe it is only advisable to engage outside consultants if the necessary skill sets are not available within the human resource pool of the enterprise. External consultants specialize in the "requirements" definition phase of any process excellence initiative and most bring a respectable approach to the effort. However, they will always be tilted in their thinking to what they know, will tend to favor processes already defined into application software they are familiar with, and, because of self-imposed cost constraints, will lack the time and incentive to truly distinguish

---

[43] More often than not the so-called "best practices" that have been built into today's ERP software solutions are simply common practices. Therefore they take a middle of the road approach to providing functionality and when implemented will deliver a workable solution. However, they seldom deal effectively with exceptional transactions, which often create the best opportunity for competitive advantage and differentiation. Further, the inability to adequately handle exceptions is the greatest cause of additional effort and promotes the creation of patch-work processes and work-arounds.

[44] The importance of data integrity to process accuracy and successful integration is overlooked by most organizations. Since data drives process, especially for transactions which are most essential for successful results, it is addressed in more detail later in the book.

the uniqueness of each enterprise that engages their services. I will concede that whenever consultants are engaged and allowed to take the time to comprehensively learn and understand the leverage points of a client's business they will incorporate *process excellence* concepts into their recommendations. Nothing less should be expected of them and the resulting consulting costs can be managed through effective negotiation. Whether the re-architected business process design is accomplished internally, with outside assistance, or some combination of the two, it should be completed prior to even considering an application software solution[45]. This will minimize fitting the entity's process to the software. The outcome of the investigative stage becomes the workflow blueprint to be used for the selection and evaluation of prospective application software solutions. Do not overlook considering modifications to the existing business system, unless it has been determined that it is totally inadequate. Preferably, the outcomes will also include the data and information flows, suggest metrics as process-level measures and define the total process without functional and organizational bias. After the software solution is determined, the process design will provide the framework for defining, installing, implementing, integrating and structuring the end-to-end business process within the new software. It becomes the plan for process design and construction much the same as a schematic blueprint is the tool for constructing a new building.

Methods of Process Evaluation and Improvement

Since the inception of computer-based business systems people have been challenged to define their business processes with the objective to maximize the advantages of automation. Early efforts leaned toward replicating existing paper-based business practices as the preferred method for configuring and implementing software. This approach facilitated buy-in from the people who would be most affected by the changes. The problem was that it rarely took advantage of all of the technical capabilities and advantages of automated solutions. Replicating an existing sub-process is never a good way to improve the overall process and may lead to excessive customization. In addition to process automation, there have been a number of fads and crazes over the past 30 years that were purported to optimize the effectiveness of process redesign. An early method [circa mid-1970's] was

---

45 Re-architecting an enterprise business process is not all about creating a requirements definition. This approach tends to give undo weight to the steps and processes of the existing business system. Rarely does a requirements definition address the priority of the requirements, nor does it consider how these so-called requirements will fit into thoughtfully defined process steps.

called *value engineering,* which was a method for identifying the non-value-added steps in a process and then eliminating them. The logic was simple. As steps in a process were eliminated the transaction cost went down while achieving the same results thus delivering "value" in the form of higher profitability from more efficient processes. It made sense and it was a precursor to the more popular trend to re-engineer.

In 1993 the book _Reengineering the Corporation_ by Michael Hammer was published and it rejuvenated broad interest in changing business processes. The tag line on the cover of the book said, "*Forget what you know about how business should work—most of it is wrong!*" There are many good ideas in the book. But perhaps the most distinguishing component was that it encouraged a focus on the points of interface with business partners to maximize the advantage that could be gained by the effective electronic interchange of data between trading partners. This concept migrated to become so-called *supply chain collaboration* which resulted in previously unheard of cooperative efforts between trading partners. Collaboration then drove the co-development of business systems to take advantage of consistent transaction information across multi-enterprise transaction processes by utilizing data from the transaction starting point whenever possible. Soon it was assumed that if there is a supply chain that can be maximized through process effectiveness then there must be a *demand chain* as well. More recently the combination of the supply and demand chains has come to be called the *value chain.* Since a supply chain and a demand chain are simply the same thing from a different point-of-view, it stands to reason that optimization for all trading partners can only be achieved when the total value to all partners is addressed in a continuous process improvement approach. Consequently the incidence of collaboration between trading partners has become commonplace.

If I am the customer and I make a change, you the supplier, may need to adapt your process to my change. Some businesses respond to this approach and some do not. Voluntary collaboration is not an option when working with some larger entities. Wal-Mart is perhaps the best example, followed closely by the U.S. military establishment. The potential benefits of doing business with Wal-Mart have allowed them to dominate the enforcement of collaboration and have been responsible for a lot of business system changes among their trading partners. Not all of it has been good and it invariably reduces the profitability of its trading partners in the short-term. However, demands for electronic integration signals the business community to get on board with collaboration, which will force process improvement initiatives to look beyond internal needs. In selected industries, educational institutions, and governmental agencies external requirements may more significantly dominate process requirements in the near future.

The historically recent outburst of collaborative thinking about process continues at an accelerated pace. It has resulted in the development of a number of new technical capabilities in both software and hardware. Technology and process optimization tools should continue to proliferate, while the acceptance of standards for data interchange will determine which of a number of alternative methods will become broadly accepted. Interfaces, file mapping, electronic interchanges are now an essential and growing part of the technology suite of products and capabilities required to engage in process improvement beyond the enterprise. However, so much attention is often paid to the benefits of outward-looking process improvement that too little consideration is given to internal process changes that will more directly benefit the performance of business enterprises that choose to make this a priority. The balance of this section presents a methodology for focusing process improvement efforts on the right things, both internal and external.

Chapter 10

Building Internal Process Capability

The Three Key Questions to Ask

From here forward our focus is on defining the basics for continuous process improvement within the enterprise with two objectives in mind. The first objective is to establish an enterprise specific blueprint for implementing new business system capabilities well before selecting the technology tools or functionality for implementing such changes. The needed functionality may come from external software, or uninstalled capabilities within existing internal software. As mentioned earlier, establishing the blueprint is best accomplished by applying the "best thinking" of knowledgeable people from within the enterprise, in an unconstrained environment. The second objective is to increase the skill capability and concept repertoire of process-responsible managers by educating them about techniques for process evaluation that can be applied in minor and major situations whenever the evidence indicates that process changes are required.

Process improvement, whether enterprise-wide or functionally specific, must start with a logical challenge to existing business practices for every process that is being considered for change. Process evaluation is not as difficult, complicated, nor knowledge intensive as the consulting world would have business leaders believe. Teams of cross-functional people within most organizations are capable of both asking and answering the three fundamental process evaluation questions that are recommended in the following paragraphs. Properly applying the three questions methodology will enable an organization to successfully challenge and re-engineer their most basic and complex processes. When the questions are used in conjunction with the ten principles of process design outlined in the following chapter, then effective process re-design and implementation becomes achievable.

A byproduct of these efforts is that people involved in process re-design become skilled in the knowledge required to promote and execute *continuous process improvement [CPI]*, which should be the ultimate goal. These newly skilled process-oriented people can become the leaders of the continuous improvement mentality for the enterprise and they will make better managers, when given the opportunity, because of their improved view of the total business.

The three-question methodology is so straightforward as to seem intuitive, but for most people it is not. I first started thinking about the concept in 1975 during a two week government executive training seminar that was focused on zero-based budgeting. One of the presenters postulated similar questions as a means for addressing zero-based budgeting. I adapted the ideas to private sector situations and since that time I have used it in a number of consulting engagements and business situations along with many of the other complimentary ideas in this document. The ideas that come from thoroughly answering the three questions always provides more in depth reasoning, which encourages new ways of thinking about process. Using the three questions in sequence will narrow the amount of work required to improve a business process, because each question will eliminate tasks from existing business practices when those tasks do not add value to the primary objective of an integrated process. Effectively applying the questions assumes that the participants have a basic understanding of their existing process, and that it has been documented sufficiently to include all meaningful steps.

Question #1: <u>Does the process,</u> or activity, you are evaluating <u>do any good at all</u>?

This is the question that most likely frustrates the people who set out to accomplish process re-design. First, because they assume that any process they are asked to evaluate has to do some good or they and their peers would not be doing it. Consequently, the process evaluator(s) has a tendency to put too many process steps into the "yes" category during their initial evaluation because they are too narrowly focused on the step and not its place in the bigger process. In reality, very few process steps that are performed within an organization stand alone. Even departmental processes are usually dependent on or precedent to other tasks. Most process steps are part of a bigger process. The process evaluator must ensure that this question is asked of all of the steps in the process and be careful to avoid sub-optimizing their assignment to ensure that they reach valid conclusions. <u>It is important not to consider jobs as process steps</u>, although in many cases process steps are grouped into tasks that become jobs and as a result they represent positions in an organization. If the evaluator begins to think of jobs rather than process steps they introduce people, usually by the names that are associated with those jobs, and that can compromise the integrity of the outcome of the response to question #1. When jobs are confused for process steps the objectivity of process evaluation becomes biased by the natural tendency to protect people and therefore the process steps that they perform. That cannot be part of legitimate process evaluation[46]. The intent of process re-design is not to determine or even consider how jobs will be structured to accomplish the new process. By eliminating any consideration or reference to jobs and people, getting an honest response to the first question is simplified although the deliberations may still be complex. Some complexity in answering the question is introduced because the desired outcomes of the yet undefined new, and hopefully better, process may not be obvious as individuals are asked to respond to this question. People only have knowledge of current outcomes, which may not be relevant or even necessary in a new process. In other words, individuals assume that they will be performing a new process with the same purpose and with the same tools that are in place today. This is rarely the case.

For purposes of making it clear about how to respond to the first question we will use the simple illustration shown in the following diagram. The diagram illustrates all of the steps required to fill a customer order from a distribution center inventory. The inventory is purchased in this example, but a similar stream of steps would be in place if the product was being manufactured. There are three primary groups of steps; one for purchasing the product, one for receiving and managing the inventory of the product, and one for fulfilling customer orders. The steps are chronologically sequenced in the order that distribution center transactions typically occur. That is, product is purchased, then received, placed into inventory, and finally consumed by filling customer orders. This illustration is representative of a typical process found in a paper-based computer system from the 1990's and earlier. Assume that the process-evaluators are considering the adoption of an automated warehouse management system (WMS). Therefore, they must use this diagram to review each of the existing process steps and answer the first question in the context of what might be, not just what is. Some process steps may be outside the capabilities of a typical WMS system, however, they should still be considered because of integration issues. In some cases, the diagram may be too summarized and successful evaluation will require that the sub-steps in some of the steps shown should be identified and diagrammed separately. For example, there are many steps that are performed by the buyers between when a system generates a recommended purchase order until an actual purchase order is

---

[46] Don't worry about jobs and people as there is always a place for qualified people in every organization. When the new process is finalized then qualified people are assigned to the newly defined process steps based on the required abilities.

created. With even a limited understanding of the capabilities of typical WMS software applications the process evaluators looking at the diagram should be able to identify that the following steps in the hypothetical current process *do not do any good at all.*

- Sort Orders – This manual step is required in the current process to group orders for different pick zones and to combine orders for the same customers. It can be performed electronically and more effectively by WMS software.

- Select Carton Size – This manual step in the existing process can be more accurately performed by the cartonization routines in WMS software.

- Deliver Pick Slips – A printed pick ticket is not required in a WMS

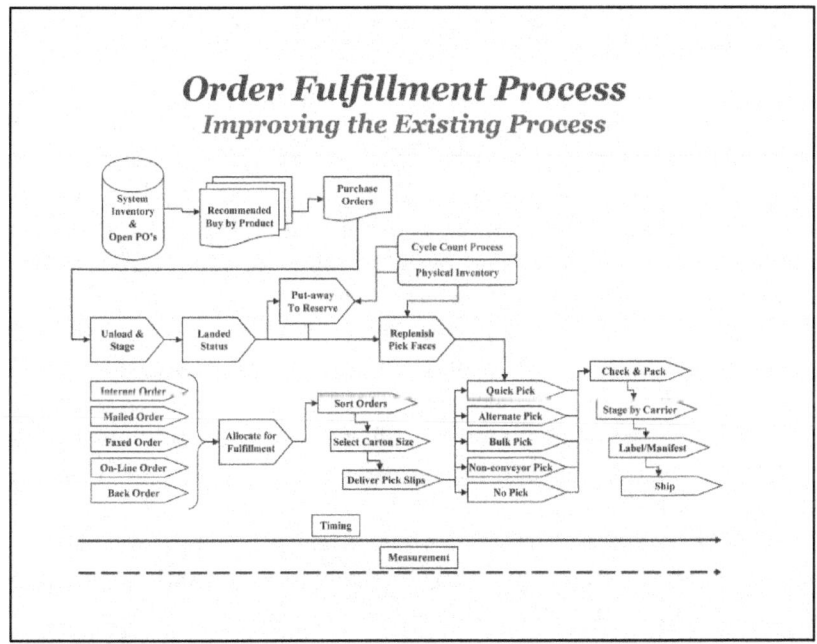

Order Fulfillment Process
Improving the Existing Process

system that utilizes radio frequency (RF) devices for picking. A handheld device with a screen will direct the order picking process and record the accuracy of the pick. Thus the printing, sorting and handling of the pick ticket is eliminated.

- Check and Pack – In WMS software the products picked and their quantities are recorded electronically and can eliminate the checking process. Orders will still require packing but other methods for validating order picking accuracy such as weight verification can be employed.

- Cycle Count Process – Because all activities from receiving to shipping are recorded electronically in a WMS environment the need for cycle counts is minimized and can be eliminated except for system identified discrepancies, which can launch directed cycle counts as needed.

- Physical Inventory – This has typically been an annual process to validate inventory accuracy for financial audit purposes. In an automated system it can be eliminated by demonstrating inventory accuracy throughout the day-to-day order fulfillment process and by utilizing system-directed cycle counts from step #5 above.

While there may be other elements of some process steps that can be addressed, these are the most obvious non-value added steps that can be eliminated by implementing a WMS solution.

It should be remembered that the purpose of every process step that does not survive the first question must be addressed in the design of the new process. The step may be simply eliminated as "not required", or redefined into the new process. The point of our example is to demonstrate that what may seem like an efficient process based on older computer capabilities will be different and can be made to be more effective utilizing state-of-the-art automation tools. Just 25 years ago very little WMS software capability even existed. Until the mid-1980's most order fulfillment processes were entirely paper-based. They relied on people to manually record completed results and actions in a computer system after all of the steps in the process were completed. Even the most effective employees made mistakes in this environment, which required additional steps to confirm order and inventory accuracy. The negative effect of incorrect order fulfillment transactions, especially in a paper-based system, is too great for any company to overlook and is a prime opportunity for process improvement.

If during process evaluation a business process or process step can somehow justify a "yes" answer to the first question, it must be further challenged by asking the second question.

Question #2: If a process step does some good, <u>is the good worth what it costs?</u>

Assuming the process analyst understands the basics of financial cost/benefit analysis, they will know that a process is rarely justified if its cost exceeds its benefit because it will decrease profitability and/or reduce the effectiveness and efficiency of people.[47] In an attempt to answer question #2, it will become clear to the process evaluator that an understanding of all three questions is helpful to be able to complete an effective evaluation of any process or business activity. Otherwise, those processes that justify an affirmative answer to the first question may have to be revisited if part of the information acquired to reach an answer to question #1 does not include process costs and benefits. Process evaluation teams will need financial analyst support to ensure a level of consistency, accuracy and reliability for the values they use to answer questions #2 and #3. To keep the analysis of competing alternatives consistent, the reviewers should use a standard format for gathering and presenting the financial and statistical data that is relevant for decision-making.

One of the difficulties that arise in attempting to answer question #2 is that the total costs of the process may not be known. Nevertheless, every effort should be made to identify, quantify and accumulate process costs, especially when the process involves multiple departments and includes several direct and indirect costs. Process cost identification is further complicated if there are departmentally allocated costs that are charged to the group responsible for the process. Unless such allocated costs are directly affected by the process they should not be included in the analysis. There are a number of cost concepts relevant to decision-making during business process redesign that should be considered in every cost/benefit analysis. We don't intend to make accountants out of process analysts, but they need to have a basic understanding of some basic cost types and which ones might be relevant to their analysis as they attempt to reach an answer to question #2.

The basic cost types that may be applicable include:

Direct Costs	*Indirect Costs*
Sunk Costs	*Average Costs*
Variable Costs	*Standard Costs*

---

[47] Typically, <u>efficiency</u> is defined as doing the job right; and <u>effectiveness</u> is defined as doing the right job right.

Allocated Costs　　　　　*Semi-Variable Costs*
Fixed Costs

A further complication to evaluating the cost of a process is that there may be other processes performed by the same group of people in the same facilities under the same management structure. Therefore, the process evaluator must be cautious and avoid double counting, or minimizing by implication, the true incremental costs of a process. The costs attributed to a process should be able to be realized as savings if the replacement process is more effective. That is why incremental or marginal cost evaluation is so important in determining the answer to this question. For those business entities that have a validated *Activity Based Costing (ABC)* system it will be easier to determine process costs at any level. By definition ABC costing has already dealt with the issues related to process costing at the activity level and has properly applied the relevant costs in a consistent way to enable decision-makers to rely on comparative outcomes. Nevertheless, as new processes are defined, ABC costing will have to be redefined to match the new process steps.

The "worth" part of the evaluation required to answer this question assumes that realized benefits will be in excess of the costs associated with the process. In some cases defining the worth or value of a process outcome is as difficult as defining its costs. For example, if we go back to the order fulfillment process diagram and focus on eliminating the *order checking* process it would be easy to determine the cost. It might be as simple as the incremental labor cost of the work divided by the number of orders checked to arrive at a checking cost per order. However, determining whether order checking is worth what it costs requires that we decide why we are doing it and therefore the value of the outcome. If we assume order checking is done to eliminate customer returns, order rebilling errors and credit memos, then it becomes obvious that there is not a direct connection between the activity and the expected benefit. By implication we would need to know the business cost impact of customer returns, rebilling and credit memos if orders are not checked. It is also a fact that the cost of the order checking process is incurred in one period and the benefits normally occur in subsequent periods making it difficult to directly relate costs and benefits. Despite these hurdles to quantifying benefits to determine process worth; the effort should be made, the procedures and analytical assumptions well documented, and appropriate measures identified.

There is no question that there is a lot of detailed work necessary to determine a valid answer to question #2. Where adequate cost and benefit structure is already in place it will be simpler even though the presentation and analysis will probably require new thinking. If an organization is not accustomed to accurately measuring costs and benefits as part of their decision-making process this step will take more time. However, the side benefit for the effort will be the development of a methodology that can be used in subsequent analyses. A "yes" answer to this question not only qualifies a process for continuation; it quantifies its costs and benefits both literally and relative to other processes. This information will be valuable when it comes time to determine the right priority among competing processes, especially relative to resource allocation.

Once the effort to answer the second question is completed, and assuming again that the answer is "Yes", the process is worth what it costs", then the third and final question for qualifying a process as essential to the enterprise is:

Question #3: If the process is somehow worth what it costs, <u>is it possible to have</u>:

1. *<u>The same benefits for less cost</u>, or*
2. *<u>Greater benefits for the same cost</u>, or*
3. *<u>Some combination of both</u>?*

Answering this question is about determining the efficiency level of the process; and then its effectiveness relative to the other processes on which it is dependent or contributory. The deeper the evaluator's analysis gets into process justification by applying the three questions the more difficult it becomes because of the complexity of process interactions, crossover integration and the impact of transactions that are not completed successfully. At the heart of the ability to determine the right answer to question #3 is an understanding of the level of productivity [effectiveness and efficiency] that is currently being achieved by the process that is being evaluated. If steps in a process can be eliminated while still producing the same outcome either the benefits will increase, the costs will decrease, or both. Therefore, that process qualifies under one or both of the first two conditions in this question. It may be that both the benefit and the cost are favorably changed to allow the evaluator to arrive at a positive response to the question by validating the third criteria. The information about the factors that were considered in answering the second question should be sufficient to determine the right answer to the third question. The detailed elements of cost and benefit should have been identified in sufficient detail to relate them to the process steps. Answering question #3 is where the evaluators get involved in breaking the process down into its detailed steps in an attempt to determine if there are any non-value-added activities within the process that can be eliminated. If there are, then it is likely that the process can qualify.

By again relating our analysis to the order fulfillment process diagram, we discover that there are other factors that should be considered in determining the answer to this question. Unfortunately, process diagrams do not divulge the qualifications of the people that are essential to produce successful results. Nevertheless, since skills and qualifications are specific to most processes we should ask enough questions to determine the right level of ability and expertise that are essential to maximize productivity. Some the questions we might ask are:

- Is the level of education or experience required to successfully complete each process task available and applied most of the time?
- Is the level of training sufficient and provided in a timely manner for the people performing the tasks? What is the experience learning curve for successful task completion?
- Is the movement and placement of products and supplies optimized to minimize unnecessary people motion to expeditiously complete each task?
- Do people understand the reason for performing their task? Do they know they are part of a total process where everyone is expected to produce an expected outcome in a specific time?
- Is there know-how about the process and its tasks that is not available within the organization?

Asking these questions may initiate further inquiry specific to each entity.

An affirmative answer to question #3 qualifies the process. The evaluation then moves into the realm of process redesign. Re-design cannot be successfully accomplished without considering alternatives to the way things are currently done. All of the reasonable alternatives for improving a qualifying process should be identified and their costs and benefits estimated. This information will allow the evaluator to recommend a solution, at least tentatively. If benefits are assumed by implication it is not likely to be sufficient. Implied results for each alternative are not the same as valid results, but valid results cannot be determined until the process is actually in place. Therefore, the implied results, particularly the benefits, should be documented with the assumptions that are used to determine them. In fact, including implied results that are undocumented is a deterrent to successful process redesign, because it nullifies the ability to measure actual outcomes after the process is operative.

The foundation of continuous process improvement requires an emphasis on regularly reviewing and testing processes to develop better alternatives. The three key questions methodology is an excellent tool for accomplishing this task. This framework for evaluating processes and process steps, defining costs and benefits, and creating alternatives should be documented and applied throughout the organization. As the methodology is proliferated everyone becomes more aware of the importance of *continuous process improvement* and how it contributes to the success of the enterprise. This awareness can create a culture that understands process, appreciates roles and responsibilities, and values process outcomes. A process-focused culture strives to create process improvements as the primary tool for gaining and perpetuating competitive advantage.

With the three key questions as a foundation, we can now move to the next chapter which presents ten principles for process improvement. After you understand the ten principles and logically group them with the three key questions, they will blend together to become a sound approach for a *continuous process improvement* effort; and encourage strategic decision-making that is compatible with process execution at all levels. The *Three Key Questions* and the *Ten Principles* presented in the next chapter are concepts that totally promote and support the objective to achieve *Strategic Decision Mastery*.

Chapter 11

Guidelines for Process Improvement

In the fall of 1986 I was to make a presentation at one of the breakout sessions for an industry software user's group. I had presented many times before and always utilized some of the tools for process development and management that I had learned and used in the past. At the time, the company where I was the divisional president was using the featured application software across over 100 locations with five different product lines. It was the second company where I had successfully utilized the software. For nearly 9 years I had been involved with this software user's group and had a significant influence in much of the functionality of the software as it developed over those years. On this occasion, the audience would include established customers and several new and prospective customers who had not yet selected or implemented the software solution. The software was an HP-based comprehensive system including order-to-cash and purchase-to-pay functionality, as well as general ledger and inventory management capability. In today's world the software would be called an enterprise requirements planning (ERP), solution built for the wholesale distribution industry. For its time it included very robust functionality that had been developed over about 10 years and was utilized by a number of industry significant companies, particularly in office products, paper and industrial distribution sectors.

On the evening before the presentation, I still had not been able to crystallize my ideas into what I wanted to be a meaningful session for the people attending. I wanted them to be able to take away some ideas and approaches for doing business that would help them immediately if they chose to follow my suggestions. I was especially mindful of the new and prospective customers because I knew that they would be facing the challenging task of implementing new software. This would mean changing their business processes and attempting to gain acceptance from employees who inherently resist change, especially the magnitude of change required to implement new computer-based systems. As I pondered about what my approach should be, it came to me what I wanted to do and I literally scrawled out on the back of an envelope what I called "*The Ten Laws of Distribution*". During the next few hours I created the presentation using *Harvard Graphics* software which was the forerunner to *MS Office PowerPoint*. I had a number of real experiences to illustrate each point and the presentation went very well. I was surprised at the number of requests I had for both copies of the presentation and for assistance to apply the concepts from two of the new customers.

Over time, after my division was sold in a leveraged buyout and I transitioned into consulting, I used these ten laws effectively with both installed and new customers of this same software solution. It was an effective means to improve their implementation outcomes and enhance their utilization of the core functionality of the solution after they had already implemented it. As I recognized that the principles were generally applicable to all types of business entities, I changed the name to *Ten Principles of Process Improvement*. The ten principles, used in conjunction with the *Three Key Questions* discussed in the previous chapter, formed the basis for planning business process improvements in a number of companies over the next eight years. After the second consulting period of my career I served as an executive with operating and technology responsibilities in two separate publicly held companies where the *key questions and ten principles* became the basis for several process improvement initiatives. I believe these concepts are successful because people in all levels of the organization can understand them.

Ideally any organization or business entity that is embarking on an effort to evaluate existing business practices and processes, with an apparent intention to improve them, would have an upfront meeting with the project team to define the approach. The ten principles list that follows can form an effective starting point for everything a process improvement team might set out to accomplish. It would be hard not to improve existing business practices when a team approaches the task by attempting to satisfy the ten principles while also developing appropriate answers to the three key questions. The *ten principles* are hard to argue with since they are logical and intuitive when considered individually. Taken together and applied in a cascading method while recognizing their interdependency will lead to sound and defensible results. The principles are presented in their logical and rational sequence in the following paragraphs including a brief explanation of each.[48] The level of detail in the explanations is limited and the illustrations simplified to be able to set the ideas in place, not to provide exhaustive "how-

---

[48] For those intent on establishing continuous process improvement, I suggest that the list be created as a large poster, adapted to reference your company, and placed in full view on the wall. It will promote the idea that all business processes should have high level objectives (principles) as the basis for their existence; and as a guide to process development and continuous improvement. It could also serve as a constant reminder to people that they have an obligation to challenge illogical practices.

to" details. Such a presentation is a work for another day and the outcome

---

Ten Principles of Process Improvement

1. Procure [Build or Buy] only products that will sell
2. Minimize the time between procurement and selling
3. Procure at the lowest possible cost
4. Sell at the highest possible price
5. Minimize the time and effort required to execute each task
6. Minimize the number of people required to perform a task
7. Do not perform a task twice for the same transaction
8. Eliminate making the same decision over again
9. Perform the task at the lowest level of decision-making
10. Only manage the exceptions

Avoid the tendency to oversimplify and underestimate!

---

will vary depending on the nature of the core business functions of each entity. The principles are guidelines that can be adapted to the individuality of each organization.

As you read and think about these principles and concepts and where they might apply in your organization's situation you will see how they build on each other. As you work down the list it will almost force you to rethink some of your earlier ideas about how any single concept might be applied to your business' circumstances. The process improvement team[49] will go through an iterative process between standalone ideas and integrated ideas until eventually they all come together to create a *blueprint* for the task at hand, whether large or small. Good processes always take advantage of the data and work from the prior steps in a process to avoid redundancy and to eliminate non-value-added process steps. As you consider each principle make some notes about what comes to mind about your own situation where you know that the principle is being violated, or compromised. [Note: Throughout this discussion the word "Product" is intended to include both

---

[49] It is not necessary to have a formal process improvement team to benefit from applying the *ten principles* to a business opportunity. As an enterprise builds a continuous process improvement culture both individuals and managers will intuitively begin to ask the *three key questions* and apply the *ten principles* to most of what they do. When cross-functional opportunities arise it may require a more formalized team to build tightly integrated processes and achieve optimal results.

tangible products that are manufactured or purchased and intangible services whether provided or contracted.]

Principle #1 –Design and procure only products that will sell!

In a perfect world every product and service that an enterprise decides to include in their product offering would be focused on what customers want. When that happens the entity only produces, purchases or staffs to deliver to customers the products they want, in the quantities they want and when they want them. The customers always buy. Everyone is happy, inventory turnover is high, profit is realized according to plan and the entity continues to produce and sell as long as the customer continues to buy, which they will do since they are getting what they want. In the real world this is not the way it happens. Customers don't always buy what companies sell because they change their minds, competitors create alternative products, and businesses make mistakes during the manufacturing, purchasing and delivery processes that drive customers to other sources. Driving an organization toward the achievement of this principle has many different aspects that affect process improvement success. Remember the objective is to build processes that promote the achievement of the principle; therefore all of the considerations outlined below should be addressed at the process level.

One of the most important elements to succeeding with this principle is the ability to accurately project what customers will buy and consume. Consequently, the process starts with product design. How entities design their products and services, including how they will be delivered to the customer, has a big impact on achieving a high degree of success with this principle. Design determines the product's ability to meet customer expectations and ideally it should be based on an identified customer need or want. New designs may be improvements or variations of existing products, or completely revolutionary in purpose and function. Forecasting the demand for new products that are similar to existing ones is somewhat easier because there is a demand history to guide the projections. When a product is entirely new and/or based on the designer's perceived interpretation or expectation of the customer's demand, then forecasting is much more difficult. New product success requires a way to quickly validate actual demand versus expectations to be able to adjust procurement to ensure balanced investment decisions. If demand exceeds projections; then too little resource will have been invested in product procurement and inventory. If the demand is significantly less than expected, too many assets will have been invested in the product. Whenever projections are not realized, whether high

71

or low, adjusting demand fulfillment resources will take time[50]. Thus, it is extremely important to have early and accurate feedback about customer acceptance at the point of consumption. A big caution is to not assume that the amount of product delivered to the selling pipeline is demand. Only product consumed by the end user is true demand and that is sometimes difficult to measure.

Because results seldom match expectations, executives and managers should want to know why. Decision-makers need to have enough information to identify why some products and services succeed and some don't. They need to know when demand is accelerating and when it is declining to make the right planning decisions and avoid the costs associated with being wrong. In some industries, the planning cycle is long enough to allow adjustments for delivering products and services resulting in a higher degree of certainty. In other industries the planning cycle is so short as to produce a high degree of variance in actual results. Business entities must have processes in place that respond quickly to both increases and decreases in demand to be able to minimize negative operational and financial results. This can only be accomplished with an effective decision information structure that is based on accurate data and delivered in a timely manner to the people who can identify cause and affect and institute appropriate change. Satisfying these needs requires a well-conceived and valid process that is comprehensive enough to consider all of the logical factors affecting demand.

A number of technical software solutions that are focused on forecasting customer demand are available to address smoothing the flow of products while minimizing inventory, lowering production costs and eliminating out-of-stock situations. The process improvement team, as they evaluate the business processes within their entity that are directed toward the implementation of this principle, must understand enough about prior failures and successes to focus on the right issues. Their challenge is to identify process correction opportunities that will improve the predictability of the flow of the right products to customers when they want them. This will require defining the data and process requirements for all of the organizations within the entity that are striving to achieve excellence by adhering to Principle #1.

---

[50] In the distribution industry it was often said that, "most of our problems can be solved in one turn of the inventory". This implied that once the wrong inventory was sold the funds would be available to procure the right products. While technically true, if you only owned buggy whips when the automobile came along, one turn of the inventory could be a very long time.

72

Principle #2 – Minimize the time between procurement and selling!

This principle is primarily about optimizing the allocation of limited resources among competing alternatives, which was explained previously. It is the principle behind the concept of Just-in-Time (JIT) inventory management systems. In some manufacturing environments it has been the most important driver for reducing product total costs and accelerating productivity improvements. The best illustration of its importance and contribution to success that I experienced was in the apparel industry. The company I worked for was able to acquire and cut fabric, ship it off shore for sewing, and receive it back as finished inventory in an incredibly short 32 days. The best our competitors could do was more than double our production cycle time. At the time, this cycle time for building and delivering product was unequaled in the apparel industry. Our success was based on principle #2, which began long before I arrived at the company and was the absolute passion of the CEO and his executive team. Our ultimate goal was to reduce the cycle time to 28 days, which we achieved occasionally but not consistently. While it was not the only factor in the growing success of the business, it was a significant contributor, especially for an apparel company without the market leverage of a top brand.

The obvious benefits of shorter cycle times, particularly in manufacturing and wholesale distribution enterprises are:
- Lower raw material inventory
- Lower finished goods inventory
- Reduced inventory carrying costs including interest, taxes and physical space
- Increased ability to adapt to changes in customer demand by product and product assortment
- Reduced manpower costs associated with handling less inventory
- Reduced costs for inventory obsolescence, etc...

The less time that fixed assets, inventory and people are required to complete a transaction, or process, the higher the financial benefit to the enterprise. Profit leverage is largely about increasing asset [plant, equipment, inventory and people] turnover, or utilization, because as soon as the task is completed the resources that it requires become available for another task. Asset turnover is the concept that makes the connection between the dollar value of assets and the time they are employed in productive tasks. It is the essence of productivity and efficiency. The more productive business assets become, through better process design and execution, the more likely is an enterprise able to establish process as a competitive advantage. And remember that a good process is the most difficult thing for competitors to replicate, thereby making it a competitive advantage.

It is easy to understand why this principle is pervasive in almost every entity, whether manufacturing, wholesale distribution, retailing, or services. It is nearly impossible to avoid realizing that this principle applies to the core business processes and therefore, should be the testing ground for continuous process evaluation. It is highly impacted by the reality of customer expectations, which will vary greatly between businesses types. Despite many who emphasize customer service as the preeminent focus of business, it is a fact is that there is such a thing as over-serving customers. For example, if product cycle time is reduced beyond customer expectations, the result is that the entity will hold inventory (products or services) in a finished form instead of a raw material form. Furthermore, idle inventories of finished goods and people abilities (as a service inventory) are more expensive than raw materials and will drive up costs. The ability to collaborate with customers, especially regarding the need to accurately forecast demand for products and services, is essential to optimize the benefits from the application of this principle. As customer-supplier collaboration continues to increase and trading partner's business systems become more integrated the ability to exploit this principle goes up. Collaboration partners are more readily able to adapt to changes in supply and demand; thereby improving their ability to optimize results and maximize financial benefits for all participants from end-to-end in the value chain.[51].

The efficiency of the so-called *purchase-to-pay* business processes will directly determine the effectiveness of an enterprise's ability to execute this principle. Almost the entire effort that has been expended since the mid-1980's addressing the idea of re-engineering has been focused on this principle. So much so that the term *supply chain execution* has come to represent how well the principle is applied by an entity. As supply-chain concepts proliferated enterprises learned that their ability to optimize their process was limited to the parts of the total process that they controlled. They realized that suppliers often controlled too many steps in their ability to

---

[51] It quickly becomes evident that the ability to measure success from changes in any business process is important to the perpetuation of the concept of continuous process improvement. Therefore, the ability to model expectations against actual results is an important capability. A methodology for accomplishing this is addressed in later chapters.

execute. This realization accelerated their efforts to pursue integration with their suppliers. Likewise, trading partners began to understand the dependency of others on their internal processes, so they gradually began to manage their business processes based on their impact on customers and suppliers. However, adaptation is always easier said than done because of the lack of common technologies between trading entities.

Over the years the ability to electronically integrate with systems outside the enterprise has gradually improved and continues to migrate from poor-man's integration (faxing copies back and forth) to full and transparent transaction-to-transaction data interchange. This will continue to be an issue for some. However, system-to-system data and information exchange is of growing importance and has become a requirement to do business with some companies, such as Wal-Mart and the military establishment of the federal government. The customer has begun to adopt, influence and set the standards for electronic integration, especially since this functionality is integral to the major software solutions available in the marketplace. Application and networking software are the tools of execution for this principle and their continuing complexity requires more knowledgeable workers throughout the stages of process execution. If enterprise leaders are not paying attention to this principle in their strategic planning, then it is only a matter of time until they will be challenged, perhaps beyond their ability to recover, by competitors who believe process is a competitive advantage and who embrace the technologies and strategies that will make it a reality. For many entities the required dollar investment will be an ongoing challenge.

Principle #3 – Procure at the lowest possible cost!

The word procure for purposes of this discussion means any acquisition activity whose purpose is to obtain the components, labor, products and services that enable an enterprise to build the products that they deliver to their customers. Products may be tangible things that are purchased, assembled, or manufactured and then resold to customers. They may be talents and capabilities that are delivered to customers based on flexible elements such as hours and rates per hour in the case of services as products. Customers may consume products in the creation of their own end user products, or they may be end users as consumers. An end-use customer to one entity is not to another. Manufacturers purchase components, add labor and build end-use products that are consumed by other manufacturers, or consumers. Wholesale distributors typically purchase finished products from manufacturers, but may also perform value-added services prior to the delivery of products to customers. Retailers are end-users to an apparel manufacturer, but people who buy clothes are the ultimate consumer. In all the transactions that occur as product moves from seller to buyer in the chain from raw material to finished goods to consumption take many forms, but they each incur costs all along the transaction stream. Procurement cost is not just what an entity pays to buy or produce products. It also includes all of the direct and indirect costs associated with acquiring and delivering the product from the time it is procured until it is sold and delivered to the customer. Everyone involved in any of the process steps required to procure, transport and control products should be aware of the importance of seeking the lowest possible cost; and look for opportunities to reduce costs by negotiation and process improvement.

This principle is about minimizing all product associated costs to maximize product contribution to gross margin dollars. Typically the focus is on the purchase price of goods and services with little regard for the incidental additional costs that erode gross margin by increasing total product cost. A properly constructed *gross margin model* for a business entity, including all of its profit centers (product revenue streams), will pinpoint the primary (hard) product costs and also the *soft costs* associated with each process step from the time of acquisition to the point of delivery. The accounting systems of most entities record the so-called *hard costs* with their related variances directly in the financial general ledger. However, a small percentage of companies isolate and manage what I call the *soft costs*. Typically, they are buried in financial accounts with direct product costs, because financial managers do not build financial systems to track them and consequently, operating managers do not understand them. It follows that anything that operational managers do not understand, they do not and cannot manage. I believe that sub-optimizing the financial information that is available to decision-makers is a more significant shortcoming than is obvious to most people. Therefore, I have provided two quite specific examples where uncovering hidden details have resulted in better decisions. Specifically the two examples illustrate some *soft product costs* that are seldom isolated and measured, thereby limiting the ability of managers to deal with them.

Manufacturing Example:

At a heavy equipment manufacturing company,[52] the total cost of welding together component parts, which was a considerable labor

---

[52] Hyster Company (circa 1970) manufactured primarily forklifts, construction equipment and heavy hauler trailers.

component of the total cost of the finished product, included a charge for "shop supplies". The amount was applied at a standard rate add-on to the total actual labor charge. The standard rate was determined by taking the total cost of all shop supplies over an annual period divided by the projected total number of units of all product models to be built over the next year. The monthly variances between actual and standard cost of shop supplies consumed in production was significantly skewed on a regular basis. Sometimes the variance was favorable and sometimes unfavorable and often by significant amounts depending on the product being manufactured. Without fail manufacturing managers were regularly asked to explain these disparate variances. Rarely did they get to the true reason for the differences because there were inherent problems between how the standard rate was computed and how the actual charges were recorded.

A new and more experienced vice president of manufacturing joined the company who was not content with the answers that were given for shop supply variances. Determined to get to the root of the issue and with an underlying objective to accurately determine true gross margin, by product line and model within product line, he made a significant discovery. Hidden in the shop supplies amount was the cost of welding rod, which from prior experience he knew to be a significant dollar amount for all of the products being built by the company. In addition, he knew that welding on a large piece of earth moving equipment is very different from welding on a forklift. He also found that the elements of production cost charged to supplies were expensed as they were purchased, and, because actual purchases of welding rod occurred quarterly, the monthly variance was high during a purchase month and much lower in the following two months. The positive and negative variances did not necessarily offset each other and were only adjusted to actual cost based on an annual physical inventory of welding rod. Further, because a perpetual inventory of welding rod was not being kept, there was no way to determine how much was actually being withdrawn for manufacturing, whether there were sufficient controls to minimize shrinkage, or how much was actually being consumed by product. To further complicate the problem there were several different types of welding rod depending on the engineering requirements of the various product models. So the question remained: what was the right solution to ensure that:

- Product gross margins were accurate,
- That cost variances reflected true differences between [engineered standards] and actual results, and

- That the right information was available for better decision-making?

It should be reasonably evident from the previous paragraph that there were three basic changes that needed to be made. These identified changes, even though inconvenient for accounting and financial people, provided better information for operating managers and resulted in a more accurate recording of gross margin by product model as welding rod became a direct product cost. These changes in this real world case made dramatic differences in how product profitability was managed which lead to lower inventory, higher gross margins [because expenses had been overstated for some products], higher selling prices for products where cost had been understated, and process improvements in the actual production processes. The following three process improvements were made.

An inventory control system was installed for managing the value of welding rod. This included a process for identifying welding rod by type, count control of the quantity including additions (purchases and returns) and reductions (withdrawals by work order by product) and periodic counts to ensure accuracy, which also facilitated a more accurate forecast of replenishment requirements. The benefits of the control system also included a reduction of total inventory as purchases by type of rod were based on near term production schedules by model.

Incidental to the process changes was the development of more accurate engineered standards for the consumption of welding rod by model by type. The standard included a factor for waste and a percentage for reworks due to quality rejects. The standard was validated to actual consumption quarterly, but only adjusted annually unless there were significant variances to the engineered standard.

The financial system was modified to establish separate accounts for welding rod and the associated usage variances. Total variances were supported by the detailed variances incurred at the work order level, which was in sufficient detail to explain where the variances were occurring and for what product models. This fostered more process attention where required and greater efficiencies were realized.

The *soft cost* in our example was called shop supplies. It was *soft* because it included both significant and incidental expenses associated with the manufacturing of heavy equipment of many types and models. Further, it was *soft* because there was insufficient information available to decision-makers to allow them to manage it, especially at the product level. Finally, it was *soft* because the expenditure pattern did not match the consumption pattern and there was no accountability for the total value, particularly the significant cost of welding rod.

Wholesale Distribution Example:

In the wholesale distribution business it is a common practice to record product cost as the purchase price. Nevertheless, to improve accuracy, the financial statements at the selling gross margin[53] level should also include the cost of inbound freight as part of product cost. In a strict GAAP accounting definition freight does not need to be reflected at the product level, but to do otherwise limits the ability of operating managers to manage product profitability as well as they could. Accountants have typically computed the freight component of product cost by applying all inbound freight charges during an accounting period to the portion of total inventory actually sold during the period. This is done by taking beginning inventory plus purchases minus shipments to arrive at an ending inventory and then applying a portion of the freight invoices paid during the period to the remaining inventory. The balance of inbound freight is assumed to be associated with the product that was sold during the period and is recorded to the financial statements as a lump sum freight cost. [For the non-accountant I apologize for the details, but all managers should be able to see the difference between the accounting way and the right way, which I hope is clear by the end of this example.] The approach described above is an acceptable way to comply with accounting requirements, but it does not consider that the lack of product cost detail limits an operating manager's ability to manage product gross margin. It also compromises inventory valuation because it does not capture actual landed product cost.

The most obvious problem associated with not knowing the true inventory cost of products is that selling prices, especially in a cost-up pricing scenario; will be set too low and gross margin targets will not be realized at the individual product level. Put another way, an understated product cost will result in an understated selling price and actual gross margin will be lower than expected. In the higher freight cost environment of recent years due to higher energy prices, this problem is exacerbated. Ideally, and especially for inventory intensive businesses, product cost should be captured

---

[53] See the *Gross Margin Model* in the appendix for a full example of the differences between invoice gross margin and net gross margin.

and managed to include in-bound freight at the SKU -level (stock keeping unit) by unit of measure. A simple example will illustrate the underpricing issue.

For wholesale distributors, there are a number of *direct* costs associated with products that are not captured and managed at the sales transaction level because they cannot be quantified accurately by product (SKU). The same is true for most retailers. Classic distribution business processes can also include a number of *indirect* product-related transaction costs. I have provided a summary explanation below of the most relevant product-specific costs to explain the logic for capturing them and to illustrate how to capitalize on the opportunity to manage them.[54] During my experience in distribution companies I preferred to call these costs "After sale product costs" because they cannot be directly attributed to products at the time they are sold. The most significant other product costs are:

Standard cost variance is typically a favorable profit variance when managed correctly. It is the difference between the actual (average) cost of products and the "expected", standard cost of the product. Generally, in times of inflation, the standard cost of product is higher than the average cost because it is based on the next purchase cost. When a standard cost is defined by product it is applied as the cost of record for sales transactions and thereby determines the *sales gross margin*. Since average (actual) cost is typically lower than standard cost during inflationary times, there will be a favorable gross margin variance for the difference between the two costs. When business systems are not set up to track a product standard cost and then measure and record the actual cost difference at the transaction level, the ability to accurately monitor and manage true gross margin is significantly limited, especially if selling price is based on average cost.

Sales invoice cost variance is the difference between the purchase order (PO) price of a product that is used to compute average cost and the actual cost on the supplier's invoice, which is applied when the purchase order is paid. Normally, average cost is calculated at the time product quantities are received and added to inventory. And, because the supplier's invoice is typically not entered into the financial system until days later, it is possible that the invoice cost will be different than the PO cost, thus resulting in a different calculated average cost. This may seem like an insignificant issue, but my experience is that it can make a 50 to 100 basis point difference

---

[54] I apologize for the level of detail required to make the explanation, but it should be instructive as the reader follows the logic.

in the actual gross margin percentage. Tracking *sales invoice cost variance* in a high transaction distribution business provides a tool for management to ensure that the purchasing, receiving and invoicing (accounts payable) processes are working as they should. If this variance becomes too large it is a strong symptom of dysfunction somewhere in this chain of related transactions. The ability to capture, track and manage this transaction variance is fully within the capability of currently available application software.

Another sometimes significant deviation from accurate gross margin reporting can be captured in an account that I always called *freight not recovered*. It is the difference between the actual outbound cost of freight, sometimes called "delivery expense", and the amount for this cost that can be captured on the customer invoice. Even though delivery freight may not be charged to the customer its cost can be captured at the sales order line level. Through the proper structuring of the general ledger interface for sales transactions, the amount of outbound transportation cost captured on the sales invoice becomes a credit to this *freight not recovered* account in the general ledger. The offsetting debit to this account is created when the freight carrier's invoice is entered for payment in the accounts payable financial system. Ideally, assuming the business intends to cover the cost of outbound freight, the two amounts offset each other. By tracking this amount in a general ledger account, it becomes possible to determine the outbound freight impact on gross margin. Whenever the amount is outside specified limits, it will once again signal that the freight tracking and accounting process is broken.

A secondary issue related to outbound freight is its impact on product prices. Many distribution businesses believe that they price their products to cover the cost of delivery. However, if there is no measure of whether or not outbound freight charges are being covered; there is no ability to validate whether or not this approach is working.

There are number of other more minor post sale transaction costs that can be captured to arrive at a true net gross margin in a wholesale distribution business. It is not necessary to detail them here, but they are covered in the appendix on the cost side of the *Gross Margin Model* discussion.

The entire point of principle #3 is that all elements of product and transaction cost that can be managed should be. If they are not isolated, particularly where they can be tied directly back to transactions, managing their impact is nearly impossible and the accountants' view of financial reporting will prevail. And unfortunately, the accounting approach aggregates these manageable transaction costs into other accounts where their collective impact is buried and where they cannot be managed at the process-level.

Principle #4 – Sell at the highest possible price!

If you were to ask, I think you would find that the typical sales person and their sales manager believes that the price a customer pays is the one shown on the customer's invoice. This misperception is generally rooted in the commission and sales reporting systems that govern sales compensation. Tampering with sales compensation is a difficult thing. An unwillingness to do so is probably the biggest single reason that it will be difficult for many organizations to adapt their processes to embrace the concepts embodied in this principle. First, sales people have no vested interest in a more accurate gauge of the customer's financial worth to the business. Second, business systems are seldom set up to track and accurately report the difference between invoice price and net selling price as outlined in the *Gross Margin Model* example contained in the appendix.

The line item selling price on a sales transaction for the products and services that are sold to customers is only one element of price management required to achieve the "highest" possible net selling price. The pricing models that companies use to ensure that computer-based business systems automatically price line items on a customer sale can be very elaborate. This is especially true in a retail sales environment, which is not addressed directly in our examples. They are typically based on a number of elements such as customer types, quantities of product sold, groups of products sold, promotions and other factors that are all linked within a pricing hierarchy. The objective of business process principle #4 is *to elevate the awareness of the people who are responsible for determining, entering and managing selling prices and customer commitments about the profitability impact of their decisions*. Almost all of what these people do and the promises they make while establishing and maintaining customer relationships have an effect on net pricing outcomes, and therefore, gross margin. Simply stated, sales gross margin is the difference between the line item selling price and invoice cost on a sales invoice. For example, if a product is sold for $10.00 and it has an inventory cost of $6.00, then gross margin is $4.00, and a 40% gross margin percent is realized. The $4.00 is considered the invoice gross margin and becomes the basis for most sales reporting because it can be directly traced to a customer sales invoice. However, in many industries there are a number of direct and indirect customer related post-sale price-side revenue adjustments associated with sales transactions that will likely reduce realized gross margin for the enterprise.

Only when the right process and integrated reporting systems are in place to record and report revenue adjustments[55] is it possible for the business entity to achieve the highest possible price. For example, in a typical apparel retail-supplier customer relationship, the retailer expects the supplier to make allowances for a number of nuances inherent in apparel retailing. As a consequence, the apparel supplier may have their gross margin decreased by retailer adjustments called over-bills; chargeback's, allowances and returns. Each of these values is a tool for the retailer to reduce their costs, minimize back-and-forth transactions for individually minor amounts, and deal with unexpected product obsolescence. Whenever the retailer benefits, the supplier's gross margin is reduced accordingly. The problem with managing these reductions to gross margin, for the supplier, is that they are not typically tracked at the transaction level and certainly not by product. Because sufficient detail is usually lacking, these charges become lump sum amounts on financial statements that relate to many transactions across multiple accounting periods. The supplier has little ability to predict the amount of these charges because they depend on the terms in non-automated customer specific contracts and sales agreements each with its own variable effective date.

The sheer complexity of multiple price arrangements, effective dates and variability by customer makes it nearly impossible for an apparel supplier to successfully challenge these deductions within the contractual timeframe. From my experience, any effort to determine whether such charges are legitimate depends on manual access to multiple paper-based customer agreements. Any ability to categorize and reconcile these charges, even when they are valid, is difficult. Yet every apparel supplier must challenge these retail customer profit reductions because retailers will routinely "charge back" unauthorized and unreasonable amounts. Suppliers normally recover about 50 percent of the retailer's deductions, but only after significant paper documentation is provided. There is no question that this process, for both parties, is the most arcane and illogical practice that I experienced in my business career. This highly suspect methodology could easily be replaced by well-designed computer-based systems that would

---

[55] I often refer to revenue adjustments as "gross margin leaks" because they literally reduce gross margin dollars and are hard to discover and fix.

produce reliable and fair results for both the retailer and the supplier.

While not necessarily as complex, other manufacturers and wholesalers also have non-standard customer-specific pricing and relationship agreements that reduce the amount of gross margin they actually realize on sales transactions. Some of the more typical examples of charges that prevent *selling at the highest possible price* are also included in the *Gross Margin Model* that is explained in Appendix I. The most obvious examples of price-side reductions to gross margin are:

- Programmed discounts, which are pre-determined discounts from "list price"
- Discounts for early payment
- Allowances for discrepancies, transaction costs, payment differences and customer disputes
- Bad Debt Write-off for uncollectible amounts that may not relate to the customer's ability to pay
- Returns (Credits) always generate costs beyond the lost revenue from taking back products.

I have long been an advocate of measuring a customer's contribution as well as their gross margin. The difference between a customer's invoice sales gross margin and their net gross margin (contribution) is the sum of these other sales transaction costs, or profit reductions. Once there is a documented awareness of the cost reductions that each customer is generating, it is rational for an organization to more effectively establish the right selling price for each customer, thereby realizing higher profitability. Further, too many executives who have the strategic responsibility for establishing selling prices have incredibly little understanding of the system-based methods for ensuring that their decisions are executed. Profitability leaks are further exacerbated because the majority of sales executives do not maintain sufficient control over the process for allowing exceptions to price policy, which means additional price reductions. Consequently, they tend to only be involved after-the-fact when forced to explain bigger than normal variances in gross margin. I can confidently state that system-based pricing is far more effective at achieving target gross margin levels than is a sales force that is given broad latitude in setting customer prices. This is even true for businesses selling highly volatile commodity products where market price changes daily, or even hourly. Those who set prices in unpredictable environments should have electronic update capabilities that are easily accessible to the sales force to ensure that an entity's price structure is current, accurate and effectively returning expected gross margins.

When any business entity takes the time to embrace this principle their profitability will increase. They can be successful by:

- Gathering the information sufficient to create their own *Gross Margin Model*,
- Determining true customer contribution, and
- Taking responsibility for aligning prices with their price policy.

From my experience in two different businesses with a wide range of market price sensitivity, we were able to achieve at least two gross margin points (200 basis points for the financial people) increase by just being consistent through the application of computer-based pricing. Another 2 to 3 gross margin points is achievable by establishing computer-based pricing that differentiates customers and products based on their contribution to the business. Each time these results were achieved, there was no measurable decrease in sales revenue due to consistent pricing. While the actual gross margin points will vary by business model, I believe comparable relative gains can be realized in any business. Other side benefits, which also improved net gross margin, included improved collections because of consistency in pricing, a reduction in the number of invoice corrections, and a decrease in the number of customer disputes.

Ideally, any decision to change a customer agreement related to selling prices, or any of the factors affecting the net amount the customer pays should be carefully considered at the executive level. Once the *Gross Margin Model* is defined for a business entity it can also be utilized to project the outcome of price policy changes by estimating the dollar impact from executing a decision to change prices. I believe establishing price is the prerogative of management. It should be established with input from the sales organization and may in fact reflect the structure they believe is most acceptable in the market. However, once a pricing agreement is established and agreed to by the executive team, the resulting price structure should become embedded in the transaction processing business system and rarely overridden. Any points of conflict with the sales organization should be resolved in the context of the price policy.

The first four principles deal with achieving maximum gross margin for the business entity. If followed, selling prices will be maximized, costs for products and services will be minimized, inventory turnover will be high, inventory obsolescence will be minimized, and financial results will be more predictable because decisions will be executed through automation.

The next five principles directly relate to creating processes that preserve as much as possible of the profitability realized by applying the first four principles. These principles drive operating expense and will directly determine people, facility, support and administrative costs associated with business operations. In a nutshell, they decide how gross margin dollars are spent and how much will be left for shareholders.

Principle #5 – Minimize the time and effort required to perform each task!

Remembering the *resource allocation concept* helps to understand this principle. It simply means that business processes should be designed to allow only necessary work to be done with the least amount of effort in the shortest time possible while not compromising quality and accuracy. The first step for improving a business process is to diagram all of the process steps to ensure that the people on the process improvement team have a clear and uniform understanding of the start to finish tasks required to accomplish an expected outcome. The side benefit of diagramming a process, which should not be overly detailed, is that each process step can be questioned to determine if it is really necessary. The *three key questions* is the preferred method for challenging the process steps from end-to-end. Those who were around prior to the introduction of the book "*Reengineering the Corporation*"[56] will recognize that analyzing a process was once called value engineering, which was focused on identifying the value of each process step. If a process step had little or no value it was eliminated. Process diagrams typically focus on tasks, or elements of work. This approach is appropriate, but it is significantly enhanced when the flow of data (information) between the process steps is also documented along with the process flow.

A fundamental characteristic of a well-defined process is the optimization of the use of transactional data as the process proceeds forward from task to task. To optimize means that data should be determined once and then move with the earlier transaction process steps to the subsequent steps, as required, to avoid duplication of effort and the delays that come when existing information must be retrieved from outside the process. It means that for certain types of transactions, there would be on-line access to detailed information about the key elements of the transaction. While such

---

[56] Reengineering the Corporation, A Manifesto for Business Revolution, Michael Hammer & James Champy, Harper Business – A division of Harper Collins Publishers, copyright 1993

information may not be visible within the transaction itself, it should be accessible via fast, accurate (up-to-date) and easy to access means. It almost goes without saying that in today's world of automation such data and detail will either be visible in alternative information windows or accessible via readily available lookup keys. The presentation format for such data should be unequivocally clear, allow cut-and-paste capability for utilizing and communicating data, and leave no room for misunderstanding in the application of the data to the process.

Wherever possible, transaction process data and information should be linked together to properly represent the actual circumstances for decision-making. Then the people who are charged with the accurate and timely completion of each process step will be more accurate. For purposes of this discussion, I choose to define "information" as the assembly of multiple points of data to create facts that are important for making valid decisions from the beginning of the process to the end of it. It should be remembered that timeliness has variable meanings depending on the nature of the process and the demands of the customer (whether internal or external). For example, most customer order processing software assumes that the customer wants the product as soon as they can get it. As a result, sales fulfillment processes assume immediate execution of the product selection and shipping process. This is not always the case. For instance, on construction projects supplies and materials are ordered well in advance of when they are required to be on site and the supplier is often penalized if orders are shipped early. Likewise, many seasonal products are to be shipped only when someone is available to receive them. Because of the variability of customer's expectation for receiving products, most good business systems have a "required date" that is entered proactively instead of allowing a default date that causes products to be shipped as soon as possible. A "required date" is just one example of a piece of data that is essential to the timely and accurate execution of a process. In this case, it is the shipping process. There are many instances in the selling and procurement processes that could be explained to make this point, but it should be clear how data and information combined with diligent and timely actions by people will promote the accomplishment of this principle.

Principle #6 – Minimize the number of people required to perform each task!

This principle is also about resource allocation. It suggests giving people enough information and tools to allow them to get the job done as independently as possible. Only involve more than one individual when necessary. Think in terms of continuous processing and add task steps to an individual's role if it is more effective than passing the transaction to someone else. This is particularly true in light of the point made in the previous principle about data and information being readily accessible during process execution. One of the biggest barriers to achieving optimum results for this principle are those created by the organizational structure of the enterprise. This is particularly true when the enterprise is organized along the traditional functional fiefdoms associated with business entities for the past 50 plus years.

A simple example based on the creation and completion of a purchase order will illustrate this point. In classic functionally organized entities the following are typical steps required for the purchasing process from inception to completion.

- Determine what materials are required – any number of means may apply such as forecasting, production scheduling, job-order material requirements, or inventory replenishment.
- Select a supplier
- Determine the purchase price and delivery requirements
- Create the purchase order
- Authorize (sign) the purchase order (PO)
- Inform the receiving department about the pending receipt via a paper copy of the purchase order (the receiving copy), or by making the PO electronically available by the time the product arrives.
- Send a copy of the PO to accounting so Accounts Payable will have a copy to match to the receiving copy when it arrives, and to support any effort the finance department may have to project cash requirements. This may also be done electronically or with paper copies.
- Receive the goods and enter the quantities received on the receipt copy of the PO and forward it to the Accounts Payable department for matching to the vendor's invoice. There may be multiple shipments per PO, which means that the probability of a one-to-one match of original PO to the receipt to the vendor invoice will not happen and the complexity of what started out as a single transaction is increased.

[Note: Some companies are so focused on having a single shipment and invoice per PO that they require the vendor to ship complete and/or only issue one invoice per shipment. The reality of this approach is almost completely illogical, except to the finance department,

88

because some products on a PO are needed before others and they may ship from different vendor locations. It prevents the vendor from optimizing their fulfillment process and invariably adds costs, which will eventually be passed on to the purchaser in some way.]

- Receive the vendor invoice for the goods received and match it to the original PO to validate prices and to the receipt copy of the PO to validate quantities received. Because most vendors invoice at time of shipment, it is likely that the invoice may arrive before the receipt copy, which will prevent the matching process from occurring as soon as it could.
- Once the invoice, PO and receipt are matched the invoice is set up for payment. Once again, depending on the level of automation available for this process, these steps may be done manually with paper copies, or electronically with no paper copies including the vendor's invoice. The payment date of the invoice will depend upon the terms on the purchase order which may be transaction specific, or default to the terms as they are set up in the supplier's master record in a computer system.
- The completion of the PO process occurs when the invoice is paid to the vendor even though it is independent of completion of the PO in the physical sense, which is when the goods arrive.

In our simple example there are at least five people in no less than three departments involved in creating and completing a purchase order within our hypothetical organization. In a typical structure it requires 2-3 people in the purchasing department, 2 people in the physical receipt process (warehouse) and 2-3 people in the finance department depending on who is authorized to sign checks. Therefore 6 to 8 people are required to initiate and complete a purchasing transaction and that assumes only one receipt and supplier invoice per purchase order.

The purchasing process should be driven by two primary objectives. One is to always have sufficient product on hand to meet demand, no matter whether demand is required for sales, inventory or production. The second objective is to minimize the amount of investment in inventory by minimizing the time between the receipt of products and their consumption. When there are 6 to 8 people involved in a purchasing process there will be mistakes, delays and duplication of effort, especially in a paper-based process. Applying the principle of *minimizing the number of people required to perform a task* to our hypothetical purchasing process can yield enormous direct benefits. In addition, there will be significant secondary benefits from the simplification that will occur.

So how do we take this complex, people intensive process and make it more efficient? The solution is a classic example of the application of technology to a formerly paper-based process. In the best of today's application software all required information is available to initiate and complete the purchasing process with a high degree of accuracy and security. A maximum of three people, instead of 6 to 8, are required because all necessary data and information is electronically accessible from inception to completion from within the transaction. Here is how I see that the process could be accomplished with three people.

One person in purchasing may be required to validate what the business system recommends for a purchase quantity [because there may be information about the demand that either is not known or has changed since the time of the electronic forecast of demand]. This same person should be capable of releasing the electronically generated PO that is then delivered electronically to all relevant suppliers. There can even be multiple suppliers and order lines per supplier on the same PO. It is not necessary to print a PO since all information on the order is readily accessible to all parties at any time via computer.

One person can physically receive products for any open purchase order via computer, or hand held radio frequency device. It is not necessary to even physically count quantities or identify products because the barcode or RFID (radio frequency identification device) tag on the shipment carries that information and it is passed to the computer by scanning either of these electronic labels. Even in the absence of the information associated with electronic labels, the receipt process can be accomplished by a single person scanning product barcode identification numbers and manually entering the quantities received to an open PO that is displayed on their radio frequency device.

One person in finance may be required to manage the cash payment process. All valid payments will have been set up for payment based an electronic *background match* of the PO, quantities received and the electronic invoice sent from the supplier. No paper PO receiving copy or supplier invoice is required. Since payment due dates are driven by either system based supplier payment terms or from override terms on the PO; the computer system can generate electronic payments (EFT – electronic funds transfer), or print checks as required. The one person is only required where the payment process requires manual authorization to meet the internal control requirements of the entity, or to respond to significant discrepancies.

This is a real world example of the application of principle #6. It clearly demonstrates the strides that have been made in this most fundamental of business processes. However, only a small portion of the total number of business entities has actually streamlined their process to this extent. There are many who have come part way and will continue to move forward. These early adopters of the technology required to improve the purchasing process tend to be the larger companies who can see the benefits and have the funds to make the needed technology investments. Even when an entity desires this type of process outcome, they will find that their partners may not be prepared to support it and, therefore, their progress toward optimization is slowed. In some cases this level of electronic processing among all business partners will take years. This high level of process automation and transaction accuracy is again being driven most notably by Wal-Mart and the Federal government, particularly as they lead the charge for the adoption of RFID.

There are two significant barriers to the application of this principle for most business entities. The first is that too many entities are still organized functionally and therefore support the territorial separation that the purchase order process structure has historically perpetuated. The second is the demand for transaction security that is driven by independent audit requirements and recent legislative edicts [Sarbanes-Oxley], both of which focus too much on an inherent mistrust of people and therefore require an inordinate emphasis on separation of duties. In an ideal world the need that these requirements have created will be met by greater understanding and reliance on electronic separation instead of human separation of the steps in a process. Despite these barriers, individual entities should aggressively pursue the application of principle #6 as part of their goal to establish a *continuous process improvement* environment and culture.[57] In doing so, they can be aggressive in resolving the real and imagined conflicts presented by organizational and legal requirements. It is

---

[57] A classic example of the benefits of continuous process improvement is illustrated in an article about Honeywell Corporation. See "*Honeywell's System Sensor Plan Declares War on 'Seven Deadly Wastes'*" WSJ, June 30, 2013.

probable that internal organizational barriers [That is, protection of the status quo.] will far outweigh the significance of legal requirements.[58]

Principle #7 – Do not perform a task twice for the same transaction!

This principle is about eliminating the hidden cost of re-work, especially when it requires the time of supervisors, managers, and executives to re-think their original decisions. It means doing the right job right the first time. Further, it means accepting the decisions that have already been made about a given task throughout the execution and completion of each step. It also implies sustaining the initiatives and guidelines that underlie all business transactions and interactions between business partners to eliminate second-guessing and contradiction. For example, if we stick with the purchase order example from *principle #6,* a poor process would require that a person who authorized a purchase order also be required to approve the payment for goods received against the original transaction. At the point the PO was approved, the approver granted permission to pay, so why ask for the second signature and review? This is especially true when the supplier's invoice exactly matches the quantity received at the purchase order price.

The two essential and basic contracts of business are the purchase order and the sales order. The purchase order is a contract between the business entity and its suppliers. It identifies what is being purchased, at what price and usually when it is required. A mirror image of this transaction is the sales order, which is a contract between the business entity and their customer and it also specifies what is being sold, at what price and when it is to be delivered. Once these two "contracts" have been accepted by both parties, no matter what level of formal approval is required, every process step from that point forward has been approved and should not be revisited. Of course, this does not include legitimate changes to either order type that are initiated during an order change process. Therefore, the business processes should be built to execute the related transactions and require intervention only when there are discrepancies. And even then, differences should revert back to and be resolved from the basic agreements.

The primary reason there are violations to this principle in process design is the lack of understanding by the people who have the responsibility for the process steps. This lack of understanding comes from either lack of

---

[58] For an excellent discussion about the organizational changes that will be required to fully employ this principle see chapter seven, "Managing without Structure" page 125 in _The Agenda_ by Michael Hammer, Crown Publishing, 2001.

training and education, and/or missing information. An effective process requires that the flow of data and information be as fast as the transaction requires for successful completion. In today's computer-based systems the interactive screens available to the people responsible for completing process steps should include sufficient data for them to successfully complete their step. With up-to-date information each step of a process can be accomplished quickly and accurately. Furthermore, each step in sequence will be compatible with the prior steps because decision information is consistent throughout and passed from step to step as needed.

This principle is the backbone of business system integration both internally between the departments of the entity and externally with the entity's business partners. It has been this way since the 1980's when barcodes were introduced on a broad scale. The initial intention of the barcode was to identify products in a uniform way. Prior to that time the same product could be identified with a different part number in every entity that used the product. UPC (Uniform Product Code) identifiers came into acceptance and new computer systems learned to recognize products by this number. The adoption of the barcoding concept is universally accepted by the retail industry. Any company selling into this industry is required to have a UPC number identifier for their products. Outside of the retail segment, the acceptance of uniform product numbers is still less than complete. Consequently, most computer systems have the capability to identify a single product with any number of so-called aliases, which enables the entity to do business with the product numbers that their systems require, and any number identifiers that their business partners use.

System-to-system business integration between trading partners, as they attempt to apply this principle, requires that each partner acknowledges that they duplicate work as they transact business without it. For example, the purchase order created by one entity becomes a sales order to the other entity. As this concept was recognized and the partners mutually agreed to exchange information the concept of *electronic data interchange (EDI)* was born. To date a number of EDI transactions types have been identified and specific data requirements defined for each. This allows the partners to electronically exchange specific business transactions with reasonable assurance that the data they require will be available for translation into formats required for them to create their mirror transactions accurately. Thus, an electronic purchase order sent to a supplier can become a sales order within the supplier's business system and be processed with greater speed and accuracy while never being touched by human hands.

93

The benefits of applying *principle #7* both internally and externally are potentially enormous. Individual entities have long recognized this, but that does not mean that they have readily embraced it. It has taken years to get disparate and often competing entities to accept the standards that are required to make each wave of external electronic integration possible. Even when there is a standard, especially in the case of EDI transactions, there are still too many business entities that violate the transfer of information by asking for more data than the standard requires, or holding back required data fields, not to mention ignoring the data sequence and format specifications. Internal to an entity there will still be competitive roadblocks between competing organizations similar to or greater than those mentioned under *principle #6*.

Principle #8 – Eliminate making the same decision over again!

This principle is closely associated with *principle #7*. It is also about eliminating the inevitable conflicts that occur when *Principle #6 [minimize the number of people required to perform each* task] is not followed. For example, whenever there are discrepancies between a purchase order and the receipt of goods, or between the receipt of goods and the suppliers invoice, the people involved in the original creation and execution of the transaction are often asked to get involved to resolve these differences. In essence, they are being asked to perform their task over again by validating what they originally agreed to on the PO. If too much time has elapsed since the initial decision, or if information must be reconstructed, it is likely that more time will be required to come to a resolution (decision) than was required to make the original decision.

The primary reason for violating this principle is the failure to pass relevant information between dependent steps in a process. A secondary reason, which also has a significant impact, is inaccurate information, particularly in the data that drives transactions. Following this principle means documenting decisions as they are made. It is usually accomplished by entering correct transactional information and communicating it to others. Everyone can relate to having been invoiced incorrectly, receiving the wrong product, or having products shipped to the wrong address. All these errors and many like them occur because inaccurate data is recorded in a transaction. Business leaders who want to successfully apply this principle will place as much organizational responsibility and emphasis on data integrity as they do on operational management and financial reporting. No one wants to be "scored" inaccurately in financial or operation measures, which will occur when this principle is violated. We all want credit for what we do and we are particularly interested in maximizing effectiveness in a highly competitive environment where the emphasis is on reaching profitability objectives.

When an entity's prices are always accurate, addresses are always precise, and product identifiers are always correct it is an indication that data integrity processes and procedures are actively emphasized and managed. When functional responsibility for data integrity becomes important to an organization, errors will be minimized, duplication of effort reduced or eliminated, and confidence between trading partners increased. To successfully apply this principle, business entities must make every effort to assure two things. First, make certain that the transaction-based interactive screens where decisions are made always display, or have available, the accurate and relevant data necessary to effectively complete each process step. Second, make sure that master data for customers, products, suppliers and prices is up-to-date and accurate. When these two things are accomplished errors will be virtually eliminated and there will be no need to reconstruct decisions. In fact, the only errors likely to occur will be mistakes made by people; and people can be further educated and trained to minimize those impacts.

Principle #9 – Perform the task at the lowest level of decision-making (ability)!

If efficiency is doing the job right and effectiveness is doing the right job right, then this principle is about being more effective. Process quality and transaction accuracy are achieved at the highest level when the people performing tasks are appropriately capable, enabled, and provided with all the information they need to do it right. Most organizations attempting to incorporate this principle may need to first address how to define what "appropriately capable" means. Too many organizations place so much emphasis on dumbing down the tasks people are asked to perform, usually under the guise of cost saving, that they prescribe failure. When this happens people are not able to place their actions within the context of the ultimate objective of what they are doing. Simply stated people are taught "how" to do a job, but they are not taught enough about "why" the job they are doing is important and how it fits into a bigger process. As is elaborated in *principle #7 and #8*, when up-to-date and accurate information is provided to people performing the tasks of a process they will perform at a higher level of effectiveness.

This principle is the embodiment of the so-called "enablement" concept. It means the entity places more emphasis on educating people and not just training them. The end result is that people not only know how to do something they also know why they are doing it, which generally means they will take greater pride in their work. In this environment people learn to react intelligently to inaccuracies as they find them, and what to do to correct them. The mode of operation becomes *"take care of the problem when it is evident and take responsibility for the accuracy of what you do."* If the problem is inaccurate data, fix it now before it affects more transactions, tasks, and people.

The essence of an entity's ability to achieve excellence by applying this principle depends on a clear recognition of the knowledge and skill levels required to perform at a high level of accuracy. Ideally people with adequate information should be able to complete as many process steps as possible. When people have the appropriate level of decision-making ability, let them perform the task. If they do not have the right education, understanding or experience to be successful, then pass the next step to someone who does. Taking this approach will simplify most processes. Non-value-added steps will be more easily identified and either eliminated or combined with other steps.

I worked for a CEO who detested the idea that people are trained. He believed that "*training is for dogs and education is for people*". I am reasonably certain he did not have principle #9 in mind when he said that, but his thought further emphasizes what it is about. Applying the principle advocates the education of people not just their training, especially as it pertains to processes and their role in the successful performance of the tasks of business. The result is the enhancement of people's jobs, more effective process outcomes, and therefore, improved business results no matter how performance is measured. Highly effective organizations that achieve success applying this principle will reap the added benefit of promoting a knowledgeable and thinking workforce that has an intuition about process effectiveness. This will make the application of the prior eight principles significantly easier because the nature [culture] of the organization can more easily absorb the purpose for each principle thereby intuitively adopting it as the standard for what they do.

Some current organizational thinking suggests that the span of control for managers must increase as a means of increasing effectiveness and lowering costs. This can be done by having more people reporting to potentially less executives and managers. This principle, as well as the entire premise for *Strategic Decision Mastery* promotes the ability to increase spans of control. I believe this will be difficult to achieve unless there is a structure for reporting performance management similar to what we have been outlining; and a culture with a strong inclination to promote and support increased decision-making at every level in the organization. A *Wall Street Journal* article March 24, 2008 on page B6 titled "Overseeing More Employees – With Fewer Managers", addresses the subject of increasing span of control. It includes some interesting ideas that are compatible with this discussion. The first is from Michael Hammer author of *Reengineering the Corporation* and *The Agenda* who says, "*If you're stuck with the traditional emphasis on checking, controlling and intervening, it takes real heroics to push as far as 12 direct reports. You need to change what it means to be a manager.*" Further on in the same article Cindy Zollinger, president of *Cornerstone Research*, says, "*I don't really manage them [people] in a typical way. They largely run themselves. I help them in dealing with obstacles they face, or in making the most of opportunities that they find.*"

Principle #10 – Only manages the exceptions!

For decades managers have been told to *only manage the exceptions*. The implication of this approach was that they would not have time to effectively do their job if they tended to every detail and concerned themselves with the outcome of ordinary every day transactions and activities. In the absence of a structure that results from applying the first nine principles, a total business process can be so complex that it will be difficult to find the exceptions. The consequence is that managers will be involved in too much financial and statistical detail, they will make too many ad hoc, independent and inconsistent decisions about similar transaction results, and they will lack the information to know what the outcome of their decisions is, or will be. In other words, everything will be an exception because there is no norm or standard. Consequently, among the ten principles, this principle is what I prefer to call *the realization principle*. It implies that process performance exceptions, after embracing the first nine principles, will be easily identified and reported. It means that managers become process oriented and will know how to fix process issues by the nature of the information they receive about exceptions.

If the previous nine principles are followed and continuously applied in decision-making to fix processes and prevent problems, this principle will automatically be in effect. Of course, a set of reports and measures must be developed to focus on reporting exceptions, preferably as they occur not after the fact. [Refer to the previous discussion about *real-time problem resolution*] The need to report or review all transactions will be gone. Patterns of exceptions will be more evident and allow process effectiveness to improve even further as their inherent reoccurring causes are identified and corrected. There will be no need to report the details of all transactions. Summary data about results will become the standard. Executives and managers will come to rely on summarized reporting of results with a high degree of confidence. The outcome is a lot less paper, more focused decision-making and less stress for everyone in the organization.

Avoid the tendency to Oversimplify and Underestimate

For anyone who has been involved in any form of process improvement, and that includes just about everyone, the greatest "gotcha" is *the tendency to oversimplify and underestimate*. Don't do it. It will be potentially disastrous for any initiative whose purpose is to bring about change because it will significantly reduce the manager's credibility for the people who are asked to implement the new process. Setting the proper atmosphere for the initiation of change is very difficult because it requires great patience and perseverance, especially at the beginning. There is inevitably the conflict between executives and managers who want to stay out of the details and the people involved in the processes who want to get into the details because they want to be heard. Allowing people to be heard does not always mean accepting their ideas, nor should it. However, it does mean listening to understand and perhaps gain a greater perspective of what the real issues are. For executive sponsors of process improvement any initiative that avoids oversimplification and underestimation will require exposing any hidden agendas or ill-conceived purposes for initiating the process change.

If a process change initiative moves too quickly and glosses over the true nature of the problems from the doer's perspective it will result in either delays or outright failure when it comes to implementation[59]. Likewise it

---

[59] In today's computer systems world, especially since the introduction of the so-called ERP (Enterprise Requirements Planning) approach to process automation, the majority of corporations involve outside consulting resources to drive the change process when it relates to the selection and adoption of new software. Inherently this is done either to add credibility to the ultimate outcome, whether good or bad, or to fill capability gaps in the organization. The approach these consulting firms take is very prescribed and staffed by generally less experienced people at the details level. While their highly scripted approach may be adapted to the specifics of the client business, it almost always results in a predictable outcome. That outcome could be characterized, for the most part, as fitting the needs of the business into the defined capabilities of existing software solutions. During implementation the significance of the divergence of needs to capabilities is identified and modifications and customizations are required to achieve an acceptable result. The result is that the project costs more than intended and once down the

cannot tolerate a slow pace. Many a well-intended initiative has failed because the team members sought for more information than was required for sound decision-making. Sometimes process improvement efforts become bogged down in so much detail that team members cannot logically assemble it into a clear cut process design. In addition, the initiative may become so focused on the importance of current process details that too many exceptions are made to what would otherwise be a well-defined process. Attempting to replicate current processes into new solutions becomes an effort to preserve the status quo while applying new approaches to old problems. It has been characterized as *paving the cow path*. The result is the preservation of old process methods (paths) where the ride is smoother, but only marginally more effective in getting from point A to point B. Where such an approach involves the adoption of new process software the realization of benefits (Return on Investment) will be significantly diminished. The reality is that most major process change over the past three decades almost always involved adopting new technology. And of course, we can't forget the Machiavelli statement about people resisting change that was referred to earlier, because it is the heart of the people problems that will likely come up.

---

path, with few exceptions, the client has no alternative but to continue. Therefore, the caution is to beware of consultants selling solutions that may not be appropriate.

Section III
Techniques for Building
Decision Continuity

Chapter 12

Dynamics of Organizational Leadership

T he next few chapters provide some helps for business leaders in their quest to get the people in their organizations performing up to their expectations. Part of the issue is clearly defining what an individual's self-styled "management expectations" really are. That definition must first take place in the head of the leader and it will require careful articulation of personal thoughts about how to solve the challenges, opportunities and problems within each leader's sphere of responsibility. The definition must be consistent with potentially higher expectations and behaviors that have been set for the entire organization as defined by its performance objectives and strategies. The first step to conveying expectations requires that the leader's thoughts be written down (documented), preferably in a logical order, and with enough clarity that it will be difficult to misunderstand them. This is an important first step for each of us as leaders because it tends to be revealing about how we think versus how we communicate. Being forced to clearly write something down will require a leader's introspection into all of the reasonable dimensions and possibilities about their performance expectations if they have any hope that they will be successfully accomplished. From this self-exercise leaders may come to realize that some of their thoughts about actionable objectives are unrealistic. It is unlikely that the initial expectations list will be the same after the introspection exercise is completed. What should emerge will be an expectations definition that is easier to comprehend and certainly more likely to be achieved. There are so many dynamics between what a leader envisions will happen and what actually gets done in a business enterprise. For that reason, this section explores and delineates some essential ideas and concepts for leaders to consider in their quest to get better at closing the gap between expectations and performance.

The Challenge – Managing the Business Process

Below is a simplified diagram of what goes on every day in most businesses. Daily transactions such as sales orders, purchase orders, production orders, pick tickets, invoices, etc. are processed using computer based systems, which also determine how the assets of the company controlled. Each day managers receive information and performance reports about the results from the transactions of the previous day. With this information in hand, they make judgments and decisions and are conditioned to react to any results that are "out of the ordinary". At the end of the month financial statements and operating reports are produced; and then an analysis of results is performed based on comparisons to benchmarks such as plans, budgets and prior periods.

The reverse arrows in this diagram suggest that feedback from our reporting and analysis determines whether we make changes to the process, or just fix transaction errors. In some organizations there is so little clarity about expectations and a general lack of principles and rules for processing that too much time is spent in the correction process. People need specifics about error prevention and correction that can be applied consistently by everyone across the spectrum of transactions. Otherwise, operations produce random results and people will make haphazard and inconsistent decisions when presented with the same set of circumstances.

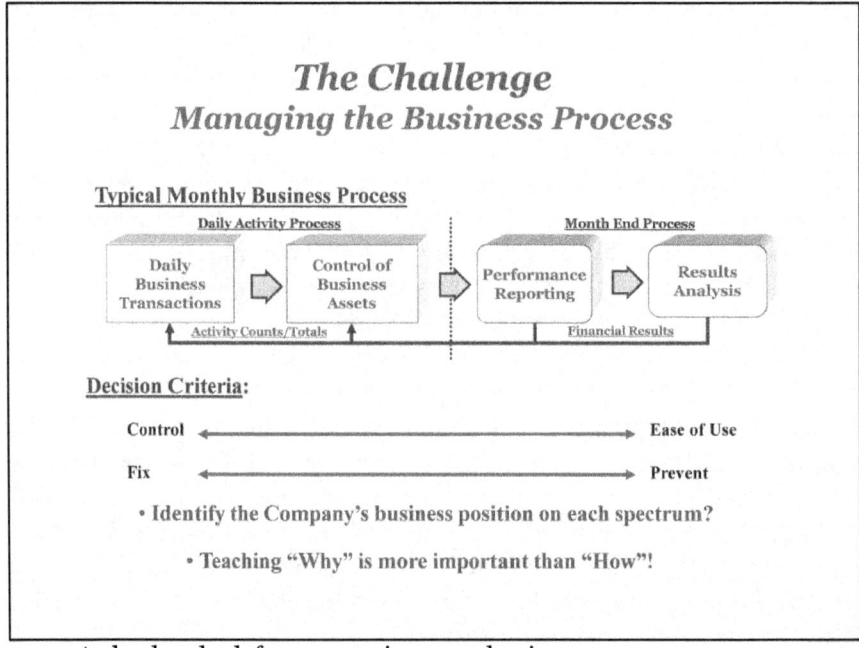

As leaders look for ways to improve business processes as a means to create a *sustainable competitive advantage* within their culture, they will have to consider and make decisions about two major issues. First, leadership direction must convey the right balance between the often conflicting concepts of "control" and "ease-of-use" as suggested in the diagram. We want to make tasks as easy as possible, but at the same time we need to control transaction results and ensure asset integrity. When people understand the controlling principles or rules that apply to each transaction type, they will find their job easier. If they don't understand or they choose to violate the applicable principles and rules, their job will be harder. Fortunately, most transaction processing software provides a significant amount of built-in control; while also presenting in a friendly user interface the information essential to good decision-making. Nevertheless, some hard decisions must be made about how to enforce control principles when they conflict with ease-of-use. Conflict resolution can best be accomplished by shifting toward an education approach that emphasizes more about "why" something is done, rather than strictly "how" it is done. People need to know where they fit in the total process and what their responsibilities are for contributing to the success of the organization. Educating people instead of just training them will help them understand how what they do affects others who follow them in a process. It will also make them aware of what has been done ahead of them and raise their appreciation for accuracy.

Second, a knowledgeable decision-maker comes to understand that most decisions fall into either a "*fix*" or "*prevent*" category as illustrated above. *Fix decisions* are non-strategic and tend to be day-to-day watching and correcting kinds of activities with a short-term impact on results. Leaders who are consciously aware of resource allocation concepts and how they are affected by the inter-connectivity between the strategic forces of profit will place greater emphasis on prevention[60]. *Prevent decisions* are generally more strategic because they attempt to more closely align processes with objectives. The need for prevention decisions becomes apparent when either a broken business process or bad data causes the same problems and errors to occur frequently. Some decisions have both a fix and a prevent element. It is imperative that leaders teach people to understand that prevention is far better than correction. Correcting errors is always an expensive non-value-added activity. A simple example will make the point. If a system price is too high, particularly for a high velocity product which would impact a number of transactions quickly, fixing the impact of the error will require issuing credits to the customers who were over charged. Preventing the problem would simply require entering the correct price in the computer system. When the error is caught on the first occurrence and it initiates an action to correct the price rather than just giving the customer credit, then a number of additional errors are prevented. Well-designed processes for ensuring data integrity, recognizing errors, fixing errors, and correcting data to prevent further errors are all essentials of a sound business process.

---

[60] Since data drives process, preventing transaction processing errors caused by bad data requires an emphasis on master file data integrity.

The fundamental challenge of a business leader is to create consistent, predictable results by promoting a culture where people *know what to do*. The following chapters present some ideas and recommendations that will improve the ability of each leader to successfully meet this challenge.

The Importance of Information Management

No matter how well defined the objectives, how appropriate the business strategy, how clear the action strategies, how effective the process goals, or how accurate the process measures; an enterprise will flounder without accurate, up-to-date and well disseminated information. Every successful business enterprise should build and pay attention to a well-defined and managed system for *information management*. In the next few paragraphs there is sufficient information to convince almost any business leader that they need to make the concept of information management a much higher focus than it has been in the past. The two primary elements of a solid information management structure are information delivery and data integrity. *Information delivery* is about getting data and information to the right people at the right time in the most appropriate medium to facilitate transaction processing and promote decision-making. Historically, in its simplified version, *information delivery* has been called reporting; and its major flaws were untimely availability and ineffective use. Leaders have mistakenly assumed that when information and analysis have been provided to decision-makers that they use it effectively. Time and again studies have shown that there are two things wrong with this assumption. First, the right decision specific data is not provided in useful formats. Second, not all managers understand the cause-and-affect relationship between processes, data, and execution; and therefore, do not know how to apply the information to their decision-making as they attempt to improve operating results. This lack of knowhow limits their ability to respond in a timely way to problems when they occur.

The second and probably the more important component of information management is *data integrity*. It is the responsibility of leaders to ensure that all transaction processing data is accurate and up-to-date if they expect transaction results to deliver the promised financial results. Having said that, it is doubtful that a high percentage of managers and leaders would clearly understand what data integrity means. To start with, it is particularly important that there is a high level of accuracy in master file data; especially for customers, products, suppliers and pricing as almost all transactions utilize this data. In far too many organizations, the important tasks of creating and sustaining valid master file data is so loosely defined that it is most certainly the cause of a high percentage of the process errors that do occur. People get most of the blame for errors and bad results, but it is more often the consequence of bad data. The lack of integrity comes from two organizational flaws. The first is that no one is specifically given responsibility to understand where data comes from, learn how it is used, and comprehend how its accuracy is maintained. Even if someone has the role of understanding the origination, flow and use of data, there is the absence of a clear method for teaching data integrity to other people. The second flaw is that too many people in too many departments can add or change master data. An important task in process design, or redesign, is to investigate, evaluate and resolve data integrity issues. Data integrity is possibly the most important factor to be addressed in process improvement initiatives. In fact, it would be wise to confirm the validity of data creation and management practices before tackling process redesign because data integrity may be the majority of the problem, not the process.

It is a subject for another time to extensively explore all of the elements essential for creating appropriate organizational responsibility for information management.[61] However, no matter what you call this process of information definition and delivery, its purpose is to educate everyone involved in process execution about the importance of the data they use and information they generate. Without the timely delivery of valid data and information during process execution, people will be prone to make decisions based on assumptions. Remember Wethern's _Law of Suspended Judgment_ ("_Assumption is the Mother of all Screw-ups_") which is the axiom that captures the essence of the problem that is created when people rely on assumption-based decision-making.

It is probably a bit of a stretch to call it a law, but the consequences can be severe enough to literally hold a business enterprise hostage while actions are taken to correct the results of assumption-based errors. A perfect example is the all too frequent failure of companies to protect credit card data. It probably happens because assumptions were made, and the recovery is very painful and carries long-term negative consequences in terms of financial losses and negative publicity.

---

[61] In the latest versions of enterprise software, particularly where there is a high level of collaboration and integration with external partners, the need to address the setup, management and delivery of data and information is accelerated. The need to establish cross-functional responsibility for data integrity is overdue. Information management organizations must have all the clout required to ensure that only knowledgeable and authorized people can enter, change and delete master file data.

Wethern's law is dynamic in its simplicity, because decisions based on assumptions are unpredictable in their severity, potentially perpetuated in their frequency, and infectious between people. It is human nature for people who don't know what to do, especially when they lack information, to suspend, or stop their effort. And, until they have more information, or they involve someone else in the decision process, they often believe they cannot proceed. When people suspend their effort productivity goes down and profitability will be negatively affected. If people have to wait too long without knowledge of what to do, they will make assumptions. Wrong assumptions cause errors and mistakes that cost money and time. Depending on the magnitude of the results from making assumption-based mistakes, there will be a fix and/or a prevent problem to resolve. Correcting errors always takes effort away from productive work. When a mistake has a strategic impact, which may lead to the reallocation of limited resources, it will have a lasting and potentially negative effect. An awareness of the reality of this little axiom will help people build processes that fully embrace information requirements for each task in every process and thereby minimize the disruption caused by mistakes. In well-designed processes lost effort is minimized, thereby increasing productivity.

It is people that do make "it" happen, regardless of what "it" is. Ensuring a valid information delivery method for every process will help people be more successful, further educate them about what *fact-based decision making* is, and raise the consistency level of performance and the result in more favorable financial outcomes.

Chapter 13

Leadership's Responsibility is to
Create an Effective Decision Hierarchy

Decision support is an interesting term, because it implies that the right information when delivered to decision-makers at the right time will help them make decisions that are supported by the evidence. In the current business jargon this would be called *fact-based* decision-making. The next two diagrams illustrate opposing decision management structures. One is desirable and the other is not. Most organizations reflect neither extreme, but are somewhere in between. The purpose for including a discussion of these concepts is to provide leaders with the logic for moving their organizations toward a more responsive and independent decision culture. These decision hierarchy principles promote an approach to decision support that is essential to enable senior executives to embrace *Strategic Decision Mastery* as a comprehensive performance management framework.

Every enterprise has a decision hierarchy; and we are not talking about the formal approval process that may be in the standard operating procedures. We are talking about how people go about making decisions at all levels of the organization in the performance of their responsibilities. Individual hierarchies determine what people's perceptions are about the level of initiative and autonomy they can take in making decisions. It defines their understanding about the difference between a small decision and a big decision and all gradients in between. Within an organization's hierarchy, decisions are categorized into one of three major types; and each has its own degree of severity relative to the impact on operations. Each decision category is defined below and then the two diagrams that follow illustrate how the categories determine two opposing decision-making styles.

- ***Routine Decisions*** are those that can be easily and safely made by everyone within their own level of responsibility. They present themselves to the decision-maker based on familiar circumstances. The decision-maker is supported by knowledge of similar past choices whose outcomes have been correct, or at least acceptable. Therefore, the risk of making a similar decision under the same circumstances has a minimal risk of being wrong. Routine decisions are typically not strategic.

- **Guided Decisions** are more complex than routine decisions because they involve more choices, affect more organizations and people, or have more volatile circumstances. Many of the elements of a guided decision situation are comparable to routine decisions, which give the decision-maker some confidence that they can make their choice based on

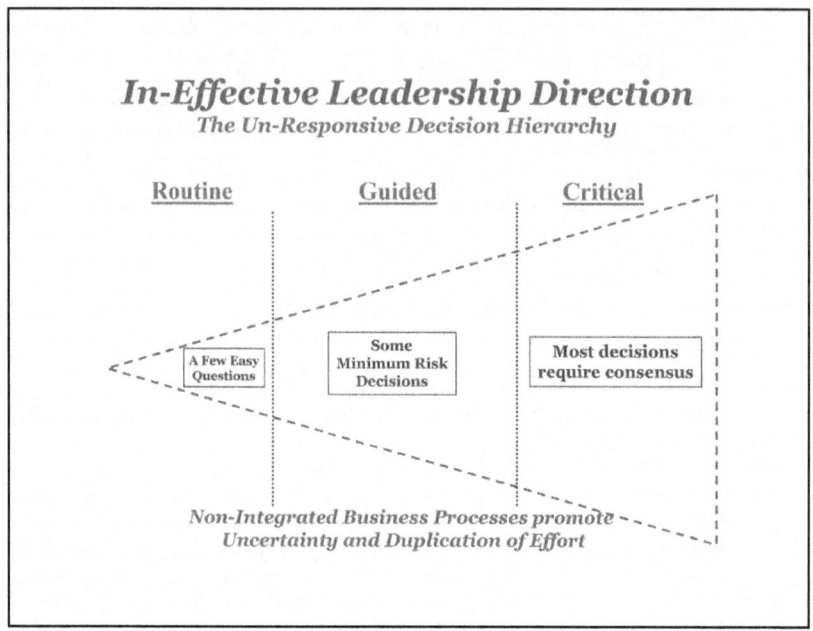

probable rather than predictable outcomes. There is proportionately more risk with these decisions, but the decision-maker relies on organizational culture to support their choice. These decisions may be operational or strategic depending on future outcomes; therefore the decision-maker must be able to differentiate them from routine decisions and evaluate the magnitude of their potential short-term and long-term impact.

- **Critical Decisions** present themselves because the circumstances of the decision environment are unique and the possible choices are unclear to the decision-maker. Making a choice based on the similarity of circumstances to routine or guided decisions is remote. All of the reasonable choices do not present any comfortably predictable result. The risk of making a wrong choice without more information, or collaboration with others, is much higher. These are clearly strategic decisions and their outcome timeframe is often beyond the near future thus making the risk highest among the three categories of decisions.

The more experienced people become at making decisions, or seeing them made by their leaders, the more confident they are at making new decisions despite incurring additional risk for potentially unacceptable outcomes as they venture into new territory. The most important ingredient for making good decisions is knowledge of the facts, which again means having accurate and timely information. Developing into an effective decision-maker depends on a combination of training, formal education and educated experience. Educated experience, in some instances, is more important than formal education alone. It may include formal education, but it is enhanced by skill, familiarity and knowledge of business circumstances. The combination of decision-making skill sets that a person has generally determines the level of responsibility that they are capable of assuming. The three decision types generally apply at all levels of responsibility within an enterprise. The magnitude of the decisions will vary, but to the decision-maker, despite their level of responsibility, the challenge to successfully make right choices is the same.

What the executive leader must create for his organization is a decision hierarchy where the majority of decisions can be independently made by people in the execution of their regular "line-of-duty" responsibilities. When a decision hierarchy is set up correctly at all levels of responsibility, people will instinctively know when to decide, when to collaborate with others, and when to elevate the decision up the organization. Almost as important, they will come to understand their performance measures in terms of the decisions they make. People will naturally be able to identify bad data and information and they will know how to correct it as they seek to make right choices and thereby minimize their mistakes and process exceptions.

Effective leadership direction depends on what type of decision hierarchy is supported by the executives and managers in an organization. Following are diagrams of two hierarchies each representing one end of the spectrum of possible environments. The first example is the least desirable and the second is the most desirable. The first diagram depicts a constrained and unresponsive decision hierarchy. In this environment few decisions are routine, some decisions are guided based on people's knowledge about how decisions were made in the past, but too many decisions are critical because they require consensus between two or more people before a choice is made. Operationally it is an *Un-Responsive Decision Hierarchy* that is characterized by slow decision-making and decisions that convey ambiguous direction. It represents the least desirable of all organizational decision structures because the decision pattern is too heavy at the top. It illustrates that of all the decisions that are made far too many are critical because the decision-maker does not want to risk bearing the consequence of the potentially unfavorable outcomes from their independently made decisions. As a result, decision making becomes collaboration because the perception of what a critical decision is has been too broadly defined by executives and managers in this structure. Either by direction or experience, individuals have learned that when there is doubt they need to get a partner before they make a decision.

In this decision-making scenario *Wethern's Law of Suspended Judgment* is fully operative and its consequences are felt throughout the organization. Processes have too many non-value-added steps and the time between the need for a decision and the execution of an outcome is too long.

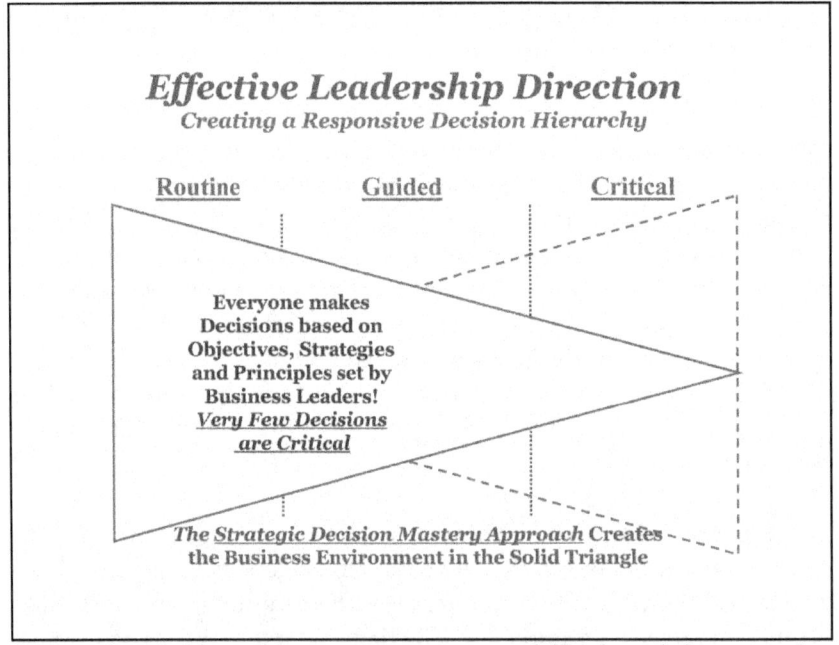

Delays are inevitable and processing norms are difficult to define. Another symptom is prolific data integrity issues because people lack the initiative to correct inaccuracies, thus resulting in unreliable period-to-period financial results. In this structure, processing costs are higher because there is an inordinately high ratio of people focused on correcting mistakes. The likelihood of this hierarchy being in place goes up significantly when business processes are not integrated effectively. Without process integration the inevitable result is uncertainty and significant duplication of effort. In fact, the *Ten Principles for Process Development* would be difficult to apply in this structure because this decision hierarchy is completely disconnected from the process design. Blind obedience is prevalent and the leadership penchant is that people are not to think, they are just expected do what they are told.

It is hard to conceive that such a decision structure could exist in the present business world. It is easy to recognize that this structure fits well in political dictatorships and unfortunately, in too many local, state and federal government organizations as well. It also flourishes in privately held companies based on the dominance of a primary owner; and in departments within larger companies where the manager or executive has an oppressive personality. Regrettably, there are still too many organizations with strong willed leaders who operate this way. Obviously it is a misnomer to call such people leaders. The problem is that such in-charge people like it this way and have a big stake in perpetuating the structure. An extensive document could be written about how difficult it is to transition an entity away from this constrained decision structure. It is nearly impossible with the same management team in place, especially at the top. It is a structure that starts with and relies on a mindset that is difficult to change. Unfortunately, it attracts people in subordinate roles who are content with the status quo and who have lower ambition and propensity to initiate change, or challenge authority.

This second diagram depicts a decision structure that is the exact opposite of an unresponsive decision structure. It illustrates a *Responsive Decision Hierarchy*. This structure is characterized by an organization with an *effective leadership communication* culture. Leaders who communicate effectively focus on creating a business decision environment that is represented by the solid triangle, which completely flips the composition of decisions from critical to routine. In this decision mode, the purposes and objectives of the entity are well understood by everyone. Consequently the majority of all decisions are routine or guided. Very few decisions are critical. In this decision culture everyone at every level, no matter what their job is, understands not only how to do the job, but why it is done that way. People understand how their tasks and assignments contribute to the accomplishment of strategic objectives. Further, underlying all processes and functions is a set of principles and objectives that are defined and measured in terms people can understand in the context of their work. It is a structure that encourages people to make process improvements and recommend changes.

This leadership communication approach is responsive because it allows people to make decisions about their work with confidence that they will create favorable outcomes most of the time. It means people can be more productive, there is a minimum of suspended judgment, and very few inappropriate assumptions are made. For that reason, mistakes and their negative impact on results are minimized. In this structure there is a high level of data integrity, information and data is readily available for decision-making, measures of performance are well defined and understood, and performance results are available to everyone. Another significant characteristic of this type of decision structure is that people understand cause-and-affect and will naturally create positive results out of even difficult situations.

In reality there are few organizations completely at this end of the decision-making spectrum either, because it is somewhat utopian and even when it is achieved it is hard to sustain. Nevertheless, it is essential that business leaders individually understand where they are on the spectrum between a *constrained* and a *responsive* decision hierarchy. It is easy to see that it is possible to have opposing hierarchies at different levels of the same organization. Consequently, it is equally important that executives know what type of structure each of their managers has established; because decision structure has such a direct impact on people, productivity and the level of staffing. It would be interesting to determine how many fewer people would be required to reach high level performance due to the increase in productivity when a decision structure moves from constrained to responsive.

In most cases, making the transition toward a responsive and organizationally enabling decision hierarchy requires a significant catalyst. Historically, one of the most significant transition enablers has been the adoption of new application software capabilities; especially where there is an emphasis on establishing the value of excellence in data integrity and information delivery. Nonetheless, despite the incentive to recreate an improved decision structure by adopting new business systems, there are barriers to making the changeover to a more responsive hierarchy. Perhaps the most obvious will be the managers who create, enjoy, and preserve restrictive decision hierarchies. They will fight the implementation of more people-enabling systems because they mistakenly view it as diminishing their authority. An entrenched autocratic leader will be hard to contest because these people tend to take the fight underground. They will publicly support process improvement initiatives while privately undermining attempts to make the decision process more responsive. In the context of Machiavelli's statement, which was explained earlier, these managers will be the lukewarm ones and they will only jump on the change bandwagon when it becomes evident that they either have no other choice, or because success is imminent.

An important byproduct of the *Strategic Decision Mastery* approach for managing an enterprise is that it promotes the creation and sustaining of a responsive decision environment. Such a structure is truly an enabling environment where everyone can thrive and succeed no matter where they fit in the organization chart. An essential objective, which may drive an entity to embrace the *SDM* approach, is the desire to have a responsive decision hierarchy. Later in the book, the components of a methodology for establishing the *SDM* business management approach incorporating all of the concepts and principles that have been offered, is presented. If the methodology is to be successfully established, it will require moving toward a predominantly responsive decision hierarchy.

Chapter 14

Implementing – The Layers of Decision Execution

After organizational leaders have come to an understanding of how their decision hierarchy works they will rediscover that *decision execution is what creates success*. Decision making is relatively easy compared to decision execution because the former is about thinking and talking; and the latter is about doing. And doing requires people and thereby the wildcard is introduced into the success equation making it somewhat less than certain. Unfortunately, people are not always predictable and therefore neither is their performance and the resulting outcome of their actions. A commonplace example of random and unpredictable outcomes is the difference between sales projections and actual results. I have never met a sales manager who did not believe that their sales team would not sell more in a future period than they had done in the past. Part of the reason is because if sales people turned in a projection for sales to be down in the next planning cycle it would be rejected outright by executive leaders. Rarely do sales people make their sales targets, but not for lack of enthusiasm. The miss is predominantly on the low side and occurs because sales projections lack sufficient substance about how projected sales growth is to be achieved. The reason projections aren't successful is almost always about the execution and a perpetual disconnect with reality.

This discussion will hopefully provide increased understanding about why there is a gap between planning and execution. I will attempt to do so by presenting a methodology for effectively building up-and-down links between planning and execution. There are five levels, which were briefly mentioned earlier, that need to be addressed and coordinated to successfully plan and then realize projected outcomes. They are:

- Enterprise-wide <u>objectives</u>,
- <u>Strategies</u> for achieving the objectives,
- <u>Action strategies</u> for executing the strategies,
- Defining <u>process goals</u> consistent with the actions, and
- Delineating appropriate <u>process measures</u> that define process success.

This methodology is demonstrated in the following diagram. The illustration should help transition from the previously presented principles and concepts to actual business practices. It depicts a structure that links all organizationally significant levels of performance management down to dependent process-level accountability. It demonstrates the cascade concept of how business objectives become strategies, strategies become actions, actions are defined by process goals, and finally, how process measures are appropriately established consistent with each process measure. In this structure, when process goals are achieved they will directly contribute to the achievement of objectives. If a business objective cannot be defined in terms of the processes that determine its achievement it is unlikely to be realized and is probably an inappropriate objective, or strategy. Effective business entities must address the construction and communication of *business execution* for all five layers if they intend to achieve their objectives by successfully executing their strategies at all levels of actual work.

There is a plethora of readily available information about delivery formats and scorecards that purport to measure operational and financial

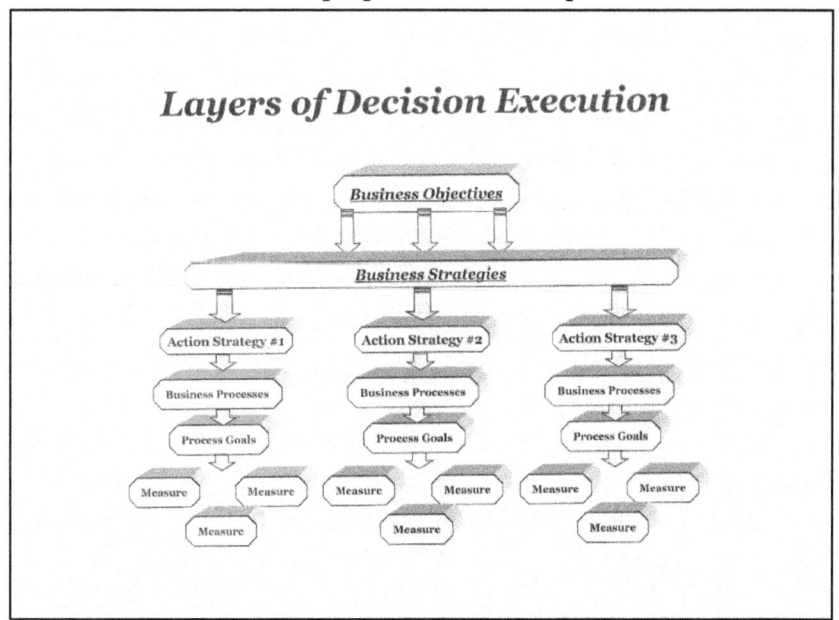

success. Whether these reporting formats define success using the right measures (metrics) has always been debatable. Consultants, authors and academicians who have focused on performance management and measures have long espoused the use of KPI's (key performance indicators). The idea is that a few carefully selected KPI's will provide executives with the information they need to know to determine if their business is succeeding.

This assumes there is a properly constructed performance management structure that includes measurement hierarchies with appropriate process level measures that support the KPI's. It seems that the KPI approach, although academically sound, has too often stumbled in execution for a number of reasons. The most notable characteristic of unsuccessful KPI performance measurement systems is the failure to tightly link process measures to overall objectives and the strategies designed for their achievement. Almost every large business entity has developed one or more so-called *scorecards* to help focus their managers on performance achievement. However, the majority of these systems does not characterize or represent the process-level heartbeat of the enterprise. Consequently, when business is not going well as measured in process detail, the symptoms of pending failure to execute strategy and achieve objectives are masked. This results in delayed reporting of difficulties and the postponement of the appropriate actions necessary to minimize the negative impacts of non-performance.

An explanation of each of the *Layers of Decision Execution* is provided in the following paragraphs.

❖ **Business Objectives** are usually stated in terms of achieving financial goals. For example, most entities state their overall objectives in terms of dollar targets, percentage growth in revenue or earnings, or return-on-investment or a similar income/asset measure such as RONA (Return on Net Assets) or ROTC (Return on Total Capital). No matter how it is defined such an objective rarely addresses how it will be accomplished. For that reason, objectives are meaningless unless they are accompanied by the definition of compatible strategies, which when executed will lead to the achievement of the objectives. Establishing appropriate objectives is *Layer One Planning*, which is a senior executive prerogative.

❖ **Business Strategies** are statements about how objectives will be achieved. For example, if the objective is to become a billion-dollar company it may be achieved by growing existing business, adding products lines, acquiring compatible companies, or some combination of the above. Each of these options is a strategy. It is up to senior leadership to determine the right strategy, but it must be compatible with what the entity already is and within the capability of the talent and resources available for its accomplishment within the specified timeframe. Once the strategies for achieving objectives are determined and clearly stated, they begin to give direction to operational managers.

They can begin to determine what actions should be taken within their purview that will support the execution and accomplishment of the strategies and thereby support the accomplishment of overall objectives. This is _Layer Two Planning_.

❖ **Action Strategies** are the specific things that must be done at the operating level to achieve the business strategies. For example, if the business strategy for growth is to "add new product lines", then the organization responsible for products needs to define how that will be done. The question is, "What actions will be taken to make this happen?" Each action must address what, who, when, how and possibly where? When specific action strategies are in place they begin to provide specific direction to process-level people about what they must do. An effective action strategy will always be linked to at least one business strategy, which supports one or more objectives. Determining essential action strategies is _Layer Three Planning_. It is also called the _Operational Transition Layer_, because it bridges the organization from mere statements of objectives and strategies on the way to defining actual operational activities that must be taken at the process level to achieve them.

❖ **Process Goals** are where the connection is made between operating performance and business objectives and their related strategies. Since action strategies are accomplished at the process level, the next layer of decision execution is to define measurable goals for each process that supports the accomplishment of each action strategy. Transaction processes are where "real work" occurs. Therefore, the goal of each process must be tied to one or more action strategies. Process goals help people who perform process work to know what is expected of them and how their process-level achievements support the strategies and objectives of the entity. When the link to process goals is in place, individual efforts begin to focus on fixing process steps that are not compatible with goals and, where necessary, re-designing processes to fit the stated goals. Setting process-level goals is _Layer Four Execution Planning_. The word execution is added to our layer definition because we are now down to the level where business is transacted and "things" really happen.

Let's consider an example of how this is done. Assume that an apparel manufacturer's objective is to improve their return-on-investment (ROI). One of the strategies for accomplishing this is to reduce product costs.

To actually accomplish this they have decided on an action strategy to reduce production cycle time from fabric-to-finished-goods. It is further decided that the process goal is to reduce cycle time from the current 44 days to 40 days. The process management team further determines that this will require that every step in the production cycle be evaluated for opportunities to reduce the cycle time. That evaluation should then define the goals for each sub-process in terms of the number of days that it takes. If, after an intelligent evaluation of each process step, the new total cycle time days are higher than the 40 day target, it may be that the goal is unrealistic. In this case there are only two possible actions. First, revisit the analysis to seek more time realistic reductions, or concede that the target of 40 days is not achievable and reset the goal. The worst thing that management can do is simply declare a target without regard for whether it is possible.[62]

❖ **Process Measures** must be defined for each step in a process that will support the achievement of the process goal. For example, continuing our example of the apparel manufacturer, the fabric cutting process has a number of steps that must be completed on time to achieve the action strategy goal of a 40-day production cycle time. Goals can be set for each step in the fabric cutting process and be supported by an appropriate measure such as, percent of fabric received on time, the time allowed to clear quality control, the time to complete the marker (how the pattern will be cut from the fabric roll), the time to spread, the time to cut and the time to pack ready for shipment to the sewing factory. In our layered example of how to go about process improvement each of these steps can have legitimate goals and measures that support an action strategy. Reducing production cycle time (the action strategy) in addition to supporting the objective to increase ROI by reducing product cost, might also support another business strategy such as increasing customer support, which is linked to a business objective to increase sales growth by 10 percent. This final step is _Layer Five Execution Planning_ and it may require little more than setting new measurement standards consistent with the process goal where appropriate measures are already in place. If the process is modified to add or eliminate steps during

---

[62] This is an actual example from my own experience. Unfortunately, the executive team always declared process-level goals by edict rather than process evaluation. Consequently, we never achieved the target cycle time. In prior years it had been significantly reduced, but had probably been milked for all it was worth without deploying faster methods of transportation with our off shore suppliers. Unfortunately, this would most likely increase cost thereby reducing profitability and work against the overall objective.

Layer Four Execution Planning, then new measures may need to be defined.

To reiterate, if any one of the planning layers cannot be stated in terms of something that can be achieved at the process level the accomplishment of the entity's objectives and strategies is much less likely. The concept of *Layered Decision Execution* is all about providing direction from top to bottom in the organization; and knowing where the company is in order to drive it to where it wants to be. Typically the CEO sets direction for the entity in collaboration with the senior management team. Correspondingly, senior managers solicit input from the people they work with and especially those who are directly responsible for process execution at the transaction level. Ultimately, after all opinions are considered and decisions are made the entire management team should be expected to promote the achievement of the objectives that come out of the planning process. When an entity's performance management model is built utilizing the *Layered Decision Execution* framework, executive leaders will begin to establish the connection between corporate objectives and people's tasks. When the framework is completely implemented people will be able to understand where they fit into the business process model; and why they are measured and rewarded when they achieve their process goals, because they will understand that the goals have been defined to support the overall business objectives.

The final element of decision execution should be the creation of an executive scorecard and measurement publication that corresponds to the approach which will regularly communicate results throughout the organization. To establish the measures without reporting results negates the positive effects from having the system in place. People want to know how things are going despite the fact that they already have a good idea of how well they are doing. Some recommended formats for communicating performance results are provided later in this document as part of the *Strategic Decision Mastery* methodology.

Chapter 15

Monitoring –Consistent, Understandable Feedback

The *Layered Decision Execution* structure is an excellent concept tool for advancing and promoting process-level performance as the best approach for achieving stated organizational objectives. After it is in place it is extremely important to follow-up with regular performance feedback. The real meaning of

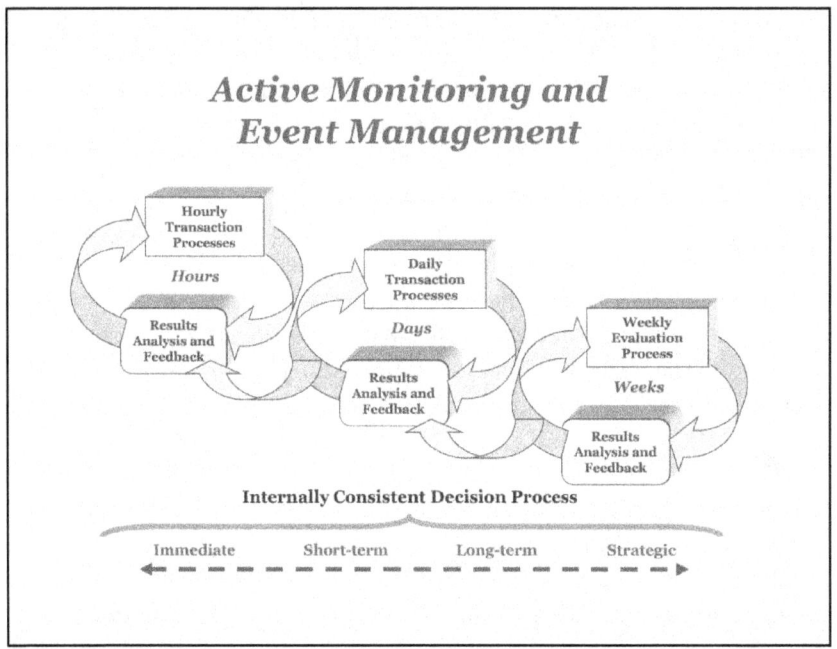

Active Monitoring and Event Management

Hourly Transaction Processes

Hours

Results Analysis and Feedback

Daily Transaction Processes

Days

Results Analysis and Feedback

Weekly Evaluation Process

Weeks

Results Analysis and Feedback

Internally Consistent Decision Process

Immediate   Short-term   Long-term   Strategic

performance achievement is to have a solid performance monitoring and reporting system. It should provide steady, consistent and understandable reporting of results, especially at the process level. There should be daily evidence of progress or failure to allow quick-response corrective efforts by people at all levels. This can best be accomplished by establishing a system for actively monitoring results and managing significant events as they occur. This graphic depicts all of the elements of what I call the *Active Monitoring and Event Management* approach. I highly recommend it. I have derived this solution from years of experience by advocating that it is a logical imperative of management to generate information delivery systems that are operationally focused. Having been a CFO, I am comfortable that accountants and financial analysts can always portray results in formats that they require for statutory and institutional reporting. But, as stated earlier, those formats, with few exceptions, seldom help frontline managers do a better job. I believe it is crucial to deliver *cause-and-affect* data and information about operating results, preferably as near to the causal events as possible. Timeliness in generating results, whether good or bad, permits judicious correction of errors, prevention of future mistakes, minimizes negative financial affects, and maximizes the realization of benefits from unforeseen opportunities.

There are some key elements of the diagram that need to be explained as a means for building the concepts, and hopefully, to convince executive leaders that this method is worth consideration as their preferred agenda for information delivery[63] (reporting). Obviously, a well-defined monitoring and event management structure works best when there is a responsive decision hierarchy functioning within an organization. Explained in the following paragraphs are three factors from the diagram that represent important concepts.

❖ ***Active Monitoring*** – A good monitoring system will report results of transactional and operational processes hourly, daily and weekly. Each timed layer contains a number of transaction outcomes whose results can be positive and/or negative relative to expectations. When reviewed in aggregate, bad results can be masked by the good results of individual transactions; and the opposite is also true. Therefore, the greater the length of time between transactions and results reporting the greater the opportunity to bury inaccuracies that should be corrected[64]. For high volume transactions it is important that hourly results be accessible for managers to review and analyze. Any unusual results can be programmatically highlighted to initiate corrective and preventive decisions and actions. This approach should initiate the correction of bad results thus minimizing their impact, and create opportunities to exploit good results by replicating and perpetuating their characteristics. In the diagram, the looping arrows between the transaction processes and the results review and analysis suggests that active monitoring

---

[63] Earlier in this document we discussed the idea of changing the concept of reporting to be "information delivery". Further, *information delivery* is just part of *Information Management* which also includes *data integrity*. I believe information management is worthy of departmental/functional status in every organization because controlling the accuracy of master data and delivery of consistent information are so important to the strategic execution and success of businesses.
[64] You should remember the earlier discussion about *real time problem resolution* and the one-degree example. We don't want the line to get too long before mistakes are discovered, fixed and prevented.

provides feedback.

The daily transaction process results review is similar to the hourly structure, but the review is typically done by different people. As shown, daily process reviews can provide corrective feedback to the hourly process review. Finally, a weekly review, which may also be conducted by different people, can provide positive feedback that continues to promote the *fix and prevent* approach to refining processes and their results. You will notice that a monthly (periodic) review is not included. It is because the hourly-daily-weekly review and feedback determines the monthly results; and the timing of traditional monthly or period end reporting will have little effect on business processes and transactions. Besides monthly report formats typically have a financial orientation and are not as operationally useful, except for comparative analysis.

❖ **Event Management** – When monitoring is active any significant extraordinary events that occur will be quickly recognized and appropriate decisions and actions can be taken. We are not talking about catastrophic events. It is the process-level anomalies, especially those that negatively affect operating results, that we are attempting to identify and bring to the attention of decision-makers through monitoring. Using our previous example, it is the wrong price or cost that we are looking for, both of which affects the customer and causes the transaction gross margin to be wrong. In this case, two actions are required to make the corrections. The errant transaction will have to be fixed; and the cost or price master file will have to be corrected to prevent further transaction errors. This error that would normally be identified in the daily review, but could be caught earlier if the financial results of transactions are included in the hourly monitoring profile that should include exception reporting. It may be as simple as reporting sales, gross margin and gross margin percent for sales order lines with an emphasis on reporting those transactions that are outside established tolerances.

❖ **Internally Consistent Decision Process** – Illustrated on the bottom of the chart is the continuum of decision-making that applies to monitoring and event management. It illustrates that decision impacts change depending on the amount of time allowed to make choices. Putting the decision-making process into the context of the "One Degree" example explained earlier helps to appreciate the relative impact of decisions. A process oriented decision-making process provides the framework for making process-level choices on an *hourly* basis [immediate decisions] that will be consistent with objectives and strategies. Similarly, short-term decisions that occur on a *daily* basis may lack a full grasp of relevant information to validate their accuracy, but they are guided by the decision hierarchy that has been developed within the organization. When all information is available short-term decisions can lead to directional changes and potentially initiate new long-term decision guidelines. Ultimately, when the monitoring and event management process exposes operational deficiencies at any of the interim levels of decision-making it may identify a need for new strategic decisions. Whenever new strategic decisions are made the methodology for ensuring that they are executed must address their impact and instigate changes for long-term, short-term and immediate decision-making where appropriate. Again, as previously explained, compatibility between objectives, strategies, action strategies, process goals and process measures is essential for consistent achievement of organizational goals.

Chapter 16

Creating a Sustainable Advantage through People

There is no question that good processes can anchor a sustainable competitive advantage. Nevertheless, good processes when combined with an outstanding people culture present an opportunity to have a *perpetual* competitive advantage; because processes can eventually be duplicated, but culture is nearly impossible to replicate. Because the people factor is so important to sustained success, it seems essential to address how organizations can approach the task of building a *sustainable people advantage*. Accordingly, this chapter outlines four steps toward achieving a culture where the people are a significant advantage. In comparison to developing leading edge processes, organizational leaders will find the people advantage much more difficult to build, nurture and sustain. Nevertheless, the increased difficulty should not deter the true leader from tackling the task.

In an earlier discussion we established the premise that the abilities of people are a key factor to successfully creating a culture that is focused on process improvement and effective decision execution. Nevertheless, the question remains, "How does an organization establish, sustain and revitalize people, since they are the primary ingredient for perpetuating excellent performance?" This chapter expands the people discussion and outlines an approach for creating a sustainable competitive advantage by populating the organization with people who have the right attitude. You might say, "Well of course we know good people make the difference between success and failure." However, just because executive leaders are aware of this fact, few of them, in my experience, actually know how to achieve a positive people culture. It is important to have an approach that will increase the probability of establishing the right mentality and consistent reliability in people. I believe there are four points to the right approach; and they can be learned and adopted with relative ease; assuming an organization has a preponderance of leaders who themselves have the right attitude. Despite adopting this approach, it will still take time for it to gain enough momentum to enable long-term success.

From personal experience I have witnessed the difference people can make in organizational achievement in both the private and public sectors. I have seen organizations that have succeeded despite poor leadership because of the talent and devotion of the people actually doing the work. Unfortunately, this type of success tends be short-lived as the incapability of leadership eventually leads to the disruptive change that comes with high turnover among the most capable managers and people. Further, because of inept leadership, these underperforming businesses become targets for leveraged buyout, restructuring and dissolution. Conversely, I have seen companies with extraordinary leaders who struggle to succeed at a high level because the organization lacks depth, ability, and dedication in their people. Leaders of these organizations face the difficult task of actually changing the culture to be able to accomplish what they envision as possible. This type of organization is also underachieving, which makes it vulnerable to dramatic change and increased people turnover as leaders attempt to hire people with the skills and abilities compatible with their objectives. In both circumstances, the time it will take to realize expectations will vary greatly. Some entities will achieve cultural success quickly and others never will make it, especially without a change in leadership.

People make a big difference in an entity's propensity for success. Actually the attitudes of people will potentially have more influence than will their talents and abilities. The recommended approach to achieving a *success-oriented operating culture* requires four essential and inseparable features. Centric to the concept is the conscious attempt to hire and cultivate people whose most evident ability is a *positive self-accountable attitude*. The four keys to establishing and maintaining a <u>Sustainable People Advantage</u> are summarized below and discussed in more detail in the following paragraphs.

Hire It!
Identify and hire people who have the clearly evident personal attributes of: Honesty, Integrity, Initiative, Loyalty and Sound Judgment.

Teach It!
Explain the organization's expectation about attitude to everyone and, *"Be an example of the attitude you expect."*

Create It!
Encourage, promote and reward people who have *"It"*

Perpetuate It!
Identify non-conformance and eliminate it.

The process oriented management and decision education concepts that are essential components of *strategic decision mastery* that we have discussed throughout this book will be harder to implement without the right people in the organization, particularly in the leadership roles. Consequently, it is appropriate that each organization make an effort to determine what might be called the *success quotient* of their existing people culture. For instance, knowing the propensity of an organization's people to assimilate the pending changes from process improvement initiatives is essential to success. Leaders need to ask the question, 'Are their people capable of adopting, implementing and supporting the proposed changes?' 'Will the collective attitude be able to lift the organization enough to abandon the status quo in favor of positive change?' Leaders must know what people are capable of accomplishing, and how fast and completely they can get it done. When the dominant attitude of people in an organization is positive and self-accountable, achieving process excellence is not only possible, but highly likely. Leadership's ability to achieve this success-focused environment can take many forms. It may require changing the culture, enhancing it, or simply supporting it where it already exists. Any enterprise expecting to achieve a sustainable competitive advantage through process excellence, by promoting continuous process improvement, must have a dominant population of people whose attitudes allow them to adapt, adopt, promote and sustain it.

Over the past three decades it has become more common place to refer to employees as associates. It seems someone decided that the term "employee" sounded too impersonal, or implied that if we were "just an employee" we were somehow slaves to the whims of an unscrupulous group of people called "managers". On the more positive side, I suppose changing what we called the people we worked with to "associates" somehow upgraded people's mentality about themselves. It was meant to help people believe that we are all in "this" together; and to status-neutralize them into believing that there is no separation between managers and the rest of us. It came along with the companion name change of the "personnel" department to the "human relations" department. As a practical matter, the titles we use for people and the organizational entities that are supposed to promote their interests, do not change the reality of the workplace. In my view, the term "associate" is not any more effective or descriptive than "employee" in practice; and neither term is any more demeaning than the other. The reality remains that there are, and always will be management and people who work for them in every organization. Similarly, the group of people who are responsible for hiring, training, paying and administering benefits within a company do not work any more effectively whether they are called the "Personnel Department", the "Human Relations Department", or any other of the newly coined titles for this functional group. It has much less to do with titles and much more to do with how people are treated and what the predominant level of respect for individuals is throughout the organization. And, it does not matter if it is a business, an institution or government entity. Wherever and whenever possible we should think about employees, associates, team members, etc. as what they are, "people". That is my preference because I have never met an executive, a manager, a company or a government. Those are only titles and labels. In reality, every time I have worked with any of these "things" it has always been a person. So people we are; and an essential element to building the right people culture is for everyone to know that they are regarded as a meaningful person, regardless of titles or labels.

It is a given that people's attitudes are as variable as they are individually diverse in backgrounds and appearance. Nevertheless, it is possible for an organizational entity to create a culture where the predominant demeanor and attitude of people is *positive and self-accountable*. To effectively utilize *Principle #10 [Perform a task at the lowest level of decision-making ability]* executive managers must acknowledge the need to ensure that the majority of the people in their organization possess the right attitude as well as ability. As a practical matter, a person's attitude is primarily formed by the influence and attitudes of their parents, teachers and friends long before they apply for employment. To change a person's approach to life, initiative, performance and responsibility is not within the ability of most business entities[65]. Therefore, achieving success relies on having people with the right attitude, which requires conceptually embracing and instituting the four elements explained below as the standard for the entity's interactions with people.

Perhaps the best known example of *attitude-based success* is the Disney Company followed closely by Chick-fil-A. Each has achieved the benefits of a positive self-accountable organization because it is an essential element of what they do and who they are. A congenial attitude is expected by Disney customers and to find anything short of it during the Disney experience would truly be out of the ordinary. Any crack in that approach would quickly result in an erosion of reputation and a decline in business

---

[65] I am not sure that a positive work environment influences a person to change their attitude toward life and work, but it can influence how they apply themselves when at work. However, such changes, if they happen at all, must come from within the person.

revenue. Southwest Airlines is another organization that has profitably thrived in a very challenging industry by hiring people with "can do" attitudes who are taught how to run an airline. Everyone is expected to be able to understand every job because they spend time doing them all. It is a culture that does not have people who pass the task to someone else. They see the customer's issues as their issues and they solve them, or find someone who can. Just as it is in these three companies, it seems essential that any business entity intending to have a *sustainable people advantage,* must develop and subscribe to people concepts that are compatible with an objective driven culture as a natural complement to their process excellence initiatives. Entities that focus on people's attitudes toward work increase the likelihood that they will be able to create and sustain a highly effective, process driven, performance focused and achievement centered organization.

Changing culture is a very difficult and long-term undertaking, but it can be done. However, it will require adopting something like the approach explained below. I recommend it as a sound approach to developing people who are and will be the culture carriers. It almost goes without saying, but it does start at the top. The executive and first level management team must have what it takes to advance this cultural emphasis as an essential characteristic for process-driven success. The four attributes of a culture where people have a predominantly *positive, self-accountable attitude* are explained as follows.

Hire It! There are several key personal attributes that people hired into an organization must have to augment and be compatible with a positive, achievement oriented business culture. I consider the most important qualities to be honesty, integrity, initiative, loyalty and sound judgment. These five character traits are both complementary and additive, which means a person who possesses all of them will be a high performing person. It will be difficult for someone to have one without the others because the first attribute of honesty generates the other attributes as a consequence of itself. The abysmal failures in organizational integrity among corporations and governments over the past few years demonstrate the consequence of having people who are not honest. The most disheartening thing about these examples is that they have been high profile people of whom much more was expected[66]. Such events should motivate an urgent

---

[66] Sadly, the parade of morally deficient leaders continues as I write. Examples of recent years include the resignation of the governor of New York and the admission of significant personal integrity faults in his successor. Perhaps for the government sector we should add *"Elect It!"* in place of hire it.

and conscious aspiration of organizational leaders to _find people who are honest_. A number of words like *truthful, sincere, candid and open* help to define how an honest person will behave in conducting their responsibilities and during their interaction with others. People, including those in leadership positions, must be congruent in their business and personal lives on this principle of honesty. If someone cheats or is dishonest in any way as they deal with people outside the workplace, they will sooner or later act dishonestly in their job and most likely when they might be depended on the most. _Add to honesty the attribute of integrity_ which means that a person's honesty is complete, not situational. Integrity implies consistency and uniformity in dealing honestly with people at all levels and in all situations.

Compatible with honesty and integrity is the personal quality of working with initiative. People with initiative will seldom fail. They may make mistakes, but they will acknowledge them, correct them, learn from them and perform more effectively when similar situations present themselves in the future. So-called self-starters grasp the reality of a situation; get the facts necessary to make a decision and then act. Teams of people who know that this is the approach that is expected of them will outperform talent and education the majority of the time. Therefore, when hiring new people it is important that a concerted effort be made to determine the level of initiative that candidates actually have not just what they say they have, or may appear to have.

Each of these five character traits is so entwined with the others as to be nearly inseparable. Therefore, loyalty is the essential trait that ensures that the entity can count on an individual to manage and balance their personal, family and business lives as to not compromise any of them. Leaders should expect people to be loyal to themselves and their families to ensure that life outside of work allows them to be loyal to the enterprise by dedicating their time to work when it is essential that they do. People with loyal attitudes do not take every opportunity to be away from work. When they are at work, they work. They devote time to their own tasks and voluntarily assist others when the opportunity, or need arises. In turn, they expect to be acknowledged for their good work and to be given progressively more responsibility when they succeed.

Perhaps the most difficult attribute to discern during the hiring process is whether people have sound judgment. Sound judgment is what allows people to progress and retain their positions because it is a demonstration of their contribution to the achievement of the objectives of the whole. People who are capable of progressively learning the details of the business, connecting performance to measures of success, and enhancing results by making and supporting good decisions can be said to have sound judgment. They are able to differentiate side issues from real issues and place their focus and efforts on the right things. They are not competitive to the point of withholding information from others to thwart their success, but are collaborative because they recognize when others win so do they.

In a perfect world, every enterprise would like to be able to rely on people who have these attributes as personal character traits. If they could, then business leaders would be able to have confidence that every well-developed business objective can be achieved. It is the challenge of all leaders to place as much emphasis on staffing the team as they do on developing the game plan. Over 50 years ago Philip Selznick, in his previously quoted book *Leadership in Administration,* made some excellent points about the true nature of the responsibilities and obligations of a leader with respect to people and the achievement of objectives. He said:

"The executive becomes a statesman as [they] make the transition from administrative management to institutional leadership".[67],

"Leadership sets goals, but in doing so takes account of the conditions that have already determined what the organization can do and to some extent what it must do. ...It means shaping the 'character' of the organization, sensitizing it to ways of thinking and responding, so that increased reliability in the execution and elaboration of policy [objectives] will be achieved according to its spirit as well as its letter." [68]

"Where implementation of policy [objectives] depends to any considerable extent on the attitudes and ways of thinking of personnel, an effort must be made to translate [objectives] into an 'organization doctrine' and to inculcate these ideas wherever necessary. Policy makers must take account of the capacity of a given organization to absorb a point of view."[69]

The challenge to create a character based organization is enormous with the possible exception of the smallest of enterprises. Ideally, a new startup business entity would address the issue of culture and the building of a character-based staff before they ever transact any business. Then, as growth occurs the positive, self-accountable people culture could be

---

[67] *Leadership in Administration*, by Philip Selznick, copyright 1957 by Harper & Row Publishers, page 4
[68] Ibid, page 62-63
[69] Ibid, page 58

perpetuated. Unfortunately, the initial focus for startup businesses is seldom on what type of people culture they want to create. Entrepreneurs are too focused on their idea or product to concern themselves with such intangible elements of success as people's attitudes. In on-going entities, especially those that are well established, the culture is what it is. Nevertheless, when culture is or becomes a significant barrier to the successful achievement of the vision of senior management, it must be addressed. The decision to change culture must initially focus on how and what type of people are hired into the enterprise. Changing the hiring profile of people to match the desired characteristics is a slow way to create the right culture; because it depends on replacing people without the right attitude with those who have it. It will require a team approach to the interview process, especially for critical positions, and some level of collaborative assessment of employment candidates against the standards established for attitude and character traits. In a character-based approach to hiring, attitude will truly become a more important criterion than education and experience. When all things are equal, among two or more competing candidates, attitude should prevail over pedigree. In this scenario, new hires will more likely fit and enhance the existing culture of the organization and quickly blend into a team approach to the accomplishment of objectives. They will be quick to adopt processes and generally begin contributing to process improvement at their first opportunity.

Teach it! – Everything that is done within an organization should reflect and demonstrate how the organization performs relative to attitude expectations. Meetings, personal interchange, group dynamics and publications should all mirror the desirability of a *positive, self-accountable* attitude. People should come to understand that the enterprise relies on their attitudes to both create and support a sustainable competitive advantage. They should know that other competing organizations can replicate their products, services and processes over time and therefore *"attitude"* is the enterprise's only outwardly sustainable distinguishing characteristic.

Executives and senior managers in particular must understand the importance of them being "an example of the attitude they expect." It has been said, "There is nothing more contagious than enthusiasm, except the lack of it". Therefore, nothing will kill the attempt to build and perpetuate the right attitudes in people than a manager who demonstrates by their actions a behavior that is not compatible with expectations. Sometimes this is a sobering challenge because incumbents who hold responsible positions may have to personally change, or be replaced if they cannot adjust.

Teaching *positive, self-accountable attitude* is not about creating the hype that goes along with motivational speakers, books and recordings. While these may be individually encouraging to those who already have the right attitude, they seldom bring about change in the people who don't. Further, this is not about soul searching in a group dynamics situation because any effect that may come from that approach will be short-lived. It is about genuinely having people who already have an internalized positive attitude. Such people will be interested in helping themselves and others to refine their work toward the achievement of objectives that they both understand and believe are achievable. Finally, teaching has an element of correction to it as well, which means when people's behaviors aren't compatible with the common good, they are quickly identified and corrected. Blame for mistakes is not compatible with the right attitude. When the culture is right, blame is replaced by personal acceptance of responsibility for errors and a proactive effort to correct them, especially when it requires soliciting the help of others. Additionally, training materials will be slanted toward teaching problem solving skills that are focused on the why of process execution.

Create it! – The creation of right attitudes among people will be significantly enhanced when the reward and performance recognition system supports it. People are driven by incentive compensation in various ways, but all people are driven by rewards that boost self-esteem and recognize accomplishment. Therefore it is important to "encourage, promote and reward people who have that elusive *positive, self-accountable* attitude". Likewise, it is important to clearly explain poor performance in the context of expectations that have been set during the hiring and teaching processes. People who have to be corrected for their lack of achievement will more likely improve when given clear reasons for their failure in the context of objectives that they have agreed to and understand. A lack of rewards will cause underperforming people to either change their behavior for the good of the organization and the achievement of its objectives, or they will leave. If they decide to leave, it will generally benefit the organization rather than harm it.

The creation of a reward-for-performance methodology should be biased toward the promotion of people who achieve and have the right attitude. The structure should be based on clear definitions of the *cause and affect* relationships between the process steps people are responsible for and their outcomes. No one should be punished for the lack of performance in an area beyond their individual or collective control. When results are based on team performance [collective results] everyone on the team should know how their individual efforts contribute to team performance. They should also understand every role on the team and how they can assist others to achieve their portion of the effort. The interesting thing about the dynamics of teams is that they will naturally eliminate people who do not contribute to expected results, especially when poor performance is attitude based. Sports is sometimes the best and worst example of people working together to achieve a common objective. And, there are a myriad of examples every year of teams that succeed because they work together, and teams that fail, despite sometimes individually superior talent, because individuals are more focused on personal achievement than on team success. In some ways, organizational cultures are similar, so it is important to have reward and recognition systems that emphasize collective rather than just individual accomplishments.

Perpetuate it! – Once the elements are in place for hiring, teaching and creating the right attitudes there must be a process for eliminating any opposing influences. Part of perpetuating the right attitude among people is eliminating people with the wrong attitude. The old adage of the rotten apple spoiling the barrel of apples is true. For that reason, it is important to have a method for identifying and eliminating the people and programs that do not support the standards for creating and maintaining the right mind-set. It is not about snitching on people, it is about making people who do not display the right attitude feel uncomfortable working with people who do have goal driven attitudes.

In the past there were many companies that had systems in place to identify the lowest performing 5 to 10 percent of their people. Most of these programs have been abandoned because they were "socially" unacceptable and a more enlightened approach suggested that using fixed percentages was too arbitrary. Many professional organizations support an *up or out* approach to the advancement of people. Those who don't advance are invited to leave and find a working environment more suitable to their talents, abilities and attitudes. Such organizations often help in the out placement of these people. Such an approach should be considered for inclusion in any initiative for eliminating people who don't fit the culture. It is a fact that most people know how well they are performing long before someone has to point it out to them, especially when they perform below expectations. In such circumstances, they assume no else knows and they try to maintain a level of performance that is just sufficient to perpetuate their employment.

These people will not be surprised if they are confronted with their non-performance. And having been coached to improve, neither will they be surprised if they are terminated because they do not improve. When honest self-assessment is encouraged at the individual level, and is coupled with fair evaluation at the managerial level, both the people and the organization win. Further, when process-level measures are accurate the achievement of results will be clear and understandable for individuals, teams and organizations.

When the enterprise comes to understand and embrace the reality that a *maintainable people advantage* is an essential element of a sustainable competitive advantage they will address all four elements of the culture building methodology. It will take longer to achieve the people culture when the current culture is far from the desired environment. And, even when the objective is to achieve a positive people culture it will require constant attention to make sure that it lasts.

Section IV
Managing Strategic Decisions

Chapter 17

A Methodology for Managing Strategic Decisions

Turning Ideas into Actions
A prime element of Process Improvement

Hopefully many ideas have come to your mind as you have read the prior chapters and thought about how the concepts might fit into your own situation. Ideally, your thoughtful consideration of the concepts has extended your view, provided new ideas that you haven't had before, and clarified some reasons to want to take a positive action that you have previously felt uncomfortable taking. Thinking about doing something and doing it are very different things. So how do we transition our best ideas into meaningful actions? Sometimes we learn best when someone else raises the question and we provide the answer. With this approach in mind, let me suggest that you consider the following questions to initiate your own action-oriented *trigger thoughts*[70] that will give you the motivation to take some risk, make a decision, and initiate some action.

"What action can I take that will help transform my organization into one that achieves more?"

"Is it possible for this business [organization] to become an entity where our strategy is truly connected to our processes, from end-to-end, or start to finish?"

"Can we be a high performance business where achievement is no longer a surprise, it is an expectation?"

"What can I do personally to initiate change to my own self-process; and then transition my new thinking to an organizational benefit that is consistent with developing a *strategy-that-works*?"

---

[70] To me a *trigger thought* is what you get when you hear a new idea or concept and have meaningful thoughts about something you want to either do personally or in your work. Such thoughts can also come from reflecting on your own circumstances and realizing that you want to make changes, or take a different approach. At the moment, your ideas may only be important to you; so you may not want to share them until you are comfortable that they make sense.

Now, assuming you have some ideas about what you want to do, the issue remains, "How do you get it done?" For most of us, it is difficult to conceptually determine how to apply our best good ideas to create practical solutions to business problems; or to capitalize on new found opportunities. It is in the carrying out of our best conceptual ideas where we most often stumble; either from lack of planning, or because we surrender to the weight of the status quo. In reality, no idea is a good idea without a way to put that idea into action. Consequently, to avoid failure and to not stifle the creativity that new ideas bring, we need a way to transition ideas into actions that produce positive results. I believe that it is far more likely that we will succeed when we have a methodology for making the transition from ideas to actions and processes.

That is what this entire chapter is all about. In the following paragraphs I will explain and illustrate my version of an _Ideas to Action_ approach, which I call *Managing Strategic Decisions [MSD]*. It is an approach for implementing the principles of *Strategic Decision Management*. *In addition, MSD* is a methodology that can be rapidly implemented in most organizations to make available a way for people to conceive, design and build a performance management system where process is synchronized with strategy. This performance measurement methodology is built on the premise that *process should be a reflection of strategy*. There are four components of the methodology. Each of the four is explained first in summary and then in greater detail in the chapters that follow. Each component can be implemented independently, in a logical sequence, as a step approach to ease the organization into becoming a process-oriented culture. When all components are implemented and operational they become the tools for building the motivation and reward system that is essential for any organization where achievement is measured, on a consistent basis, as the realization of objectives, strategies and actions.

The *MSD* methodology puts the meat on the bones of the concepts and ideas presented in the previous chapters. The intention is to provide sufficient information and explanation about the methodology to permit you to create an *MSD* -like performance management system utilizing the unique capabilities and information structure of your organization. *MSD* is a means for developing and implementing a process management and decision-support approach that permits any enterprise to more successfully achieve or exceed their financial performance goals and expectations.

After much consideration and countless revisions, the preferred tag line for the *MSD* approach is:

"*Accelerating organizational performance by connecting strategic objectives to decision-making and operating behavior.*"

The object of *SDM* is to enhance each decision-maker's ability to make decisive, highly accurate decisions that engineer predictable operating performance results through process refinements and improvements to data integrity[71]. When process-level operating behavior is connected to business objectives, by means of an understandable performance system where highly accurate data prevails and process refinement is expected, the probability for

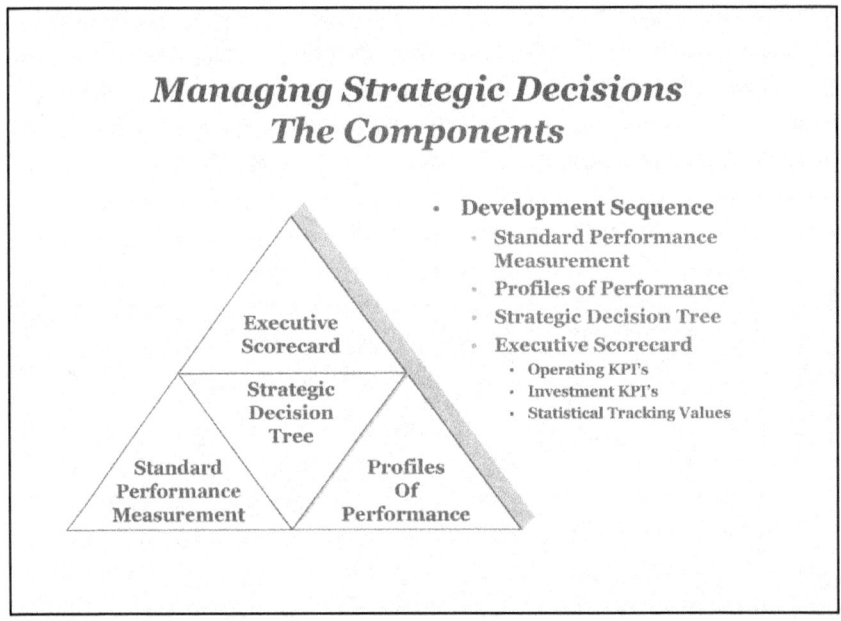

success increases appreciably. The components within *MSD* constitute a methodology for delivering information, not just data, to organizational decision-makers when they need it. When fully adopted it helps executive leaders become more focused on their role to deliver performance; and on their obligation to improve process effectiveness based on a high level of data integrity.

---

[71] It is a fact that no business process, or suite of processes in a comprehensive system, can succeed without significant attention to the validity of the data used by those processes. It simply cannot work. Therefore, as alluded to in prior chapters, the concept of data integrity must be elevated to a higher priority within most organizations and should have executive/manager level responsibility attached to it.

It might be argued that so-called "business intelligence" (BI) software already provides all of the capabilities necessary to develop a comprehensive performance measurement system. That is only partially accurate. Under the BI software umbrella there are a number of excellent tools which provide information to decision-makers using the latest technology for desktop presentation, but with limited flexibility and interaction. However, the missing ingredient in most BI solutions is a meaningful process-oriented architecture behind the presentation formats, which thereby limits the information delivery from being as useful as it could be. I believe *MSD* solves this important issue. By using each element of the *MSD* tools it is possible to create direct associations between decision opportunities and the information that is relevant for making right choices. Effective information delivery can be accomplished from the highest level objectives to the lowest level process steps by carefully constructing the *MSD* components to focus on appropriate business actions and their associated process goals and measures.

An Executive Overview *to Managing Strategic Decisions*

As depicted in the *MSD* diagram above, there are four elements to the approach. Three of the four components are specifically targeted to meet the need for defining appropriate decision information in support of the achievement of strategic objectives. The fourth element is a scorecard summary of the data from the other three components in formats uniquely tailored to the preferences of executives and primary managers. Following is an executive-level summarized explanation of each component.[72]

Standard Performance Measurement (SPM) – This component is focused on providing up-to-date information about operating performance based on actual results compared to previously established expectations that are defined as *standards*. *SPM* utilizes financial and statistical information taken directly from available transaction-based sources within the enterprise and the accounting general ledger. *SPM* can accommodate multiple standards each built to achieve a logical performance target as determined by the executive/management group who are interested in a specific outcome. A number of financial and statistical variances in performance are tracked with an emphasis on pinpointing where performance deviates most from expected (standard) performance. The elemental line item standards are defined in terms of their dependent operating factors whenever possible. If there is no direct dependent

---

[72] A more complete explanation of each *MSD* component is in the following chapters. For those who are visual, the illustrations are included to provide a summary picture of the concepts.

operational factor, one or more logical factors are selected and defined as performance ratios.

Performance Profiles (PP) – There are three key business factors, or informational groups, that are significant to the successful performance of any enterprise. The three factors are *customers, products*[73] (including services as products), and *suppliers*[74]. Accurate data about each of these factors is essential to the successful completion of all business transactions, especially those that are automated. By profiling each product, customer and supplier it is possible to objectively rank them based on their relative contribution to the business. Properly constructed profiles will suggest what the primary metrics should be to develop appropriate contribution rankings. Once the profiles are established they can be used to determine how customers, products and suppliers should be managed based on their relative contribution to revenue and profitability. For instance, to treat all customers the same will not allow business to be optimized for any of them. The same is true of products and suppliers. There are a number of operating decisions that become far more effective when the contribution profiles are known. For example, on the customer side the business approach to pricing, credit management and delivery cost recovery can be managed more effectively based on customer contribution profiles. There are similar profitability elements for products, services and suppliers.

Strategic Decision Tree (SDT) – This tool defines and tracks all of the elements of the income and investment sides of whatever primary measure the business chooses to use to define success. *SDT* is the radar map of entity performance because it highlights areas of operational concern and provides the total picture of performance based on a periodic snapshot. Examples of common high-level measures that would be in the center of the decision tree are return-on-investment (ROI), return-on-net-assets (RONA), return-on-equity (ROE), and economic-value-added (EVA). The visual presentation of the decision tree shows the primary measure in the center and the increasingly detailed layers of the profit impact decisions to the right. The layers of investment decisions are presented on the left. (Sample decision trees using ROI as the primary measure are provided in the Appendix II.)

---

[73] Whenever the term 'product' is used it is intended to include services as they are generally revenue generating factors.
[74] Realistically there is a fourth factor. It is employees. And, just like customers, products (services) and suppliers, people can be ranked in terms of their relative contribution to the success of the business. However, since the people factor is discussed in a previous chapter it is excluded here.

As an example, if increasing ROI is an entity's primary objective then the right side of their strategic decision tree would show all of the elements of the income side of this equation, up to three layers deep. It would include all of the operational actions that can be taken to increase income and thereby increase ROI. On the left side, in a similar structure, the tree would show all of the investment elements that can be enhanced to decrease investment and consequently increase ROI. Ideally, on both sides of the tree each income and investment element might be color-highlighted depending on that component's relative opportunity for contributing to the overall goal to increase ROI. As executive leaders come to understand their *SDT* diagram it will help them define where special emphasis should be placed in the decision-making process to focus the organization on improving underperforming factors, since they represent the greatest opportunity to improve ROI performance.

Executive Score Card (eSC) – Almost all executives take confidence from knowing that they have the right performance management system in place to help their managers meet or exceed performance expectations. However, they seldom want the details. Consequently, the final element of *MSD* is a customized executive scorecard that presents a succinct view of all of the entity's primary measures of success. Typically the scorecard would show operating results for up to 15 key performance indicators for a specific reporting period. A well designed executive scorecard does not exceed two pages, may have charts, graphics and numbers, and clearly highlights areas of achievement and under performance. A well-defined *eSC* pinpoints and quantifies, by target measure (KPI), the difference between current performance and the goal, as well as the remaining dollar opportunity for contributing to the achievement of the overall objective, such as increasing ROI results.

It is not the intent to provide enough specific information to suggest how to build an air tight *MSD* structure within the methodology. However, there is sufficient detail to allow anyone with the proper initiative to conceptually apply this methodology to their specific and unique organizational circumstance. Perhaps, the best characteristic of *MSD* is its simplicity. In addition, it can be easily adapted to changing circumstances, particularly for growth enterprises where acquisition integration might be a priority. The *MSD* structure and reporting formats can be applied to evaluating prospective acquisitions and for quantifying internal growth initiatives by modeling prospective results to support essential decision-making.

Chapter 18

A Guide to Managing Strategic Decisions

This chapter explains the particulars of *MSD* for those who might be interested in pursuing the approach within their own organization. For those who are not prone to enjoy specifics I suggest you skip to the next chapter which includes a sample executive-level scorecard that is created from the *MSD* components. For everyone else, there is value in going through the thought process about how the methodology might be applied in your organization. In the next few pages a more comprehensive explanation of each of the *MSD* components is provided along with selected illustrations to help you more fully understand and get a picture in your mind about what the end products are. Along with the full sample of an executive scorecard there is a sample *strategic decision tree* in Appendix II. It would require too many pages and a lot of explanation to include a sample of *standard performance measurement* so it is not included. However, the accompanying explanation of each component should be sufficient to help create a conceptual model of how *MSD* can be applied to any entity.

Standard Performance Measurement

The foundation component of *SDM* is *Standard Performance Measurement (SPM)*. Essentially it presents financial and statistical information about operating performance that compares actual performance to any one of many standards of performance. A standard performance presentation format restates results, by applying operating ratios from one or more "standards" to regenerate actual results in a "what if" scenario. Operating results at standard are then compared side by side with actual results and the variances between the two are shown in a third column. A spreadsheet application such as MS Excel is a good tool for accomplishing both the calculation and presentation of standard performance results, although it can be accomplished with any number of available tools. Taking the *MSD* approach, versus strictly comparing period results against a plan or prior period, allows performance variances to be more easily explained in terms of the informed assumptions that were made to develop the operating standard. There are three recommended options for setting standards. Each is explained as follows.

Establishing a *Performance Standard* is an effective way to develop a profit plan or budget using *MSD*. It involves selecting a set of operating ratios for each meaningful financial and statistical element of the performance reporting structure of an entity. Standards can be established at any level in the organizational structure by making defensible assumptions about projected operating performance. Setting the standard requires the planner to make informed assumptions about each component of the income statement and balance sheet based on its dependent operating performance

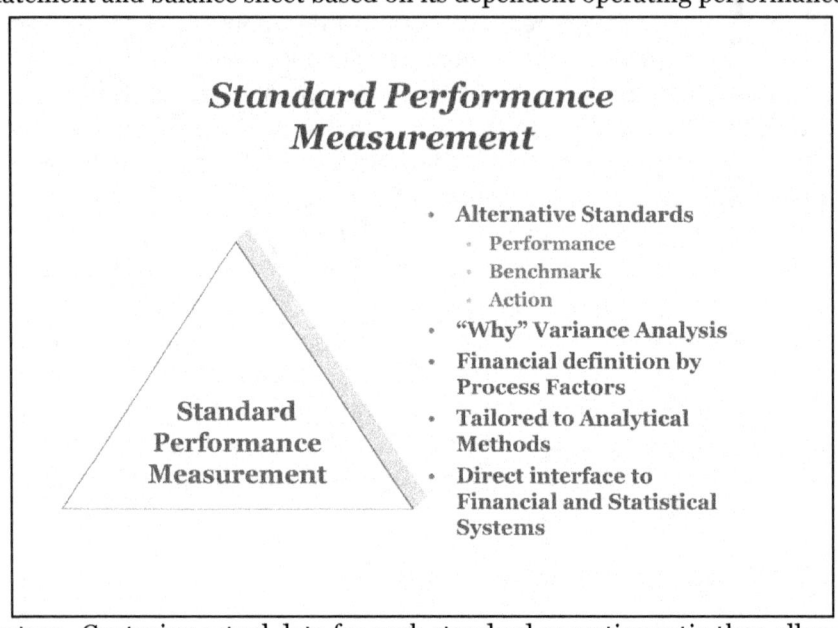

Standard Performance Measurement

Standard
Performance
Measurement

- Alternative Standards
  - Performance
  - Benchmark
  - Action
- "Why" Variance Analysis
- Financial definition by Process Factors
- Tailored to Analytical Methods
- Direct interface to Financial and Statistical Systems

factors. Capturing actual data for each standard operating ratio then allows actual and standard performance to be more effectively compared. The quantified unfavorable variances will pinpoint where the greatest areas of focus should be to more effectively manage toward performance goals. It will also highlight where performance has been exceeded, which may suggest opportunities to further accelerate successful initiatives. Using this standard, *MSD* effectively becomes the profit planning, or budgeting application.

For a *Benchmark Standard,* operating ratios are set at current operating levels to allow the going-forward actual results to be more accurately compared to the benchmark thereby clearly establishing improvements and shortfalls from a point in time. It differs from the *performance standard* in that it can be kept in place for a longer period of time to reflect longer-term gains. It is also possible to have more than one *benchmark standard* operative at any one time. In addition, the benchmark can be compared to both actual results and the *performance standard*.

Setting an <u>Action Standard</u> allows an entity to use *SPM* as a method for modeling operating results for potential major decisions, including impending acquisitions. It is a very effective way to measure initiatives of any kind that are expected to have an impact on operating results. An *action standard* is determined by setting the operating ratios based on informed assumptions about what is likely to occur if a pending decision is made. By applying the new ratios to historical actual operating results the differences can be quantified. Running *SPM* with prospective operating ratios permits the potential costs and benefits of initiatives to be isolated for decision making.

SPM provides the decision-maker with the capability to conduct "why" variance analyses, define financial results in terms of process factors, and tailor the output to the preferred analytical model of the reviewing

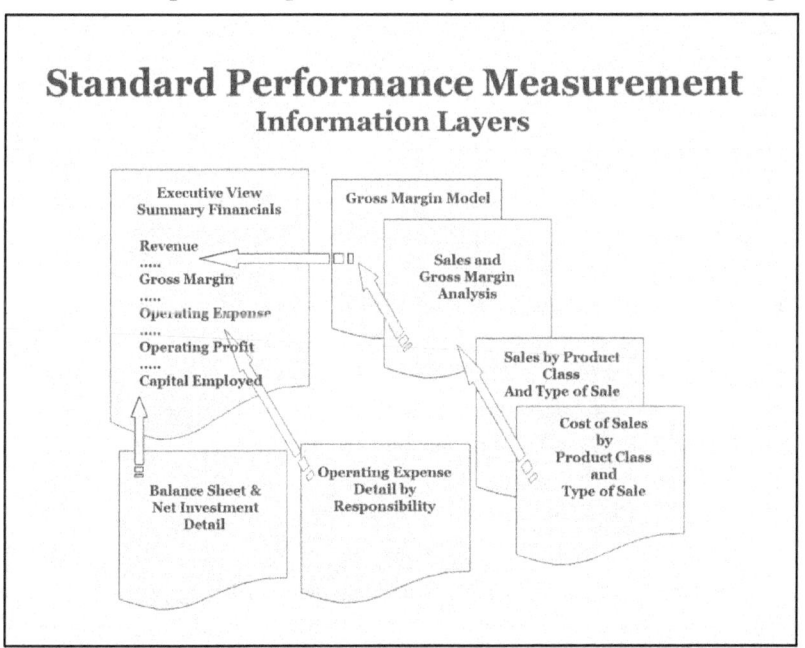

audience. It is should be directly interfaced to transaction level data to ensure an accurate reflection of results and to make certain that it is consistent with general ledger financial information, which is typically reported on a regular basis in numerous financial statements and reports.

145

An example of a layered structure for *SPM* is shown in the previous diagram. While the *SPM* model can be constructed at the summary financial statement level, it is preferable to build it at the lowest level of financial responsibility. This allows the reviewing decision-maker to start at the summary level and then move down to the details as required. In the example shown in this diagram, the executive summary format is built up by first providing significant gross margin level detail by product line and method of sale. Operating expense detail by expenditure type, or profit/cost center provides detail for the sub-totals shown in the executive summary. The balance sheet detail is constructed to match the preferred analytical model, such as ROI.

A highly recommended addendum component to *MSD* is the development of a company-specific *Gross Margin Model*. This tool presents an analysis of the company's ability to manage gross margin by measuring the entire set of price and cost decisions that determine net gross margin. A *Gross Margin Model* provides insight into how revenue and cost decisions affect the net realizable gross margin for an entity. This may include projecting best-assumption details of pending decisions. In the model there is a line item for all of the revenue side and cost side factors that impact net gross margin. It is particularly important to build a well-designed model because of the significance of gross margin to overall profitability and cash flow. As stated earlier, gross margin dollars, and not sales or revenue dollars, are the only dollars that can be spent to conduct business. Unfortunately, this is not a common perception for many business leaders, particularly those on the revenue generating side of the entity. Most of the line items in a well-constructed gross margin model require strategic decisions because they often have long term impacts even though they are only measured periodically. Sample gross margin models are included in Appendix I to more clearly illustrate the concept.

Performance Profiles

As previously explained, there are three Key Business Factors [customers, products and vendors] that have a direct impact on profitability. How each of these critical elements of commerce is managed, throughout the transaction process, will determine how successful the enterprise will be, especially in terms of revenue and profitability. Financial results will be maximized when the factors are managed to leverage their strengths and minimize their weaknesses in the course of operational performance. The performance profile concept measures and ranks the relative contribution of each customer, product and supplier against the total population of each group.[75] Performance Profiles are the leverage component of *Managing Strategic Decisions* because the data contained in system master files for each of the key factors drives the results of every business transaction. A summary of the key points about the performance profiles is shown in the accompanying diagram. Reliable information about customers, products and

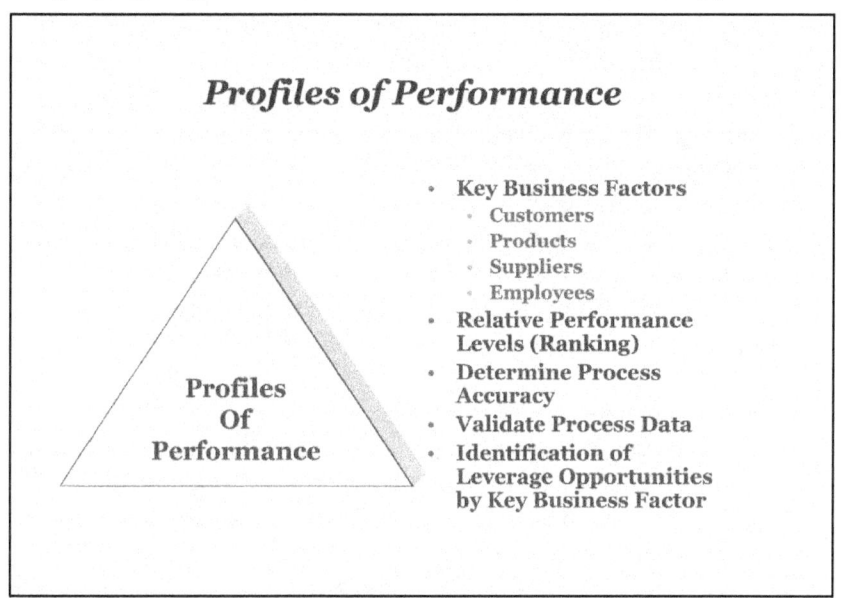

Profiles of Performance

- **Key Business Factors**
  - Customers
  - Products
  - Suppliers
  - Employees
- **Relative Performance Levels (Ranking)**
- **Determine Process Accuracy**
- **Validate Process Data**
- **Identification of Leverage Opportunities by Key Business Factor**

Profiles Of Performance

suppliers delivered at the right time, and in the right way, to decision-makers helps them design, monitor, and adjust business processes to maximize profitability and asset productivity.

The profiling of the key factors can be based on one or more data elements. The initial profile should focus on identifying which customers, products and suppliers provide the highest contribution to profitability. Ideally, with these profiles as a tool, management can make decisions about pricing, costing and process focus to exploit the greatest opportunities and eliminate the most significant weaknesses. The key to such profiling is to select profile measures that reflect the operating goals of the entity and contribute to the achievement of objectives and strategies. The report formats for presenting the profiles should be designed to help executives and managers accomplish all of the following.

---

[75] As previously mentioned people are the fourth key factor. In this discussion, however, the emphasis is on the first three, since the importance of people is covered in the earlier chapter about how to establish a sustainable people advantage.

- Validate the information about each of the key business factors to insure that the processes using the information will be executed successfully.
- Determine process accuracy by clearly providing the results of transactions in formats that promote quick decisions to fix inaccurate data and operational issues; and facilitate decisions that will prevent further process errors.
- Demonstrate the relative performance contribution of individual elements of the key business factors to make possible timely and appropriate decisions that will improve operating results. Well-designed contribution profiles tend to suggest how to structure processes to more effectively utilize profile data during transaction execution. In addition, profiles flag data elements that are inconsistent with operating objectives so they can be corrected more quickly.

One of the more advantageous characteristics of the *MSD* methodology is the ability to provide predictive decision information as well as reflective data. Profiling helps to quickly determine what decisions will allow the entity to more effectively leverage profitability and identify asset utilization opportunities. It will also provide focus for all efforts designed to fix data errors in both processes and measures.

Strategic Decision Tree

The executive presentation component of the *MSD* approach is the *Strategic Decision Tree (SDT)*. It is called this because it utilizes information taken from *SPM* and the *Performance Profiles* to focus decision-makers on the most critical areas where significant strategic and some tactical decisions need to be made. The *SDT* can be built and presented to any level of management where there is responsibility for profitability and asset management. It will concentrate the attention of profit center managers on the areas that require their attention. The *SDT* is built for each entity based on their decision structure, emphasis, and strategy and is upwardly cumulative between responsibility levels. Decision-level information is provided to managers in the context of the entity's overall measure of success, such as ROI. Therefore, an obvious first step is to find the right measure.

Once the right measure has been validated, *SDT* facilitates the identification of the right key performance indicators (*KPI's*) and then presents them in terms of investment and profit opportunities at a summary level. A ranking leverage is applied to each element of the decision tree to insure that decisions and efforts are focused on those opportunities and issues that have the highest performance improvement leverage. Since the calculation of each element in each layer of the tree is based on information

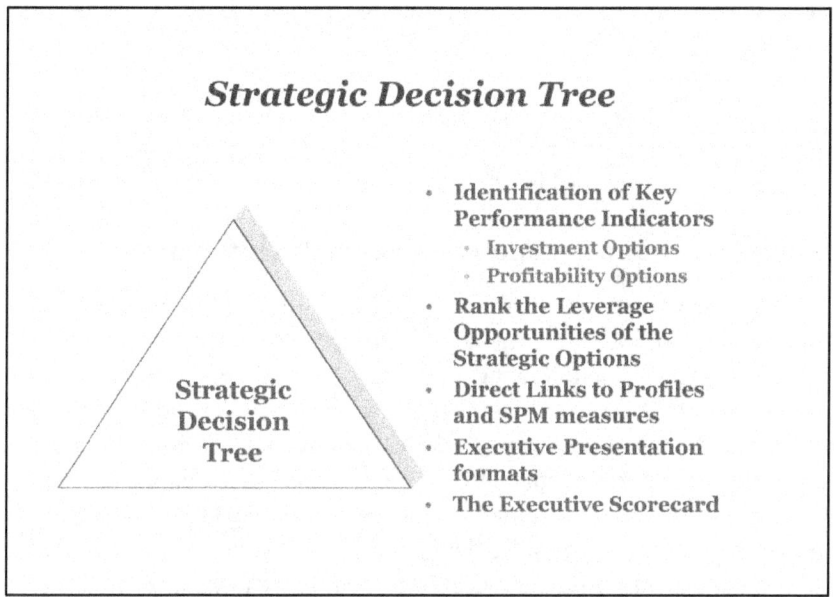

that comes directly from the data in *SPM* and the *Profiles* it is internally consistent within each reporting period. The ability to present consistent information across all of the elements of *MSD* is a distinguishing feature of the methodology and a confidence builder for the executive/managers that use it. Specific *SDT* presentation formats focus on delivering appropriate information at each level of profit responsibility.

The Executive Scorecard

Monitoring the Progress of Key Performance Indicators

The final and optional component of *Managing Strategic Decisions* is the *Executive Scorecard (eSC)*. A well-defined scorecard provides a quick view of the primary key performance indicators and their progress toward attaining established goals. The presentation view of performance indicators is in the preferred formats of each executive user. It is directly linked to the other elements of *MSD* to continually ensure the consistent presentation of data for each selected reporting period. One of the advantages of the *eSC* is its ability to start with any executive level key performance indicator (KPI) and then drill down, from any responsibility level, to the key business factors and processes that may require decisions and actions to improve performance. Ideally, the model is accessed from a personal computing or mobile device where the maximum amount of information and flexibility is available for presentation, inquiry, communication and resolution. However, since personal computing devices are not always available or appropriate, the scorecard can be printed for use and reference in an off-line environment whenever the need arises.

The best way to explain the *eSC* is to illustrate it with an example. Therefore, after a brief discussion of the *MSD* database structure, I have included a sample scorecard in the next chapter.

Managing Strategic Decisions – System Architecture

To be able to complete a working concept of *MSD* the would-be practitioner should find it helpful to get a clearer view of the recommended system architecture. The following diagram is a picture of the basic architecture for *MSD* from a systems point-of-view. To determine what an entity-specific architecture should look like requires addressing both sides of the diagram. The left side represents the "inventory" of available data and information sources as determined by surveying existing legacy systems. If the information outcomes require data from outside sources they would also be defined here. You cannot skip this step because without knowing what information is readily available it will be difficult to define logical measures. On the far right side of the diagram are drafts of reporting and presentation formats, which necessitate specific identification of the information required to produce them. The required output information is then reconciled with the data sources to ensure that the presentation formats can be produced and delivered in a timely manner. If data is missing, then additional effort will be required to capture the missing data points, or the output formats will have to be modified.

In order to avoid the potential errors that can occur from human intervention during the data collection process, it is preferable that electronic transfer be the primary method of data capture. This means data extraction processes and interfaces between the *MSD* database and all data sources will be required. Since it is not particularly complex this should not be an issue in today's world of high reliability data extraction capabilities. Ideally, information will be gathered from valid sources of transaction level data. Such original data normally includes financial values, logical data attributes, and related statistics that are used in separating, ranking and profiling *MSD* information.

In a working *MSD* system, data is periodically extracted at intervals that match the specified reporting period-ends. It is then stored in a relational database that has been designed to match the structure of all of the *MSD* components. This financial/statistical database should have an

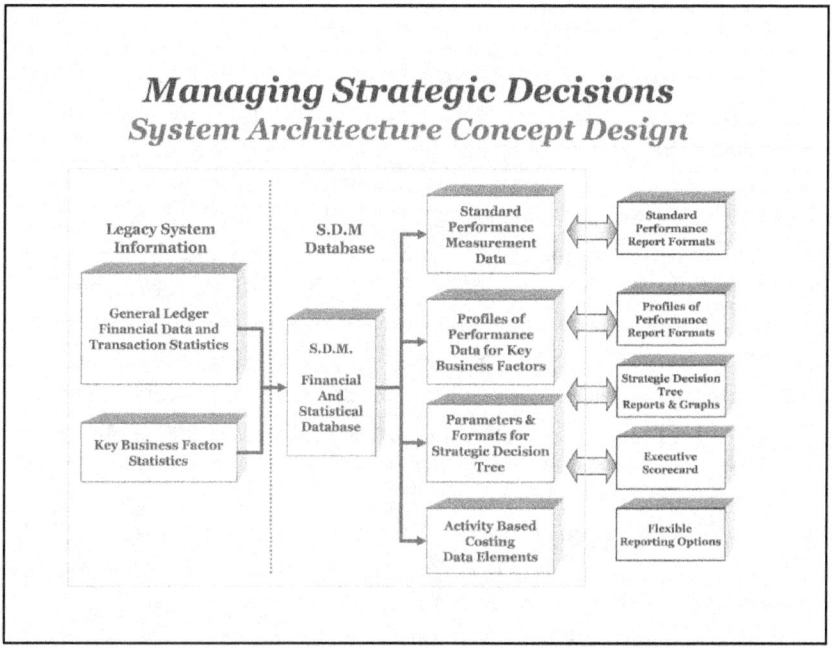

architecture that will facilitate the production of the information formats and data relationships that are required to support both periodic and ad hoc reporting requests. It is assumed that the database architecture will be designed to last and only be modified to accommodate new data elements that were not available during the initial design. As illustrated, the *MSD* database may include report-specific data marts to allow more diverse access to meet the reporting needs of different organizations.

Chapter 19

A Sample Executive Scorecard

The intent of this discussion is to heighten awareness about how results are determined and the factors that most directly affect them. This sample scorecard is designed to communicate the performance of a hypothetical business entity based on fifteen[76] KPI's. In the example, the KPI's have been selected to focus on each of the principal business objectives of the company as determined by a strategic decision tree. The hypothetical entity has defined return-on-investment (ROI) as their primary measure of success. By definition this determines the two primary elements of the strategic decision tree to be investment and profitability, or in other words, the income statement return on the value of investment[77]. Therefore, progress is measured by an increase in profitability or a decrease in investment and, most likely, some of both. Each *primary* component of investment and profitability are measured by a KPI that demonstrates progress toward the achievement of the target ROI. The actual baseline value of each KPI is captured and a target level is defined. The *Executive Score Card (eSC)* then periodically measures the current value of each KPI and compares it to the baseline and the target. The components of the sample scorecard are shown separately in the following discussion to more easily describe them. In an actual scorecard they would be combined into 2 to 3 pages. The sample that follows illustrates the investment side of the ROI objective under a section of the scorecard titled "Net Asset Productivity" where each investment element is tracked. A section of the scorecard titled "Profit Performance" tracks the income objectives for ROI.

In our example two additional KPI groups are included to illustrate that there may be other measures, as defined by executives, which do not directly relate to the achievement of ROI objectives, but are deemed to be contributing factors. In our example, entity management believes strongly in

---

[76] Ideally, an organization will not define more than 15 KPI's. There is always the tendency for each manager to have their preferred measures, but usually when these are further examined they tend to be process level measures that support one or more higher level KPI's. When the KPI concept is properly explained during the definition and implementation phases of *MSD*, only meaningful KPI's that support business objectives will be utilized.

[77] Included in Appendix II is the *Strategic Decision Tree* from which the KPI's were determined. In includes a three-level tree to clarify how KPI's are connected to process level performance measures.

measuring and tracking customer satisfaction and has defined four (4) KPI's to track it. The assumption is that when these objectives are achieved customers will be more loyal, will buy more, and will choose the entity as their preferred supplier[78]. These KPI's are separated on the scorecard into a section called "Customer Satisfaction Performance".

A second indirect group of metrics is included in the sample scorecard under "Business Activity Measures". These two measures are what I would call sentimental favorites among old school business managers. In our example, neither of the two measures (orders per day and order lines per day) can be said to directly contribute to the profitability side of our ROI equation, nor indirectly to the investment side. After all it is possible to have more orders per day and sales would decline. Likewise, more order lines per day does not necessarily mean more revenue. The actual validity of these measures as contributors to improvement in sales, profitability and investment is entirely dependent on the nature of the business. Nevertheless, the measures are included because they are important to our hypothetical executive team. A brief explanation of each of the KPI's by business objective for our sample company follows.

It is important to note that it is critically important to measure the trend of performance measures because it is far more important than the absolute value of any metric at a point it time. The trend can be defined relative to the base period or the last reported period, or both. In the sample, the trend is reported as the difference between the current value of the KPI and the last reported value. In addition, the impact of that trend is presented in terms of its dollar impact on performance. In many businesses there is some seasonality to operating results. If the seasonality is extreme then a measure might be modified to allow for a seasonal factor to be able to measure months and quarters in a more realistic context relative to an annual goal, especially for the dollar value of the trend result. There are no seasonal factors included in our example.

Key Performance Indicators of Investment:

In our example, the investment side of the ROI equation is defined as net current assets, which is the total of <u>accounts receivable</u> plus <u>inventory</u> less <u>accounts payable</u>. In the first section of the scorecard these three

---

[78] It is nearly impossible to measure whether or not customer satisfaction directly contributes to business improvement, especially in the same period the measure is captured. Nevertheless, in companies that track such metrics the secondary benefit, and perhaps the most important, is an increased customer awareness among the people who are responsible for determining whether or not a customer is "satisfied".

individual components has a measure and the total of the measures determines the overall achievement of the investment objective. At the end of this section of the scorecard is the Net Asset Summary which provides the summarized outcome to-date and the remaining opportunity for improvement based on target levels. The summary shows the beginning position, progress year-to-date, target amounts and the remaining opportunity. The opportunity amount for investment is calculated as if an entity is operating at target levels. A further explanation of each investment component and how it is measured follows.

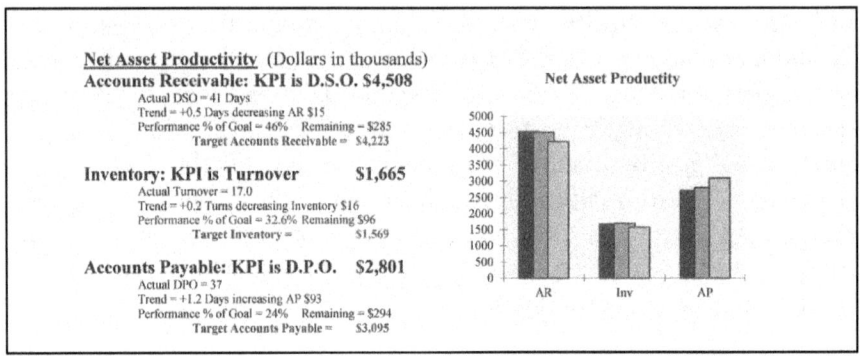

Accounts Receivable – In order to increase ROI, the objective is to reduce the company's investment in accounts receivable (AR) as measured by Days Sales Outstanding (DSO). The scorecard provides current period information about the value of AR investment, the progress toward meeting the target DSO objective and the trend (favorable or unfavorable) since the last reporting period. It also indicates the remaining planned improvement based on the target. This information is provided for each of the KPI's where appropriate and when the right information is available.

Inventory - The ROI enhancement objective is to reduce the company's investment in inventory as measured by inventory turnover

Net Asset Summary:

Investment	Beginning	YTD +/(-)	Target	Opportunity
Accounts Receivable	$ 4,751	$ 242	$ 4,223	$ 285
Inventory	1,711	47	1,569	96
Accounts Payable	2,708	294	3,095	294
Net Assets	$ 3,754	$ 583	$ 2,697	$ 675

(Turns). Inventory turnover is a generally accepted measure that allows for an increase or decrease in inventory relative to the sales level supported by that inventory. While turnover is an adequate measure, there are higher level measures of inventory effectiveness. One is gross margin return on investment (GMROI), which factors in the gross margin percent times the number of turns. This is a better measure because a product that turns four (4) times and makes 35% gross margin contributes more to ROI than another product that turns the same number of times but only has a 25% gross margin. An even higher level measure is GMROI factored by the sales velocity of the product, where velocity is defined as the number of times the product is sold. Obviously, a product that sells more times generates more profit contribution when the turnover and the gross margin are the same.

Accounts Payable - The Company's total investment in working capital is reduced to the extent that current assets are funded by suppliers as measured by the dollar amount of accounts payable. In our example, the KPI measure for accounts payable is defined as Days Purchases Outstanding (DPO). Where applicable, for calculation purposes, the total dollar amount of accounts payable should include the amount for accrued purchases, which is defined as inventory received but not yet invoiced. Since the inventory investment value includes all received goods, accounts payable should include the associated value of the liability regardless of whether the invoice is entered for payment.

Key Performance Indicators of Profitability

In our example, there are four KPI's for measuring profitability performance at the executive level. Since the business objective is to increase profitability and thereby ROI, the selected KPI's address sales growth, gross margin percent increase, and the reduction of operating expense as a percent of gross margin. Also included are two secondary measures whose achievement supports the related primary KPI. A subset of sales is *Catalog*

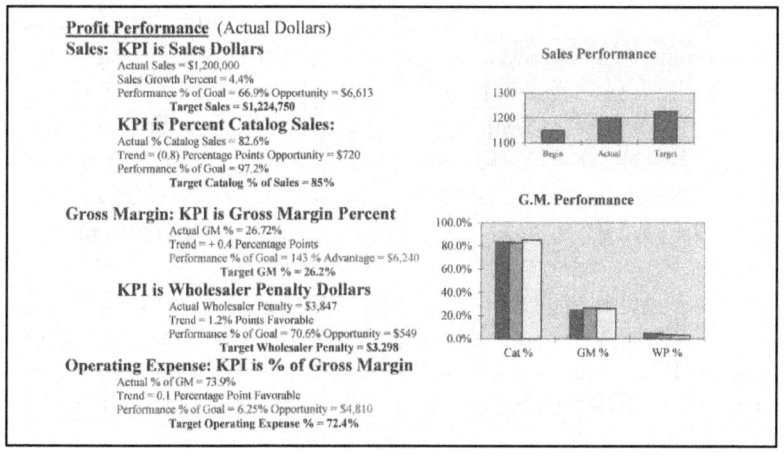

155

Sales Percent because our company has determined that this is a specific sales channel to be targeted for growth. Secondary to the *Gross Margin Percent* KPI is a measure called *Wholesaler Penalty,* which is a wholesale industry specific profitability factor that depletes gross margin dollars when products are not in inventory and must to be purchased from secondary sources to fill customer orders. Therefore, it has been selected by our Company because it needs to be improved by reducing the dollar amount of penalty relative to sales.

The scorecard again presents the beginning position, the year-to-date progress; the target value, and the profit opportunity for each KPI. Once again, profit opportunity is computed "as if" the company was performing at target levels. At the end there is a summary of profitability performance after the individual KPI information. The explanation of each specific KPI is as follows.

Sales Dollars - Sales dollars is a key measure because it is the gauge of increasing or decreasing business volume and thereby gross margin, which is the actual measure of profitability. In order to determine progress, or the lack of it, sales dollars as a measure is only meaningful when compared to prior periods, and/or target levels. In most entities, total sales dollars has many subsets such as sales by product line and sales channel. Therefore, the effectiveness of the overall sales process is determined by a number of process-level metrics at the subset level. In our example, it has been determined that a strategic sales channel is *catalog sales;* therefore it becomes a KPI-level measure instead of simply a process-level measure.

Catalog Percent of Sales – A major sales initiative in our sample entity is focused on increasing catalog sales. It has been determined that the higher the percentage of catalog sales the higher the potential profitability because the company is able to take advantage of purchasing and pricing programs that increase gross margin on catalog products. A secondary profitability impact is lower selling costs, especially in an online sales environment, because there is no sales commission involved for products sold through the catalog; and customers typically pay for delivery costs, which is not the case when products are sold through other channels.

Gross Margin Percent – Since the value of gross margin dollars retained from total sales dollars is measured by the gross margin percent this is a significant KPI. To improve ROI the objective is to increase the gross margin percent. This is most often easier said than done. Since there are a number of factors that must be effectively managed to increase selling gross margins, several departments (people) are involved in executing this action strategy. The factors include customer pricing, product costs and sales channels to name the most obvious.

Gross Margin – *Wholesaler (Alternative Source) Penalty* – Our sample entity has determined that they need a better process for stocking products sourced from their primary suppliers to minimize product costs and thereby increase gross margin. For our entity, whenever a stocking product is purchased from a secondary supplier to fill a customer order the profitability typically goes down because the product cost is higher from the alternate source. Therefore, the business objective is to minimize the loss of gross margin when buying from alternate sources. This metric is also associated with and contributes to the outcome of the KPI's to "increase *gross margin percent*" and "*reduce inventory*" since they are both affected when the percent of orders filled by products sourced from primary suppliers increases. The objective is to reduce the cost penalty that is incurred when inventory stock-outs occur and products must be purchased from secondary suppliers to fill customer orders. Success is measured by computing the gross margin difference between products sourced from primary suppliers versus secondary suppliers. The KPI is the amount of dollar penalty.

Because this metric also affects the other two metrics, there will be an overlap in the initiatives required to accomplish all three of the strategic actions. There may be conflicts that need to be resolved. For example, increasing inventory turnover conceptually runs counter to the idea of increasing stocking levels to satisfy this metric, which may be required to eliminate purchases from secondary suppliers.

Operating Expense Percent of Gross Margin – The final profitability KPI is a broad measure of operating expense control. Gross margin dollars minus operating expenditures is earnings before interest and taxes (EBIT), also sometimes called operating profit. EBIT is a closely tracked number by the financial and investment community as it most accurately reflects the profitability results from the operations of a business entity. In our sample company, operating expense management is tracked by reporting the dollar amount of operating expense as a percent of gross margin dollars. And, since sales dollars are not spend-able and gross margin dollars are, this is a better measure than operating expense as a percent of sales because it more accurately reflects the consumption of the entity's spend-able dollars.

Obviously, there are number of expenditure components in total operating expense including people costs. In a *Strategic Decision Tree* a

Profit Summary:

Profit Element	Beginning	YTD (+/-)	Target	Opportunity
Sales: Growth	$1,150,000	$50,000	$1,225,000	$6,613
Catalog %	83.4%	(0.8)% Points.	85.0%	720
Gross Margin: %	25.0%	+1.72 % Points	26.2%	(6,240)
Wholesaler Penalty	$5,067	$3,847	$3,298	549
Operating Expense %	74.0%	+0.1 % Point	72.4%	4,810
EBIT	$74,750	$83,687	$88,582	$ 6,452

breakdown of the most important operating expense categories would be reflected. In the *Standard Performance Measures* model all of the expense elements would be separated and tracked based on the processes that affect them.

As with the investment section of the **eSC**, at the end of the profitability section there is a summary table (shown above) of the primary data for each metric, as well as a their total impact on EBIT.

Key Performance Indicators - Customer Satisfaction

Our hypothetical executives have determined that the level of satisfaction that customers feel when doing business with the company is important to sustained long-term success. Therefore, four KPI's have been selected to measure, as objectively as possible, this difficult to define and somewhat intangible endeavor to maintain a high level of customer satisfaction. At the end of this section the company has developed a customer satisfaction rating. It is a composite of the satisfaction scores for the four KPI's, which are then subjectively weighted to produce an overall customer satisfaction score. The specific measures of customer satisfaction are:

In-Stock Fill Rate - A published marketing objective of the company is to have a 99 percent[79] fill rate for customer orders. This is measured by the in-stock fill rate. It implies that sufficient inventory will be on hand ready to ship when the customer's order ship dates require it. Obviously, higher inventory levels that may be required to meet this objective could negatively affect the objective to increase inventory turnover, which is one of the primary investment objectives. Any failure to meet the 99 percent fill rate is

---

[79] A 99 percent fill rate is a highly unrealistic target for most business, especially those with a high number of SKU's. If it is to be achieved it will require a highly disproportionate investment in inventory which would be a challenge to achieving a higher ROI.

believed to be detrimental to customer service and, therefore lowers customer satisfaction. [80]

Returned Lines Percent of Total Lines - A primary measure of customer satisfaction is the number times customers return product. The KPI is calculated as the number of returned order lines as a percentage of the total order lines. It is assumed that the lower the percent of returned sales order lines, the higher the customer satisfaction. There are some intangible elements to this measure. First, customers may have gotten what they wanted and ordered, but they changed their mind after receipt of the product and returned it. Second, the return of product may not match the same

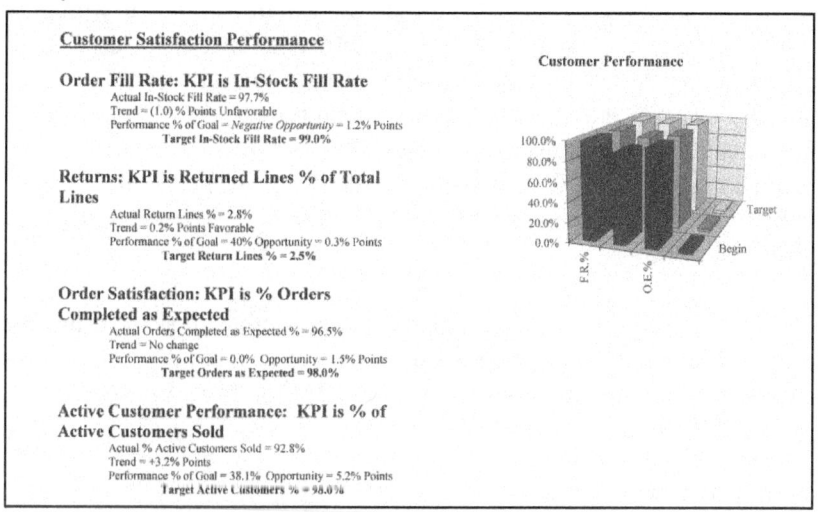

Customer Satisfaction Performance

Customer Performance

Order Fill Rate: KPI is In-Stock Fill Rate
Actual In-Stock Fill Rate = 97.7%
Trend = (1.0) % Points Unfavorable
Performance % of Goal = Negative Opportunity = 1.2% Points
Target In-Stock Fill Rate = 99.0%

Returns: KPI is Returned Lines % of Total Lines
Actual Return Lines % = 2.8%
Trend = 0.2% Points Favorable
Performance % of Goal = 40% Opportunity = 0.3% Points
Target Return Lines % = 2.5%

Order Satisfaction: KPI is % Orders Completed as Expected
Actual Orders Completed as Expected % = 96.5%
Trend = No change
Performance % of Goal = 0.0% Opportunity = 1.5% Points
Target Orders as Expected = 98.0%

Active Customer Performance: KPI is % of Active Customers Sold
Actual % Active Customers Sold = 92.8%
Trend = +3.2% Points
Performance % of Goal = 38.1% Opportunity = 5.2% Points
Target Active Customers % = 98.0%

accounting period as the original order; and connecting actual returns to the original order can be technologically difficult. Finally, to lower returns (improve the KPI), it would be advantageous to track a reason code for the returns, but reasons can be highly subjective and therefore may not contribute to a solution.

It is also worth noting that the volume of returns, especially when the product is added back to inventory, will affect the inventory turnover metric,

---

[80] The number of percentage points difference between actual and the 99 percent target fill rate determines the customer satisfaction score in the Customer Satisfaction Rating (CSR). The CSR scores are: (5) if actual fill rate is greater than or equal to 99%, (4) if less than one percentage point difference, (3) if greater than one but less than two percentage points difference, (2) if greater than two but less than three percentage points difference, (1) if greater than three but less than four percentage points difference, and 0 if over four percentage points difference.

net sales dollars and gross margin dollars.[81]

Orders Completed as Expected (Promised) - There are any number of elements to each order that determine a customer's expectations and therefore, their satisfaction. They include, but may not be limited to, the timeliness, completeness, and accuracy of the delivery of the total order, accurate delivery address information, accurate delivery instructions including packaging, pricing of products, and customer identification information. Our sample entity has determined that they will measure the percentage of orders shipped *on time and complete* as the KPI. This obviously does not account for all of the possible reasons an order may not meet customer expectations, but it is difficult, if not impossible, to gather and manage all of the elements of an order to enable more specific measures. Nevertheless, an accurate customer master file that contains all of the customer order preferences, including shipping address, delivery and other customer specific requirements is essential. Measuring *on time and complete* should not be difficult because the entity controls the data elements, especially where a state-of-the-art warehouse management system has been deployed.

There is a third element to having orders completed as expected and that is accuracy. Did the customer get what they ordered in the right quantities? However, measuring *accuracy* in addition to *on time and*

Customer Satisfaction Rating:

Satisfaction Measure	Target Level	Actual Level	Satisfaction Score	Weighting
Order Fill Rate	99.0%	97.7%	3	25
Return Lines %	2.5%	2.8%	4	25
Orders as Expected %	98.0%	96.5%	3	30
Active Sold %	98.0%	92.8%	0	20
Combined Score			2.65	

complete is a challenge because it requires customer feedback to identify lines shipped in error. It should also be recognized that orders may involve multiple shipments for a single order which may further complicate the accurate tracking of this KPI.[82]

Percent of Active Customers Sold – In our sample company, the products are consumable by the customer. Therefore, it is assumed that active customers will order regularly in a predictable pattern as long as they

---

[81] It is easy to see why understanding the strategic forces of profit concept helps executives and managers learn how some KPI's are dependent on each other, for the same operating results.
[82] Accurate and timely information is essential for reporting KPI performance. Therefore, any proposed KPI must be validated by determining the data requirements, the calculation method and the timeliness of accurate data prior to selecting it for inclusion.

are satisfied with our company and our products. Consequently, our executives want to measure how many active customers buy from us during each reporting period. When active customers order regularly executives believe it implies that they are satisfied with the company's service level and products. Therefore, the percent of active customers ordering in any given period is the KPI that measures success for this component of customer satisfaction. Utilization of such a measure requires that a benchmark (where we started) be set; and that there is a definition of what an "active" customer is. Ideally, active customers will be flagged in the information system to make it easier to record and calculate the metric.

Key Performance Indicators - Business Activity

The number of orders and order lines represent historical measures in our sample company. Executives believe that they are important indicators of activity that can be directly tied to business opportunity and profitability. In addition, they are contributing components of some of the other KPI's. Even though they do not directly represent results that contribute to ROI performance, they are included to give managers a general indication of business activity trends. They also become more meaningful by trending comparisons. An explanation of the two measures follows.

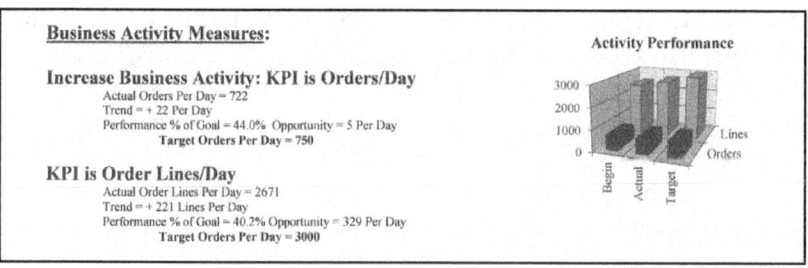

Business Activity Measures:

Increase Business Activity: KPI is Orders/Day
Actual Orders Per Day = 722
Trend = + 22 Per Day
Performance % of Goal = 44.0% Opportunity = 5 Per Day
Target Orders Per Day = 750

KPI is Order Lines/Day
Actual Order Lines Per Day = 2671
Trend = + 221 Lines Per Day
Performance % of Goal = 40.2% Opportunity = 329 Per Day
Target Orders Per Day = 3000

Activity Performance

Orders Per Day - This is simply the number of customer orders processed in an average day over specific reporting periods. Orders processed may be defined as orders entered, released, picked, shipped, or delivered. It depends on the purpose of the measure. For our sample company the number of orders shipped is tracked because it is the best representation of sales revenue. However, the other optional definitions for this measure may be equally valid, but they are generally tracked as lower level, or function-specific measures in our sample entity.

Order Lines Per Day - As with the number of orders per day, the number of lines can be defined in multiple ways. However, for each definition of orders, the number of lines should correspond to the lines on those orders. Therefore, for this KPI, the order lines per day are the shipped order lines. It is implied that the higher the order line counts the higher the sales dollars and therefore an increased potential for profitability. Obviously, this depends on the products, the product costs and a number of indirect costs including shipping and handling. Nevertheless, in our sample entity the historical inclination to rely on order line counts as a business measure is preserved, at least for now. It might also be suggested that longer term trends in this metric are more meaningful and perhaps an even better long-term trend would be order lines per order.

I have intentionally created a sample set of key performance indicators for our hypothetical company that includes six metrics that really have little direct effect on the objective to increase return-on-investment. The customer satisfaction (4) and business activity (2) KPI's represent what I would call hold-over measures from a prior performance management system. As the *Managing Strategic Decisions* approach to performance management is initially constructed, most entities will have some of these holdover measures. They can safely be classified as "memo" KPI's because of their indirect, or missing, influence on the outcome of ROI. Over time, as entities improve the use of the *MSD* model, holdover measures, if they survive at all, will be properly placed lower in the hierarchy as process-level measures. Another point to make prior to concluding our discussion of the executive scorecard is this: *Many elements of business activity affect multiple specific measures and KPI's.* Therefore, it will take a significant front-end effort to properly define and associate outcomes with the most appropriate activity measures. When this is done it literally allows the *MSD* model to become not only a reporting tool, but also an excellent forecasting and planning tool with built-in connectivity to actual results.

The Composite Scorecard

At the end of the sample scorecard, is a summary of all of the KPI's, by category, with a simple plus or minus sign to show whether they are

Composite Scorecard:

Investment	Score	Profitability	Score	Customers	Score	Activities	Score
Accounts Receivable	+	Sales- Growth	+	In-Stock Fill Rate	-	Orders/Day	+
Inventory	+	Sales Catalog	-	Returned Lines %	+	Order Lines/Day	+
Accounts Payable	+	G.M. Percent	+	Orders As Expected			
		G.M. Penalty	+	Active Customers %	+		
		Operating Expense	+				

improving or declining relative to expectations. It is provided to give the operating manager a quick glance at how well an operation is doing relative to expectations. An alternative use of the scorecard is to conduct performance reviews with upper level managers. The scorecard can be used to focus on specific tasks and to guide executive level decision making for each of the dependent processes. This sample of a scorecard built on the measures in our example, including optional graphical representations for selected measures,[83] provides the concept. It is up to each entity to build the components of a scorecard that best represents their performance objectives. This is just a sample for a hypothetical company, but it reflects reasonable results for each of the KPI's as they have been explained above. There is a lot of information, which taken together gives the executive a clear view of how the entity is progressing toward the stated objective to raise ROI for the company. The sample is just one possible format and each organization that adopts *MSD* as their tool for managing and reporting performance will no doubt do it differently. Other popular overall measures include RONA (return on net assets), ROTC (return on total capital) and EVA (Economic Value Added). All principal measures may have several methods for defining what is include in the primary values. No matter how they are defined, the key is to be consistent in order to make comparing period data most meaningful.

---

[83] The graphics have been developed for those who like this format and they are optional. In this example, they are copied into the report after being developed from the supporting data using a spreadsheet application.

Section V
Performance Planning
Methodology

Chapter 20

Strategic Decision Integration
Utilizing Business Performance Planning

Background and Introduction

This chapter presents a "how-to" methodology for analyzing operational performance and communicating the results to people throughout the entity. Nearly forty years of post-education business experience that included working for six different business entities and consulting with many more has taught me countless lessons. Perhaps the lesson that stands out above all others is this: *few businesses operate with a clear and uniform strategy that is well understood among the members of the leadership team.* The corollary to this is that *the strategic significance of daily decisions and process actions is either absent, misunderstood, or only partially effective at the transaction level.* The lack of strategic execution is further compounded because *most businesses do not employ a methodology for performance reporting that is synchronized with leadership direction [strategy], nor reflective of consistent business practices.* The most energetic top executive who has a personal view of where the enterprise is and where it needs to be is rarely able to disseminate that vision beyond their closest senior managers. Consequently, people at the operating level who are responsible for executing daily business transactions perform with limited strategically focused decision-making ability. They generally lack sufficient understanding about how what they do contributes to, or detracts from, the achievement of strategic goals and objectives. Nevertheless, the existence of established policies and procedures ensures that a majority of decisions and their results are acceptable.

In the absence of clear strategic direction, how are the people in an enterprise able to succeed as well as they do? I believe one of the predominant reasons is that transaction-level activity is generally guided by well-defined computer-based business rules, priorities, and alternatives that are supported by reasonably accurate and up-to-date data. For that reason, it is logical to conclude that transactions will generally accomplish their intended outcome for both the business and the customer. Beyond computer-based systems performing to expectations, consistent and reliable success depends on the quality and clarity of the instructions that have been given to people coupled with their own intuitive understanding of what seems right for the enterprise. When things do go wrong, it is unlikely that causal feedback about actual results will reach people in time to help them correct and improve their on-going performance. Even if feedback is timely, most people will not be able to remember the specifics of their mistakes when it is reported to them. It is almost certain that people will only hear about the transactions that went wrong. As a consequence, in an unreasonable effort to avoid blaming wrongdoers, error correction and process modification often takes a generalized form that leaves everyone wondering whether they have contributed to poor performance. In other words, out of the ambiguity of random information about performance successes and failures is born change without understandable reason. And, change is always disruptive. The magnitude of the disruption depends on the degree of the required process modifications.

Sporadic financial results, which randomly reflect the achievement of strategic goals as they were envisioned by the executive team, are a consequence of the entity's failure to clearly link strategic initiatives to performance management. The phrase, "a well-oiled machine" is often used to describe teams, families and organizations that work well together and deliver noticeable successful results. It implies that everyone is "on the same page", meaning each individual understands their role in the collective achievements of the enterprise. And team members assume with confidence that everyone else also understands. Each player presupposes that everyone is giving full effort to achieving the objectives that are clearly understood by all. In a competitive world, the likelihood of achieving consistent success is relatively low unless there is a process for defining effective strategies and promoting their influence throughout an enterprise. It is essential that there be a means for directing people at all levels in the enterprise toward the achievement of common objectives. It is equally important that there be an established performance measurement system that provides timely and effective feedback to everyone.

I believe it is imperative that every success-driven executive pay attention to the methods that the organization has in place to promote the uniform definition, understanding and effectiveness of business objectives and the strategy for their achievement. Managers must be aware of the total enterprise strategy and adapt their organizational group to focus on the achievement of that strategy. Ideally, leaders will participate in the continuous definition of appropriate strategy. Further, they will provide meaningful feedback, especially where the tools [processes, data and reporting] at the transaction level are not adequate to facilitate achievement of the desired outcomes. They have the responsibility to fully engage their co-workers in the focused achievement of organizational results consistent with enterprise-wide goals. It means organizational leaders must:

- Know the processes they manage,
- Clearly define and understand the metrics for measuring success at each process step,
- Educate the people about the "why" of their tasks, and
- Ensure that all processes are properly defined and driven by accurate data.

To be fully effective, entities should establish and leverage a performance management and measurement system as means for the achievement of objectives throughout the chain of strategies, action strategies, process goals and process measures.

As an executive, or as an advisor to executives, for the last fifteen years of my active career it has been my conscious emphasis to do all I could to focus my organization and other executives and their teams on the quality and effectiveness of their collective business process. I was particularly interested in challenging several somewhat complacent leaders who perceived that their existing business processes were adequate. I also found that it was reasonably easy to expose the absence of a meaningful performance measurement system. I expected such systems to be useful for motivating people toward achieving the enterprise's stated strategic objectives. I knew from experience that with the explosion of computer-based processing in the 1980's and 1990's most entities had implemented new software. Unfortunately, transaction processes, procedures and practices were only as good as was built into the new software when it was implemented. I found too many processes that were implemented to closely replicate previously existing transaction methods. In the software business this is called "paving the cow path". It means that the new path may be smoother, but it is still crooked. The consequence of taking this all too common approach to software implementation is that the productivity gains and improvements that were expected when the decision was made are seldom fully realized. Finally, because so many companies outsourced the majority their implementation to third party providers, they were left with too few internal people who understood what their systems were capable of doing beyond what they were initially set up to do. As a result, businesses learned to live with the way they had initially built their systems. Coincidentally, business leaders with their limited understanding of technology were left scratching their heads in frustration and trying to resolve their gut feeling that there was more to be had from such significant technology investments. These circumstances left me with ample opportunity to assist businesses in improving business practices and defining new processes to take better advantage of the software capabilities that they already owned. After clients achieved the obvious process improvements we turned our attention to developing and implementing more effective performance management methodologies that were compatible with the new processes.

Introduction to Performance Planning

As an independent consultant working with large and small enterprises, both publicly and privately held, I developed a method for delivering a high value take-away for my clients. It was born from observing the striking similarity between the circumstances of the entities I worked with regarding process and performance management. While my concepts and approach pre-dated the publication of *Reengineering the Corporation* and *The Balanced Scorecard,* they were essentially concentrated on dealing with the same core business issues that are addressed in these books. When I worked with consulting clients I called my initial engagement *Business Performance Planning.* I am certain, given my own time working as a business consultant with Deloitte Haskins and Sells in the mid 70's, that most of the larger consulting firms were doing something similar. But I felt that, given the opportunity, I could deliver a sound solution for my clients and do it on a much more personal level, especially when I worked with the primary decision-making executives. I expected to leverage my comparable industry experience and my knowledge about how to apply technology to the development of better business processes. It worked. I could help them. And I soon developed a method for documenting my work, leaving behind a knowledge base they did not previously have, and it was done quickly and at a reasonable cost. I was convinced that this approach would leave me in good stead with the client executives and benefit us both over a period of years, and it did. I rarely did for clients what I believed they could do for themselves. I was a coach to the people in their organization and often had a continuing relationship as an advisor occasionally doing small limited engagements. It was never my intention to sell my next engagement by pointing out other work that I could do for them. I believed that when the opportunity arose they would call if I could help.

The _Business Performance Planning (BPP)_ approach that I used was initially focused on wholesale and retail distribution enterprises that were using a specific enterprise software solution. As previously mentioned, I had deployed the same application software in two different enterprises as the chief operating officer. Because I was responsible for successfully operating both companies I was very involved in the implementation process. I learned the capabilities of the entire software suite and made configuration decisions during the course of defining, building and implementing this new application software solution. Consequently I knew what the capabilities of the software were and had observed, through interchange with other users, the multiple ways it had been deployed. Working directly with the software company, I conceived and designed a number of enhancements to the software suite to accomplish specific process needs of our businesses. These were the early days of packaged software solutions and we worked closely with the software company to "computerize" every part of the business process that we could in order to achieve predictable results. Extra effort was spent on the quality of the data that drove the business processes as it was the one thing that we found directly determined an acceptable outcome. The software suite was tightly integrated so that the financial impact of every transaction was directly posted to the accounting system. Detailed records in the master files could be reconciled to financial accounts enabling little human intervention in the closing of the books for each accounting period. It was truly an enterprise requirements planning (ERP) system long before SAP, Oracle, J.D. Edwards and PeopleSoft created such systems for the masses.

My early career background was in finance. I had been tutored well by the CFO of a Fortune 500 company in the art of financial analysis long before the personal computer was available as a speed tool for doing what we did. Initially, everything was done manually. There was little room for error in what we did because the amount of time it took to manually rework the solutions was onerous. Then, based on self-taught programming skills, some processes were gradually transitioned to simple computer programs that were run in a computer time share environment. From these experiences I learned to understand the cause and affect between processes and financial results; and learned to recognize obvious disconnects between financial performance and processes. Leveraging this experience, we modified the software suite to include a number of internal financial variance accounts to provide focus on selected financial results that were tied to specific processes. Daily monitoring of these specific accounts helped to identify process and data problems and allowed them to be corrected before their impact increased or accelerated. It was truly a real-time processing environment that did not wait on monthly results to fix issues. For its time, this software product included a costing capability that was very robust. It allowed the accurate tracking of actual product cost while introducing a traditional manufacturing standard cost into the wholesale distribution environment. This standard costing method introduced a new tool for managing and increasing gross margin and allowed more appropriate cost definitions depending on the characteristics of each product.

Upon surrendering my position as president of a large multi-product division to a leveraged buyout; and armed with a knowledge of how business processes and transactions translate to financial outcomes, I created the *BPP* approach after just a few consulting engagements. A *BPP* consulting engagement was designed to assist companies by evaluating their current business practices as the basis for recommending logical improvements. It was accomplished by conducting an end-to-end review of the core business processes and then conducting a two day executive manager's seminar to review findings, prioritize initiatives and obtain consensus among the top managers regarding strategic actions. The two days were broken into four sequentially congruent sessions. The intended outcome was a prioritized list of a few strategic initiatives that could be implemented to improve operating performance. The four parts of the seminar were:

Part I – Review of the findings from the end-to-end process analysis of the business. The analysis was normally performed in a just a few days depending on the size and complexity of the business. An additional 5 days was required to digest and summarize the findings into a presentable format for the seminar.

Part II – Present selected applicable business concepts to each client. These were concepts[84] that each manager should be aware of and consider in decision-making. It can safely be assumed that not all managers understand fundamental business concepts the same way. Therefore, this segment was intended to promote common understanding of some basic and applicable business concepts. The session was very interactive and included many references and examples to the specifics of the business. The purpose was to help the managers begin to form consistent conclusions that would be required to get the team focused on process improvement.

Part III – From the prior discussions, develop a list of potential actions that should be taken to improve on the company's business process and address the deficiencies found during the process evaluation. The objective of this segment was to identify no more than 8 action strategies that

---

84 Many of these concepts are included in section two of the *SDM* document.

would support the business objectives as defined by the CEO or COO.[85]

Part IV – The final four hours of the second day were spent with the entire team prioritizing the list of action strategies from Part III using the concept of paired comparison. A single sheet of paper was prepared for each of the possible action strategies that included a brief description of the action and a rough estimate of its costs, timing and potential benefits. I then acted as moderator for the team as they ranked each action alternative against each other alternative one at a time as if only those two things could be done in a constrained time and resource environment. Once all actions had been ranked against all others the scores were tallied. The actions were listed from the highest to lowest score, which represented the sequence in which they were to be implemented. Together they become the action strategies for the business.

One of the most revealing findings gleaned from this process was how disparate the range of understanding was among executive team members regarding the most important business initiatives. In more than one instance the management team was pointed in a completely different direction than the CEO or COO. Some people were entirely focused on short term financial performance improvement without any understanding of the changes to the business process that would be required to achieve their target level of performance. As always, others assumed that increasing sales would cure all ills. However, there was no consensus about whether that meant selling to more customers, selling more products, some combination of more products and customers, or pricing. Those who advocated reducing expenses did not understand their company's ratio of gross margin to operating expense enough to comprehend what expense reductions might mean to overall performance. For the few who thought about long-term performance (beyond the current year) tended to do so in the context of minor tweaks to current business practices rather than radical change. To my recollection, no one looked at *process as the potential solution*.

The *BPP* methodology evolved with each engagement as my understanding and discernment about the variability and uniqueness of business processes and management thinking expanded. It became clear that the possibilities for process improvement depended upon the unique circumstances of the customer, product and service orientation of each

---

85 After some less than successful attempts to perform this engagement without senior management, I determined that I would not do performance planning for any company without the involvement of either the CEO or COO, and preferably both.

client's business. Often the opportunities for change were limited by the capabilities and level of integration of the enterprise's software solutions. In time I diagrammed the process into a presentation slide that was used to promote the concept to potential clients. I also used it to introduce the *BPP* seminar to the participant managers, which helped them understand what the on-site activities and outcomes were expected to be. Eventually the consulting engagements ended and I returned to being an employee for two publicly traded companies in executive roles. This presented a unique opportunity to apply the lessons learned from the consulting engagements to real situations in two very diverse businesses. I often discussed the same concepts and ideas with my executive counterparts in an attempt to bring more emphasis to process change and performance management as tools for improving results. Coincidentally, both companies were going through changes associated with implementing new enterprise-wide business systems. This was a good news, bad news situation. The good news was that we had the opportunity to start over and define our business processes utilizing new computer-based capabilities. The bad news was that it would take a long time to achieve desired results because of the time it takes to overhaul business systems end-to-end; and then recover from the disruption that such changes inevitably cause.

All my experience taken together has convinced me of the validity of the ideas and the practical nature of the *BPP* methodology. It is a viable approach for companies to accelerate the achievement of their objectives and strategic initiatives. While previous chapters provide the basics of the concept of *SDM* as a strategic performance management methodology, this chapter provides an approach to getting the initiative off the ground by getting senior-level managers involved. I have included sufficient detail to once again provide self-starters with enough information to begin utilizing the *BPP* approach without assistance. However, someone needs to assume the role of organizer, interviewer, analyzer, presenter and moderator much the same as I did as a consultant.[86] As you read the details of *BPP* in the following pages it would be a good exercise to pause after each subject and think about how it might be done in your entity and within your span of authority.

---

[86] I am willing to support and assist entities that have a sincere interest in pursuing the adoption of the methodologies explained in this book. There are undoubtedly multiple ways to make this happen.

The Business Performance Planning Methodology

Transitioning a business to process orientation can be initiated, or reinitiated, for any one of the following three reasons.

- *New Business System Implementation* – In this scenario the business enterprise is changing a process to conform to the capabilities of new software. It could be a completely new suite of software, for example a so-called Enterprise Requirements Planning (ERP) solution. It may be implementing new functionality from an existing software solution as a result of a new release, introduction of a new solution from another software vendor that will be integrated to the existing suite, or simply the first install of new functionality from an existing software suite. These process changes could be taking place for the enterprise, in a specific business unit of the enterprise, across a specific functional organization of the enterprise, or in a department or physical location of any part of the business.

  Change for any one of the above reasons and for any part of the enterprise will take time and require a detailed execution plan to realize maximum benefits. The magnitude of the total effort will depend on the extent of the change, the ability and willingness of the people in the organization to participate in and embrace the change, and the time required, or allowed, from start to finish[87]. Reaching the *Customer for Life* phase, as shown in the diagram, should include full documentation of the new processes and their related procedures, as well as the often overlooked education and training plan. Good documentation becomes the basis for the development of the right education tools.

- *Correction of Operating Deficiencies* – In this case, process improvement actions must be taken to correct an existing business process or practice that is not delivering acceptable performance. The breadth of the possibilities of this type of change is wide. It may be something as simple as how products are packed for shipping or something as complex as how the physical layout of a distribution center is configured. The first example may require some study of how to best pack a product, but the change can be easily made once a decision is made. In the second instance, it is a complex task to

---

[87] As discussed in a previous chapter, resource allocation is an important part of every process change. Ignoring the complexity of this issue has been the root cause of many failed projects.

rearrange the physical layout of a distribution center, especially while continuing to fulfill customer orders from the same facility. This project will clearly require more effort.

Major process change is more about the physical dimensions of a process and may require extensive capital investment depending on the solution. In some cases, corrective changes may be mandated by regulatory requirements with timing constraints. A perfect example is the Sarbanes-Oxley compliance efforts that so many companies were forced to go through during 2005. Not only was the effort difficult because of the lack of definitive understanding about what compliance meant; it was exacerbated by a general lack of employees with the proper skills to get the job done. In most cases, the required changes significantly constrained a number of existing business practices and other initiatives, particularly in information technology (IT) organizations. It touched almost all employees and required work by many people in addition to their regular tasks.

- *Implementation of Strategic Initiatives* – This is the most desirable, opportunistic and optimistic of all business process change situations. Success assumes the strategic change is well conceived by the executive team, thorough in its definition and breadth of impact, does not conflict with existing initiatives, and is meaningful to the people who will be required to make the changes. Those are some big assumptions. The *BPP methodology* is a complete tool for process change formulation and management that can help formulate the necessary valid assumptions. It is a integral part of the *Strategic Decision Management* approach for successfully developing a continuous process improvement culture.

All three types of process change are best accomplished within the context of a clearly understood strategically focused operating environment that is internal to the enterprise. Regardless of the size of the company or organization, a strategically focused environment promotes process orientation. In addition, greater flexibility for making strategic decisions and successfully executing them is more easily achieved when existing business processes are supported by sound, stable, and well-conceived application software. An effective application software solution that is also flexible enables strategic thinking to be focused on creating, executing and correcting business processes. When there are limited system constraints process can more quickly become a competitive advantage.

The *Business Performance Planning (BPP)* methodology is represented by the following diagram. This illustration was used on many occasions in a business seminar environment to help people understand what happens

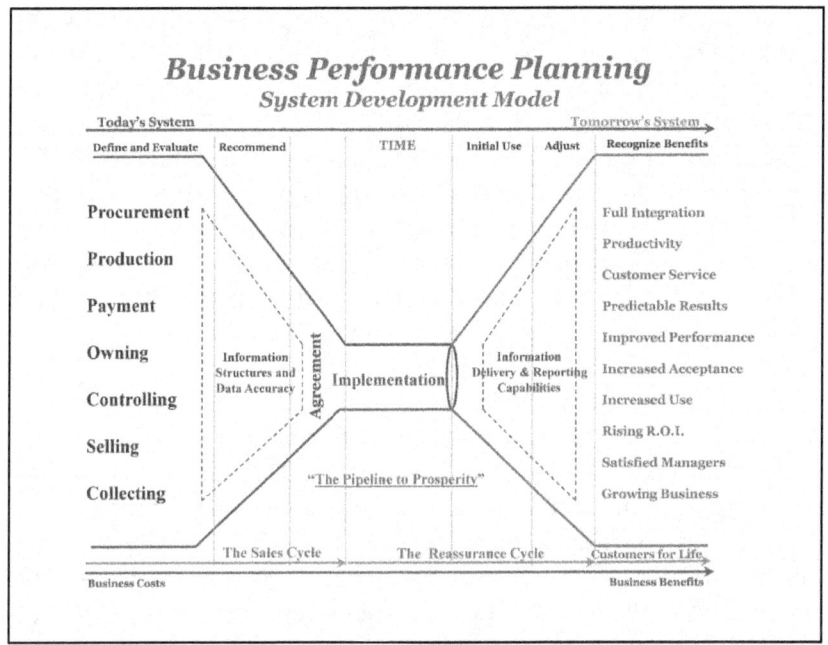

whenever there is a change to existing processes. No matter how large or small the contemplated change may be, this method for planning, evaluating, monitoring and measuring the change can ensure a more positive outcome, and it can be accomplished in less time. The amount of effort required to prepare the change plan will depend on the magnitude of the change.

An explanation of the meaning and symbolism of the performance planning diagram should help clarify how it can be used. It provides a useful guide for any enterprise management team that is willing to undertake the task of transitioning their business toward a process oriented focus. It is important to understand that all of the elements must be included in the project plan to realize the full benefits of the change. The primary points to understand in using the diagram are explained in the following paragraphs.

The transition from left to right represents the progression of time and is demonstrated in two ways. First, on the top of the chart are the words, "Today's System" and "Tomorrow's System". The descriptors on the line, with the arrow at the right, imply movement from today's business process toward a new operating paradigm that will become the new business process. Second, on the bottom of the chart are another set of lines with arrows suggesting rightward movement, which illustrate that there are three distinct segments to any process change. First, the *Sales* Cycle is an essential step to communicate with people and familiarize them with what is going to happen and, hopefully, obtain their buy-in. Second, once the new system is launched there will be a time period when people will need to be assured that things are working as expected. I prefer to call it the *Reassurance* Cycle, but it is the same thing that we often refer to as the 'learning curve' period. Finally, as the expected gains from the change are beginning to be realized people will become *Customers for Life* when they have not only accepted the changes they become proponents and begin to see continuous process improvement as the right way to do business. Each phase is essential to a successful project and will vary in detail and duration depending on the nature of the change.[88] These phases are further explained later in this chapter.

It is important to understand the cost-*to-benefit* element of process initiatives. The concept is represented on the diagram by the last right-arrowed line labeled "business costs" on the left and "business benefits" on the right. First, for most projects benefits are seldom realized in proportion to actual costs as presented in the original proposal. In fact, many business initiatives fail, or achieve less than anticipated financial success, because of a misunderstanding about the basics of project costing. Whenever a project is proposed, people seem to perpetually underestimate the dollar costs and seldom calculate the human and business disruption costs. Assuming that it is not done out of malicious intent, it most likely happens because the estimates are based on believing that optimum conditions, circumstances, timing and the availability of people will prevail for the duration of the project. This is almost never the case.

Since every initiative incurs costs well before there are any realized benefits the monitoring of both is essential to keep executives committed to the initiative. The longer the duration of the project the greater the potential for missing cost and benefit targets simply because business conditions change. Nevertheless, every initiative that is outside the normal work pattern of an enterprise should only be undertaken after the total costs have been accurately estimated and the potential benefits projected using defensible assumptions. It is assumed that no initiative would be undertaken unless the

---

[88] While it is essential that change is planned, executed and measured well, each stage should match the magnitude and impact of the proposed change (project). Over planning is sometimes as much a risk as no planning and may have a heavy cost in time, money and morale.

benefits will exceed the costs and deliver the minimal acceptable returns that have been defined for the business[89]. A proposal with a high probability for success, including a reasonable hedge for unexpected events, should be required of every significant initiative. This will provide executive leaders a reasonable assurance that the benefits will be realized within the projected timeframe, because they know that it is a certainty that the costs will be incurred at the estimated level or beyond.

A directional axiom for business initiatives is "*Start right, follow through and end well*". This idea is suggested by the three phases shown at the bottom of the diagram. Since they are essential to successful process initiatives I need to further elaborate on what they mean. All business process change initiatives go through each of these three distinct phases so it is important to give them full consideration throughout the planning, execution and completion stages.

The *Sales Cycle* is the time that an initiative's sponsors take to develop the idea, quantify the costs and benefits and prepare the proposal for presentation to the decision executives. Where the enterprise operates utilizing a *responsive decision hierarchy*[90] with appropriately defined procedures for making capital commitments, then business initiative decisions will be easily made and effectively completed within that structure. However, that is a little bit like talking about utopia, it is hard to explain because it is seldom seen. The level of detail and accuracy to "sell" a proposal to management depends on the magnitude of the expenditure, the breadth of the proposed change, and the number of people affected by the change. People who sponsor change must understand that their success depends on a comprehensive understanding of the initiative and its financial, organizational and timing impact on the business. A successful sales cycle ensures a good start to the execution phase of any project.

The *Reassurance Cycle* begins as soon as approval is granted. It includes the time during which the actual change is being made, the near term initial use of the new process, and a period of time for making minor adjustments to the process in order to gain full effectiveness. The total time required for this phase is determined by the magnitude of the initiative. For well planned and

---

[89] Some changes may be required for statutory compliance, which may preclude measuring benefits.

[90] We have already had a full explanation of what constitutes a responsive decision hierarchy in an earlier chapter. Essentially, it means that most decisions are made based on the guidance and direction given by enterprise leaders, consequently people at all levels feel little risk of making mistakes.

executed projects there should be no surprises when the process is put in place. Nevertheless, the reassurance phase embraces by default the time for making the final determination about whether the change will survive, or be reversed. If, for whatever reason, the change is not effective in delivering substantially all of the expected benefits, or if it negatively impacts other elements of the business more than can be tolerated, it will most likely be reversed. That is why almost all good system initiatives have a recovery plan. When the project is effective, as measured by the evidence, then it is fully embraced by all of the affected departments and organizations and it becomes the operational standard.

Properly defining measures of success can be a difficult challenge. All benefits cannot be quantified in financial and statistical ways. On the other hand, executives look for tangible benefits and they are most typically defined in terms of financial and productivity gains. However, as suggested by the sample benefits shown in the diagram, there will be intangible benefits from most projects. Whenever possible, an effort should be made to capture at least a sense of the intangible benefits of change perhaps by surveying employee feelings and opinions about the changes. Just as a flexible and highly capable application software solution facilitates change, a well-defined performance management system will make measurement easier and validate benefits. If both systems are in place the enterprise can more readily embrace process improvement as a focus for competitive advantage. In such an environment defining, planning, executing and measuring process change will be expected. Resource allocation will be effective, efficiency will be the norm, and managing to expectations will be self-inflicted throughout the organization.

Once the pattern of successful process change based on well-defined initiatives has been established people become converted and they buy-in to the concept of consistent positive change. All of the "customers" inside and outside the organization become *Customers for Life*. However, it should be understood that processes are like products they can have very short life cycles, or they can last for a long time. Sustaining an effective process change climate in an enterprise will require vigilance, especially when there is too much reliance on the old way of doing things to the detriment of operating and financial performance. Another scenario that will end or block an effective process change environment is when enterprise business leaders believe they are done. In the business systems world, whether processes are computer automated of not, change will always be occurring. Executives should assume that their competitors are always making positive changes and constantly looking for best practices and organize accordingly. They should also realize that hanging on to the successes of the past is not part of a process-oriented company. The final caution is, make sure that the majority of the changes that are being made are strategic. The level of vigilance about change will depend on the competitive environment and the nature of the business enterprise; and leadership must embrace the view that process is the last opportunity for creating and sustaining competitive advantage[91].

The center portion of the *BPP* diagram is intended to illustrate the actual course an organization must go through in order to create and manage business processes toward establishing competitive advantage. The number of tasks and the amount of effort required to complete important projects may discourage the impatient executive. In particular, far too many executives believe that information technology projects should take less time and deliver more benefits. If management pressure is applied to drive process improvements with this mentality too many compromises will occur and the results will slide toward ordinary or mediocre. Such an approach will eliminate process excellence as a tool for competitive advantage in that management environment.

There are seven steps to the *BPP* approach to process improvement and they all require well defined tasks, prudently estimated time, and reasonable resource allocation assumptions. A brief explanation of each of the steps and their subtasks follows.

Step One – Define and Evaluate – In manufacturing, distribution and retail businesses the primary transaction processes can be defined in terms of a few *basic functions*. The first step in the *BPP* work plan is to examine these basic functions by interviewing the people who actually perform them daily. This discovery process pays particular attention to the level of integration among dependent processes and documents the availability and integrity of the data requirements. A summary of the findings are reviewed with the participants to ensure that the processes have been documented accurately. An explanation of these basic process transactions or functions of business follows.

---

[91] As discussed earlier in this document *process as competitive advantage* is an important strategic emphasis. In fact, without it there is little reason to make changes to business processes until they are forced upon us.

Procurement – These are the process activities that are required to ensure that materials are on hand to support production or that products and services are available to sell and deliver.

Production – Whether a company's products are tangibly manufactured or services that are to be delivered, there is a strict set of process requirements for executing this step. In addition, warehousing and distribution logistics processes are included in this category. The logistical processes for inbound product movement, storage and handling, and outbound delivery are critical to the success of most entities. This is especially important for wholesale and retail distribution companies, and particularly in the current environment that demands effective supply-chain integration. So-called production processes are typically rife with opportunities for change and improvement as machines, methods, and technology are constantly improving.

Payment – These are the closing transactions for all procurement and production activities. For procurement it usually means paying providers whether inside or outside of the company. For production transactions payment may simply be passing the accumulated production costs to another product or inventory. To be timely and accurate, payment transactions depend on accurate data being passed from the initiating transactions step-by-step through to completion with tight integration. All parties to the workflow of each transaction must be timely and accurate in completing their tasks if the payment process is to be optimized.

The first three functions constitute what is typically called the **purchase-to-pay** process cycle. In today's world of supply chain and value chain integration there are many opportunities to make this process seamless between multiple business partners when their computer systems are integrated. In addition, paperwork can be reduced significantly, or totally eliminated. For example, there is no need for a supplier to invoice a customer because the customer has the purchase order and can pay the agreed price for products or services received without a paper invoice.

Owning – After products and/or services are acquired, whether purchased or produced, there are a number of processes required to effectively own and manage these assets for their useful life to the business. The ownership sequence of transactions (process steps) includes taking ownership (receiving), accurately valuing these assets (cost tracking) during the period they are owned, and carefully managing asset locations (put-away to inventory) while retaining their full value.

Controlling – Processes that control revenue generating assets for the business should be focused on clear identification, tight control of the placement and movement of assets, and well documented release of assets when they are sold, or transferred.

Selling – The sales process has always been the focus of most effective business enterprises because it is customer centric and therefore, should be as efficient as possible.. In its simplest form it is how the customer takes ownership of the product or service. It may simply be presenting a product to a cashier who utilizes a barcode identification that determines the price. When the customer presents an acceptable payment method then ownership changes hands. In its most complex forms it can take a long time, be highly customized, modified a number of times before the sale is complete, and be contingent on conditions outlined in contracts. The more complex the product or service the greater the need for a well-defined work flow oriented sales process.

Collecting – Performing the settlement function for sales transactions can take many forms as well. It can be instantaneous at the time of sale when cash equivalents are used, or it can extend over many months and years when installment payments and final approval are required to complete payment. Highly effective integration of the sales transaction to the settlement solutions is an imperative to optimize productivity and accuracy. Full sequential accessibility to all customer interchanges regarding each transaction vastly facilitates the ability to conclude transactions and maximize customer satisfaction.

The **order-to-cash** cycle includes the selling and collecting activities. In the past few years almost all software functionality and consulting work plans are focused on this cycle and the *purchase-to-pay* cycle. While the logic and work flows for both are basic, the uniqueness of each business makes it challenging to ensure that the processes are established to capture the distinctive nature of each company.

All significant process improvements will involve one or more of these basic functions. When the basic functions are integrated, all of the points of integration between the functions will require validation or adjustment any time there is process change in any one of them. In this first phase of *BPP,* after defining the existing processes and their points of integration, one of the more challenging tasks is to select the most significant opportunities for process improvement because there always seem to be more opportunities than there is time to accomplish them. Once the highest impact projects have been selected their effect on functional processes and departmental integration has to be fully evaluated as a prelude to developing a recommendation. Even after the list has been shortened there are often more opportunities to make meaningful changes than there are resources to get them done in the designated timeframe. Because of time and resource constraints, I recommend a self-imposed limit of no more than eight initiatives for presentation to the management group.

 Step Two – <u>Recommend</u> – After evaluating the impact of the proposed process improvement initiatives an appropriate recommendation must be developed. Being able to combine all of the proposed process changes into a recommendation that makes sense to the executive team is critical to the success of the venture. The proposal must be developed as a comprehensive end-to-end package. It cannot be a set of standalone changes that will fail during implementation, especially at the points of integration. A recommendation to be defensible will require the availability of accurate process data from within the existing information structure of the business. For example, if a proposed process change requires a single additional piece of customer information it may impose a significant change to the existing data file structure. This may not be feasible. Whenever a proposal causes more difficulty or impact than anticipated, it may require an alternative solution.

 This phase also focuses on assessing the proposed new processes respective to the acquisition and flow of data and work between the affected transactions. With the new processes in place, the data flows and work flows for the total business process must be well defined to maximize the benefits from the improvements. From a consistently designed, comprehensively integrated business solution the company can:
- Achieve effective communication throughout transaction execution,
- Report the timely disclosure of discrepancies as they occur,
- Successfully complete transactions on time, and
- Avoid duplication of effort.

 Step Three – <u>Agreement</u> – After the proposed initiative has been clearly defined and the necessary statement of costs and benefits is prepared as a recommendation, all of the information should be in place to present the proposal to the appropriate executives for their approval. It is rare that a strategically significant process improvement initiative would not cross organizational responsibilities. Therefore, approval to proceed presumes agreement among the senior business leaders from all of the functional disciplines.

Ideally, the proposed initiative will be evaluated within the context of existing, and perhaps competing initiatives, to resolve any conflicts that it might cause. In reality there is no stop and start for business initiatives that coincides with the reporting of financial and performance results. Just as financial reporting does not coincide with point-in-time accounting period-end dates; capital spending does not stop and start with budget periods. In this "moving target" financial reporting world there is a void of good methods for developing the costs and benefits of major initiatives. As a result, a means for evaluating initiatives by isolating them for analysis and decision-making is an important element of the strategic decision-making process. After the costs and benefits of an initiative are determined they should be applied to base period data to reflect the combined result. In this way, duplication of either costs or benefits can be avoided and the cumulative benefits of all initiatives will not be overstated.

I believe executives are more likely to approve major projects when the numbers supporting them take into account ongoing projects with their anticipated costs and benefits. They will want to know what the cumulative costs and benefits of their decisions are going to be. Unfortunately this is not the typical financial analysis approach. The primary reason is that most performance reporting systems do not have the capability to adjust actual performance for the impacts of business improvement initiatives, particularly over time. It is this lack of accurate financial management and project reporting that is the cause for never quite achieving planned benefits. Whenever there are many initiatives in play at the same time, and this is almost always the case, the timing of the execution of the several initiatives will impact the realization of benefits. There is even more added complexity because the recognition of costs and benefits over the project duration will vary greatly depending on the nature of the initiatives. It is certain the costs will be incurred so it is imperative that the benefits be documented and reported as they occur. And, benefits do not always require completion of the project, which makes interim tracking and reporting essential.[92]

---

[92] As previously discussed, the *Standard Performance Measurement* concept is a proven method for regularly reporting financial results while also tracking the costs and benefits of initiatives.

Finally, the last consideration that executives should evaluate before giving approval to process improvement initiatives is resources. Does the company have the financial and human resources to do the project in the proposed timeframe? No organization has endless resources. Consequently, project decisions are often constrained by the proper allocation of limited resources and time. Resource allocation and realistic time expectations are often overlooked or underestimated as meaningful factors in strategic decision management. The most successful entities know how to deal with it appropriately through proper prioritization of competing initiatives.[93] The importance of executive agreement cannot be overstated. When all of the elements for strategic decision-making are part of the structure of an organization this phase will be easily accomplished. Without the proper structure, decisions will be unpredictable.

Step Four – *Implementation* – After an initiative has received the approval of executive managers the implementation phase begins, hopefully immediately because nothing ensures continued support more than early visible action. The more complex and broad the initiative the more important is the necessity for collaborative detailed planning. The implementation plan must include realistic resource allocation, dedicated commitment of people's time, and the definition of achievable completion outcomes. There are myriad books and articles written about how to effectively plan for the implementation of business initiatives, especially information technology projects. As well, there is now a much more defined and organized role for so-called project managers who are given the responsibility for the successful completion of large projects. The project manager's role has literally expanded as a business discipline in the last 15 years primarily because of a number of well publicized failed ERP implementations. There have always been people who managed projects, but now the role is much more about insuring that every task is defined and accounted for, assigning responsibility to people, determining deadlines, and holding people accountable. In the former world what project managers do was encased in the so-called *critical path methodology (CPM)*.

In the *BPP* diagram, the implementation phase is intentionally depicted as a pipe. It is meant to imply that all of the affected organizational entities of every enterprise that undertakes process improvement initiatives will literally go through an intensive and focused course of action that can be

---

[93] It may help to refer back to the discussion of resource allocation and the need to prioritize competing projects based on their strategic significance.

compared to "stuffing" large amounts of people's time and company resources through a very narrowly defined sequence of events that are intended to create a beneficial expected outcome. The effective execution of the planning phase is essential and will be as varied in scope as are the projects that come out of the *define and evaluation* phase.

Step Five – Initial Use – After a project "goes live" there is an initial use period. It is the time from when the initiative is completed and launched (becomes the new process) until it is declared a success. It may be hours, weeks or months depending on the magnitude of the project. During this phase there is close monitoring of the execution of the process and careful reporting of attitudes and outcomes. Organizations should be cautious to not overreact to the initial negative feedback from process users during this phase as this is a normal and expected reaction to change in any circumstance. Negative initial feedback can be minimized by increasing the level of involvement and teaching for the affected people during the planning and implementation phases. During the initial use period there may be minor changes to procedures within a process to remedy obvious errors and to take advantage of opportunities for improvement that were not discovered during implementation training. When all of the prior steps have been done well there is minimal chance that an initiative will fail. Therefore the initial use period will be short and general acceptance will occur more quickly. Further, the learning curve will be accelerated and comfort levels will be achieved more quickly. The hands-on users will become advocates and pull the skeptical users along until the new process is fully embraced.

Step Six – Adjust – A properly conceived, planned and executed initiative will require only minor adjustments to realize the expected outcomes. During the *adjust* phase the process corrections identified during the initial use period are evaluated as to their complexity and probable effectiveness. The evaluation determines which changes are appropriate across the organization to avoid making changes that negatively affect one group to the benefit of another. Proposed changes should be made only after ensuring that there is consensus among the affected organizations. If the magnitude of change is so significant as to consider the original initiative a failure, then this is the point at which the change can be rolled back until the major issues can be resolved. The probability of high impact roll-backs from process changes should be very low when all of the prior steps have been accomplished. However, it is always prudent to have a rollback plan.

Many an organization has experienced second guessing in the late stages of process improvement initiatives, particularly when top executives succumb to the cries of a few pieces of misinformation and/or expressions of discontent from a few people whose motive is to defend the status quo. Even though executives should "buy in" during the *agreement phase* they can still allow their enthusiasm to wane, especially when they are not technologically savvy. Whenever the wavering of executives and managers is a threat to undo weeks and months of thoughtful and diligent effort on the part of the project team, every effort should be made to quantify the impact of aborting the project to put the complaints in the proper perspective. Process changes should only be rolled back when they create issues that have a significant unfavorable impact on performance, customer perceptions, or business results. Every effort should be made to define what is significant, and only executives should be able to make that decision.

One of the key elements during the initial use and adjust phases is the delivery of information about process and transaction performance. Process measures should have been well defined during the planning phase including the formatting and timing of reports. Reported results, whether financial or statistical, will be the primary evidence of success to the executive team. For example, if a new general ledger system is the initiative and financial period closing and reporting does not at least meet or exceed the timing of the prior system, no one will be convinced that the new process is better. In fact, it is my experience that accurate and timely reporting will calm the most skittish manager even when results are not perfect and it will allow reason to prevail until the new process becomes fully effective.

Step Seven – Recognize Benefits – As soon as the adjustments to process improvements have been made, which means the new initiative is fully launched and is the process standard, it should be possible to continuously measure whether the expected benefits are being realized. Listed on the right side of the diagram are some of the typical business benefits that can and should be expected from any significant process initiative. All of the benefits do not apply to all projects and will depend on the magnitude and nature of the change. Assuming the initiative was to adopt a completely new business system, then all of the listed benefits should apply and perhaps a few more. The measures are not mutually exclusive and more than one will typically apply to every initiative. Some measures are more tangible than others, but all benefits should be measurable.

The proper ratios that represent each measure can be defined in general financial terms or company specific preferences. The metrics may have variable time periods to make them meaningful. For example, the number of orders processed can be measured by the hour, but day's receivable outstanding is typically measured monthly. All measures should be congruent at all levels. The sample measures on the diagram are representative of what could be called *key performance indicators*, each of which will have multiple process-level measures that support them.

The Pipeline to Prosperity – this phrase is displayed in the middle of the diagram, which is a tongue-in-cheek depiction of the fact that business initiatives always seem to be perceived as the solution to under-performance, particularly for companies struggling to achieve financial success. To the extent that initiatives are truly strategic, meaning that they are focused on addressing structural deficiencies, transaction inconsistencies, performance weaknesses, and customer preferences; they will improve the effectiveness of any business. Successful and growing enterprises always have a *pipeline* open which means continuous process improvement is their focus. As a result, they will always have a "pipeline" full of initiatives aimed at more prosperous business results no matter how prosperity is measured.

Conclusion

I believe that any organization that wants process effectiveness as a competitive advantage will succeed more quickly using the *Business Performance Planning* approach. As alluded to earlier, much is being written to suggest that in today's business world, where it is so easy to replicate products and ideas and where shared information is so prolific, that the only distinctive competitive advantage that an enterprise can call its own will be its processes. Effective processes run by quality people are the keys to continual and consistent long-term success. Hopefully, the idea that your organization cannot be competitive without addressing process improvements should provide the incentive to further explore the adoption of *Strategic Decision Mastery* as an effective way to get it done.

Epilogue

*S*trategic Decision Mastery (SDM) is a methodology for establishing and achieving a process-oriented decision-making culture. It addresses how to overcome the issues and barriers that organizations encounter as they transition from their predisposition to be tactical instead of strategic in decision-making. It includes valid solutions and methodologies to move toward operational execution based on strategic direction. It can be effectively utilized in at least three ways:

- As a guide for executives in determining the current strategic tendency of their enterprise,

- As a tutorial for educating managers and executives within an enterprise, especially where leaders are determined to perpetuate and proliferate the concepts among the managerial ranks, and

- As a textbook-like model for students of process analysis to learn what strategic decision management is and why *SDM* is more effective than more traditional approaches.

It is an insurmountable task to assimilate the collective written wisdom of the best writers and educators of the last century and apply their best concepts to the unique circumstances of any enterprise. It simply can't be done. There is just too much. However, I believe *SDM* is a structure for managing that is flexible and can adapt to new operational approaches. It is a sensible method for incorporating a number of sound organizational practices under a single concept-like umbrella about how to strategically manage an enterprise; without being overly complex. It is a sound solution for facilitating the establishment of process-centric operational style.

As we have already discussed, it is difficult to embrace new ideas and even more challenging to adopt them. The best intended executive leader must weigh many factors before undertaking the sponsorship of a major change initiative, especially when it is focused on process improvement. After all, there are far more glamorous and outwardly acceptable things for an executive-leader to do than to focus on process. Process responsibility is not generally considered one of the arrows in the quiver of an organizational leader. It is somehow relegated to lower level managers, which is probably why it is less effective than it could be.

There is another factor besides the unglamorous side of process that I believe affects an executive's failure to adopt a process focus. It is the limited time they spend in their roles. The span of time that top executives are in their roles is sometimes so short, either because of age or other factors, that process change is probably not in their suite of things that they want to accomplish in the time they believe they have been given. The *time-span-of-control (TSC),* as I like to call it, tends to cause executives to think short term, let's say less than 5 years. What's more, it seems intuitive that we all like to finish what we start. Consequently, when an executive's *time-span-of-control* is too short, they forego making sweeping changes because they either fail to see the short-term benefit, or they believe the benefits are so far into the future that they will leave it to their successor. It is only the leader that can look to the long-term of their organization and ignore their *TSC that* will recognize when they have a prime opportunity to be a catalyst for positive change and do something about it. Such insightful leaders don't feel that they have to be around to see the ultimate results of everything they initiate, or to take credit for the full benefits. They just know it is right for the organization and they do it.

Appendix Materials

Appendix I – The Gross Margin Model

In my estimation, one of the most revealing presentations of the financial performance profile of an organization is the *Gross Margin Model (GMM)*. Whenever I have constructed a *GMM* for a client it has always received more executive interest and inquiry than I ever expected. The first thing this tells me is that too many senior executives do not know how much of the sales dollar evaporates between recording the sales invoice gross margin and the net gross margin reported in the financial statements. I will take time to explain in reasonable detail the first of two sample models shown below in the hope of alerting each of you, as existing

Apparel Manufacturer's Gross Margin Model

The Price Side	Company Profitability	The Cost Side
Gross Sales		
Programmed Discounts		
Invoice Sales	Invoice Gross Margin	Invoice Cost (Standard)
		Royalty and License Fees
		Production Cost Variances
		Contracting Variances
Customer Profit Reductions:	Sales Gross Margin	Net Invoice Cost (Actual)
Returns		
Allowances		
Chargebacks		
Overbills		
Net Sales	Net Sales Gross Margin	After Sale Product Costs:
		Product Recoveries
		Inventory Adjustments
		Samples
		Provision for Value Fluctuations
		Provision for Business Fluctuations
	Net Gross Margin	Net Product Cost

and potential executives and managers, to the potential prospect to more proactively determine ways to improve your entity's *Net Gross Margin*. Hopefully, you will also realize that gross margin retention is the quintessential duty of business leaders. It is the kernel of operational profitability and, as a result, should be the heart of strategic significance for most profit-oriented entities. The tale of profitability and the significant decisions that shape its outcome is captured in a thoroughly constructed *GMM*. The illustration demonstrates the descriptive model, but the actual reporting of the financial statement values behind each of the elements along with its percentage ratio to *gross sales* is the *GMM* results model. While the results view is not shown here, it is generated as part of the *SPM* component of the methodology.

Explanation of the Gross Margin Model

The *GMM* could just as appropriately be called the profitability framework of the entity. It is a framework for profitability because it includes the financial outcome of all of the business practices of the entity relative to how they manage the price and cost side of their revenue generating transactions. The model assumes that the entity is selling a product or service, which leaves investment entities for another discussion. I have chosen to provide one sample model for apparel manufacturing and one for wholesale distribution because it allows me to use firsthand experience. However, a company-specific model for any business enterprise would not vary significantly in principle and only the descriptions of the price and cost side line items would change. I choose to separate the model into two sides. As illustrated, there is a price side and a cost side. All elements on the price side either directly generate or reduce revenue. On the cost side are recorded all of the elements of direct and indirect costs associated with revenue transactions. The *GMM* is a reflection of the decisions that have been made about how the entity chooses to do business with its customers. It also mirrors the process level operational practices of the entity with their corresponding accounting and financial treatments. In an ideal structure, at least from my point of view, the *GMM* will be oriented toward operational performance not financial performance. The importance of distinguishing between these two approaches was explained earlier in this document. A brief definition and explanation of each of the elements of the apparel manufacturing *GMM* follows. As you read ask yourself, "What is the appropriate measure(s) for each element of the model in my organization; and what decisions and processes underlie its definition?"

Price Side Gross Margin Elements

❖ **Totals and Sub-totals** – there are three different amounts on the price side that represent levels for totaling profitability. Each is significant because it represents a grouping of strategic decisions.
  ○ *Gross Sales* is the first sub-total, which is a number that will never appear on a financial statement because it is a derived number. It is the *Invoice Sales* sub-total plus the *programmed discounts*.
    ▪ *Programmed Discounts* are the cumulative difference between the list price of the products and services sold minus the actual price at which these same products and services were actually sold. It is included to quantify how much potential profit is lost based on the customer discount structures that are typically programmed into a computer-based system. Such discounts are the derivative of all customer price arrangements based on the pricing strategy that has been adopted by the entity.

For example, assuming the list price for a product is $100 and the customer has a standard discount of 25 %, the actual selling price would be $75. Therefore, the value of the programmed discounts for this transaction is $25. In most businesses, the price structure can be much more complex than a simple customer discount. It might include volume discounts, promotional discounts, product category discounts and any number of other variations. When there are multiple layers of price concession it is difficult to determine the impact of each of them individually. The more complex the price structure the less likely anyone is able to determine how much gross profit is lost by simply applying the discounts to the actual sales values by product by customer. The point is that these gross profit dollars are gone before sales transactions ever occur.

The solution to minimizing gross profit loss from programmed discounts is to project the effect of proposed price changes before they occur. This can be done very effectively using programmed discount reporting for the most recent quantity sales by customer by product. The value of *programmed discounts* in the *GMM* is simply calculated by multiplying the product quantities sold by the list price of those products and then deducting actual sales revenue.

o   *Invoice Sales* is the second total value and it is the actual sales invoice dollar value of customer transactions as recorded in the financial statements. It is the starting value for gross profit from which all of the price and cost side values are deducted.

o   *Net Sales* is the second sub-total. It is *invoice sales* minus what I call the gross profit leaks that primarily occur because of customer arrangements beyond the sales transaction; and depend on the internal processes for collecting invoiced sales dollars. In our apparel manufacturing example the primary deductions from invoiced sales are:

- *Returns* by the customer. Product returns can be a significant value for an apparel manufacturer. There are a number of contractual arrangements with customers that affects the total value of this amount. The problem in apparel is that any product returned can rarely be completely recovered and sold to other customers. Even when it is sold it will be at a significant discount. The solution to controlling this amount is managing the contractual arrangements with the customers. Therefore, it is important that customer price negotiations deal with acceptable parameters for limiting customer returns. This is where a customer contribution profile is valuable in setting limits based on the overall customer value to the enterprise.

- *Allowances* are simply deductions without product returns. These are again negotiated by customer and should be limited based on each customer's total contribution to the profitability of the enterprise. An allowance is typically in the form of a small percent of total sales for each customer and may even be fractions of percentages. It should be obvious that the amount will vary significantly based on which sales number it is based on. For example, is it invoiced sales, or invoiced sales net of returns?

- *Charge-backs* are, as I previously mentioned, one of the most fabricated and arcane business practices I ever came across in my business career relative to customer pricing. It is an amount that the customer charges back to the apparel manufacturer because they did not adhere to the labeling, order delivery, packaging and shipping methods specified by the customer. I was convinced as were most people on the manufacturer's side, that larger customers made a profit center out of charging back to their suppliers. As with the previous two amounts this value can only be controlled by how the customer contract is negotiated. After considerable effort the manufacturer usually recovers approximately 50 % of the amounts the retailers charge back. However, it requires good record keeping and a significant manual effort to match documents to the amounts charged back to convince the retail customer that charges are not legitimate.

- *Overbills* are nearly as unreasonable a practice as are the charge-backs. These are amounts held back by the retailer from invoice payments based on prior agreements. They are normally percentages of total invoice dollars loosely connected to issues associated with apparel retailing. The manufacturer will agree to provide retail support for such things as an advertising allowance, margin support, product markdowns, defective merchandise and fixtures. The amount of these sums is usually a fractional percent of total invoiced amounts often by style. All retail customers do not receive all of the promotional grants and for very large customers they are simply accumulated to a total percent without specific identification of the reason for the allowance. Needless to say, when the customer pays their invoices short for these amounts it becomes very difficult to track and determine the legitimacy of each charge. Limiting such gross profit deductions starts with the customer contract and ends with the process for validating the amounts allowed by promotional program, or reason.

- *Net Sales Gross Margin* is the value determined by subtracting the total of these specific price-side deductions from the *Sales Gross Margin*, which will be explained in the cost-side discussion.

Cost Side Gross Margin Elements

- ❖ **Sub-Totals** – there are two sub-totals on the cost side that represent different groupings of additional costs associated with sales transactions. Similar to the price-side the individual elements of the sub-totals are the result of strategic decisions.
  - *Net Invoice Cost (Actual)* is the first sub-total and it is the invoice cost at standard cost minus three specific direct product costs. These costs should be factored into the product standard cost, but by their nature will not be specifically tracked to the

actual products sold in a given reporting period.

- *Royalty and License Fees* are contractually connected to the products that are sold. Each is typically based on a percent of the sales price of the product, but may be a dollar amount per quantity sold. In some cases it is the sales price before any discounts and allowances and in others cases it may be the price net of one or more such amounts. It may or may not be reduced by returns of the affected products. Once again, the sum of this cost increase is determined long before the product is sold; and because of the nature of branding and labeling such arrangements can be complex.

- *Production Cost Variances* are the difference between the standard and actual production costs for each element of production that has been factored into the product standard cost. The amount may be positive or negative depending on the accuracy of the process for setting standard costs and the environment for tracking labor and material production costs. Depending on the sophistication of the production costing system this total may be made up of several specific variances that can be tracked and managed. In our apparel example, these are the costs specific to and under the control of the manufacturer's processes.

- *Contracting Variances* are the difference between the expected contracted cost for the products sold and the actual cost paid. Once again these costs are factored into the standard cost, but actual costs can vary depending on the variable allowances granted to each contractor. In my experience, the contractors were primarily sewing piece goods that were cut by the manufacturer. This can be a favorable [negative] variance, but is typically an unfavorable or additional cost amount.

o *Net Product Cost* is the difference between *Net Sales Gross Margin* and the sum total of a number of indirect product and sales related costs that cannot be attributed directly to specific products. I prefer to call these costs *After Sale Product Costs* and the ones attributable to apparel manufacturing are explained below.

- *Product Recoveries* are the products that are rejected during quality inspection that can become first quality by applying sewing or other corrective measures. However, since they were rejected and therefore not paid for as first quality product they never become inventory until after the corrective effort. This is typically a favorable cost amount because the cost of rejects is included in the standard product cost and in the *contracting variance* where the cost of rejects is charged.

- *Inventory Adjustments* normally are associated with physical inventory and cycle counts. It can be characterized as inventory write-downs which can be either lost or damaged product. The amount of this number will depend on the quality of the inventory control processes. Losses can occur on an interim basis and then be recovered during an annual physical inventory process, but this is the net amount.

- *Samples* are a legitimate cost for apparel manufacturers. Product samples are provided for sales people for customer presentations; and to customers for evaluation prior to adopting the product for the retail sales floor. The total of this amount will also depend on policy and practice as well as the level of control within the entity. It will reduce gross margin, but cannot be directly associated with the sales revenue in any given accounting period.

- *Provision for Value Fluctuations* is an arbitrary value that is determined by management to factor for unanticipated, usually customer related, costs of doing business. Frankly, in the company I worked with, it was a way to insure that we met our profitability objectives and could truly be called a cost hedge, which varied depending on the selling environment over a fiscal year. It is similar to a load factor that is used in developing discrete manufacturing costs. It was generally built into the standard cost. However, the amount charged to this account was determined based on management's discretion. Ideally, this account will always be a reduction to product cost, thereby increasing net gross margin.

- *Provision for Business Fluctuations* was another profit hedge factor the sum of which is determined at the discretion of management. As the description implies it was different than the prior amount because it depended on the retail sales climate. For example, if sales were down for specific styles for specific customers and necessitated additional allowances for markdowns, then this amount would be the repository for adjusting product cost. Again, it was built into the standard product cost and then depending on the business climate management could adjust accordingly, either up or down. Typically, this was also a favorable product cost adjustment that increased net gross margin.

Once an entity has designed their gross margin model it presents an opportunity to evaluate and perhaps redefine the emphasis on capturing and retaining maximum gross margin dollars. Most businesses will find that some of the metrics for measuring each of the elements of the *GMM* will need to be changed. Remembering the discussion of the *strategic forces of profit* will help to guide executives and managers to a more complete understanding of their entity's profit potential. In particular, I recommend that all of the processes associated with each price and cost element be challenged to ensure that it is appropriate for limiting reductions to gross profit. Obviously, it is also advisable to look carefully at how customer prices are determined with the objective to limit *programmed discounts* because they automatically occur every time products and services are sold. You may recall that I explained how just consistently applying a price structure, while limiting price overrides, will add more than one margin point to gross margin dollars. From my experience in two companies, consistent pricing added an average of 2 ½ margin points [250 basis points]. In addition, being creative with pricing by customer by product group has the potential to add more gains in gross margin resulting in lower programmed discounts.

I have also included a sample *GMM* typical of a wholesale distribution company, which is sufficiently detailed to suggest other

---

Wholesale Distribution Gross Margin Model

The Price Side	Company Profitability	The Cost Side
Gross Sales		
Programmed Discounts		
Invoice Sales	Invoice Gross Margin	Invoice Cost (Standard)
		Standard Cost Variance
	Sales Gross Margin	Net Invoice Cost (Actual)
Customer Profit Reductions:		
Terms Discounts		
Allowances		
Bad Debt Expense		
Net Sales	Net Sales Gross Margin	
		After Sale Product Costs:
		Sales Invoice Cost Variance
		Inventory Adjustments
		Physical Inventory Adjustments
		Freight Not Recovered
		Minor Price Variance
	Net Gross Margin	Net Product Cost

---

price/cost side elements that may be applicable for other types of entities. Several of the *after sale costs* were explained in a previous chapter.

Appendix II – The Strategic Decision Tree

Following is a more detailed explanation of the concept of the *Strategic Decision Tree (SDT)*. The tree is a visual picture of the operating and financial results of all the interactions that are part of the *strategic decision mastery* methodology. In a single picture an executive manager can visually determine where the operational performance of the entity is meeting, exceeding and failing relative to the accomplishment of its planned objectives. The picture can be viewed at the summary (KPI) level or at the detailed level. In this sample *SDT* there are three views. The first illustration, shown below, is a combined summary decision tree. The other two illustrations show the details. The first is the detailed investment decision tree; and the second is the detailed operating (profitability) decision tree.

In this example, the primary measure of success, as depicted in the

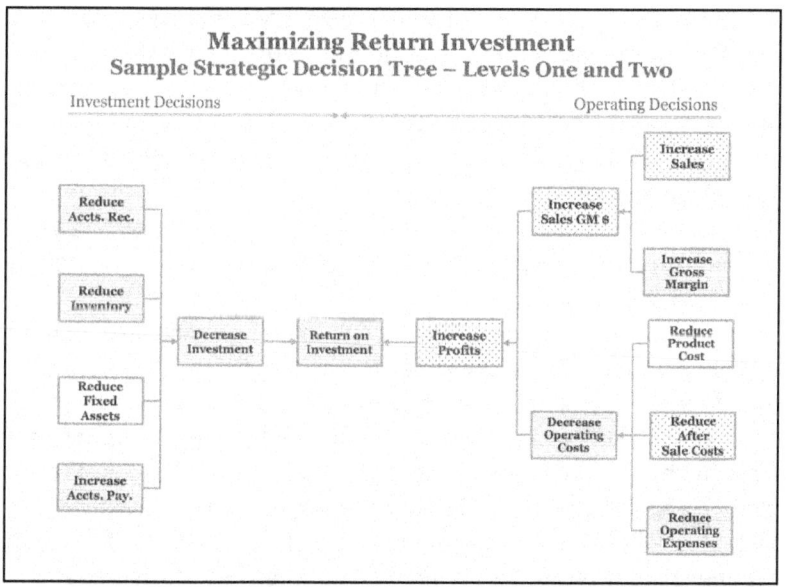

center of the diagram, is return-on-investment (ROI). The typical ROI ratio is profitability divided by investment. Therefore, to improve ROI an enterprise can increase profitability, decrease investment, or some of both. Since both profitability and investment are made up of a number of other values and ratios, which are the results of operational and investment decisions, the ability to improve either of these numbers is dependent on managing the individual components. In the summary decision tree the primary components of profitability and investment are shown as the second layer. Each of these values is a significant factor in determining what ROI will be and are therefore measured by their own KPI. For example, the KPI for accounts receivable is typically days-sales-outstanding (DSO) as a measure of the relative ability of the entity to collect sales revenue from customers who buy on account. As the number of DSO's goes down so does the investment in accounts receivable thereby improving ROI. Likewise on the profitability side, gross margin dollars is customarily measured as a percent of sales. Therefore, if the gross margin percent goes up and assuming the same sales level, profitability will increase and ROI will go up. Likewise, each block on the decision tree has a primary ratio or measure whose movement up or down will affect ROI. The process level measures should always be compatible with the primary objective, which is to increase ROI. Surprisingly, this may not always be the case and such incompatibility will result in inconsistent results.

The outside level of the summary *SDT* is where objectives are typically set as the approach for achieving the overall objective, which is to increase ROI. Since the *SDT* presents the results of operations for both investment and profitability, it can only hint at what the business strategy is for achieving a higher ROI. This is a results achievement picture for the enterprise relative to expectations; and is supported by actual performance numbers, which are not shown in the tree[94]. It is important to remember that all of the components of *SDM* are dependent on the same financial and statistical information. Despite the absence of actual numbers, the relative success for each component can be shown on a customized presentation diagram by using accents, such as shadowing or color, based on actual results. For example in the above diagram the darker (horizontal lines) highlighted boxes represent the most significant areas of underperformance relative to expectations and therefore, also denote the greatest opportunity for improvement. In other words, these are the areas which should receive a strategic focus and offer the best prospect to improve ROI. The lightly highlighted (small dots) boxes mean the performance measure is exceeding expectations. Finally if there is no highlight it means the measure is performing to expectations and there is little opportunity for improvement. Initially, a tool such as MS PowerPoint with hyperlinks can be used to move between different levels of the SDT analysis without creating elaborate

---

[94] The *Executive Scorecard (eSC)* provides the actual numbers that would typically correspond to the *SDT*. An executive with both reports in hand should be able to have a comprehensive picture of performance and be comfortable that they consistently present performance information. The scorecard also provides the target level, the trend, and the remaining opportunity between where the measure is and where it is expected to be.

programming. Once the format and content become established it may make sense to 'program it' for ease of use and presentation.

While the summary level decision tree is an effective tool for demonstrating where strategic focus and decisions are required, it does not represent the process level actions that need to be taken to actually improve performance. Therefore, the action strategies, or process level objectives and measures, are provided in the detailed decision tree. An example of the operating (profitability) side detail is shown in this illustration.

The real world of operations is revealed in this level of the decision tree. Similar highlights are used in this illustration and the one that follows. For example, in the summary tree it is clear that the objective to "reduce operating expense" is not being met. As the detailed layers clearly show, there is work to do for all three primary process-level measures that make up the composite measure for reducing operating expense. In both the summary tree and the detailed tree you will also notice that a higher level composite

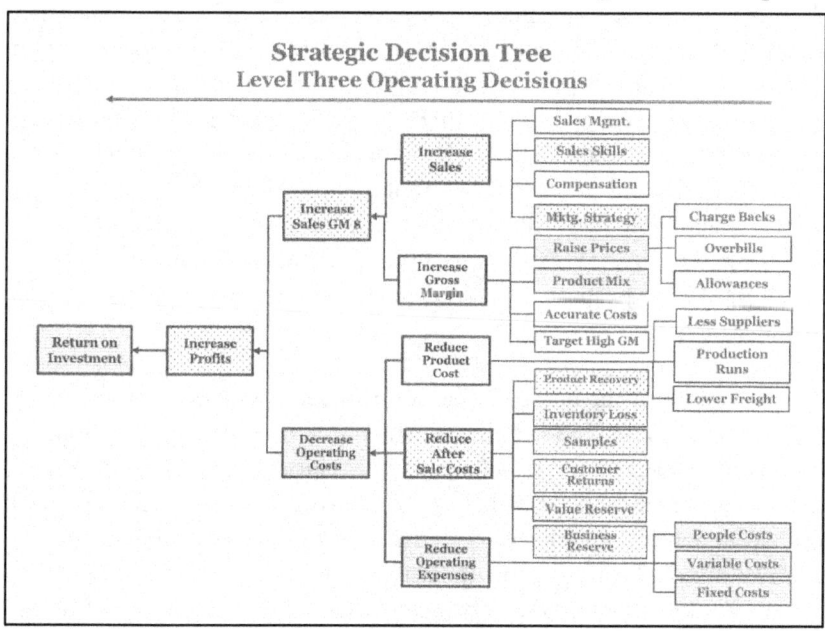

measure may be positive (small dots), but a lower level measure that is a component of the higher measure is underperforming. In our example, the target for increasing sales gross margin dollars is positive, but it is because there is an increase in sales dollars; while the target to increase gross margin dollars on sales is not being met. Specifically, the two strategies to increase gross margin dollars, namely raising prices and selling a more profitable product mix, are not being achieved. As a side observation, these operating results represent an executive's best-of-both-worlds' situation. Sales are increasing therefore presenting a more favorable condition for still having the opportunity to raise prices and improve product mix. However, it may be that sales are increasing because neither the price increases, nor the promotion of more profitable products has been achieved. These conditions present some interesting opportunities for evaluating strategic decision making. In such circumstances the decision-maker should make sure they have all of the relevant information before making a different decision.[95]

Ideally, decision-makers should be motivated to make strategic decisions that will exploit the market conditions that are allowing them to meet or exceed sales objectives; and at the same time, improve gross margin dollars on sales by some combination of selectively raising prices and promoting higher gross margin products in the sales mix. This is where we go back to our strategic information to make sure we have enough facts to make the right decision. In this case, both the customer and product profiles should provide the necessary information to make the right decisions. And, assuming that *standard performance measurement (SPM)* is operational it is the right tool to project probable outcomes by implementing alternative approaches for managing price and product mix. As you can see, knowing what is shown in the *SDT* will logically point the executives and managers to the business operations and processes that are most in need of their attention. Prudent leaders will be almost as interested in why they are succeeding as they are in why they are failing. Sometimes exploiting our successes, or at least perpetuating them as long as possible, is the most important strategy.

By looking at the detailed decision tree for the investment side as shown below, it is possible to again see which of the process level action strategies are successful and which are not. In our example, it is interesting to note that we are missing our objectives for investment in inventory for one reason; we have not been able to reduce the quantity. Based on current demand, we simply have too much quantity on hand for the products in inventory. For example, this simply means that there is a quantity of 10 on hand in inventory when a quantity of 5 is sufficient to cover demand during a product order cycle. Too much quantity on hand for any given product is

---

[95] You will remember one truth about the *strategic forces of profit* is that any decision to change any one of them will affect the others. In our example, moving ahead with the action strategy to increase prices without considering its effect on sales will most likely reduce the trend for increased sales that is already being realized.

usually caused by overstating the requirement for so-called safety stock. It is the increment of quantity on hand that is planned just in case demand unexpectedly increases. And since by definition it never sells under normal circumstances, it must be carefully controlled. The typical solution for reducing product quantities requires a more effective forecasting capability. And, as is the case with most of the investment side components of ROI, it will take longer to achieve expected results. For example, getting down to a quantity of 5 (five) may require ordering none in the next order cycle (the

prevent solution); and it may take two order cycles to sell off the excess (the fix solution). Ideally, the next purchase receipt will occur just in time to meet customer demands.

In our example, the investment in accounts receivable is not meeting our target performance, also for a single reason. The accuracy of orders is below standard and is causing our customers to pay slower. I don't even want to get into all of the possible solutions for this problem. The reasons for inaccurate orders could be many including, but not limited to, how the order is taken, how it is priced, order filling accuracy, and invoicing. Needless to say each possible cause is related to specific processes and both the fix and prevent solutions will be found at the process-level.

All layers of our sample enterprise *strategic decision tree* can be shown in a single chart, which would be too large to show here with sufficient clarity. I am a proponent of seeing the whole tree because it is such a good communication device. I believe it should be publicly displayed perhaps even on the wall in public areas as a means to communicate and emphasize what the strategic focus to everyone in the organization. It is the pinnacle measurement tool, to which all other measures from top to bottom in *SDM* will be consistent when it is properly constructed based on actual results.

Table of Illustrations

www.ingramcontent.com/pod-product-compliance
Lightning Source LLC
Chambersburg PA
CBHW051455170526
45166CB00001B/252